Translating the City

6/10/2017

To Prof Paul,

Hope this will be the
beginning of future collaboration

best.

[signature]

Translating the City
Interdisciplinarity in urban studies

Stephanie Vincent-Geslin, Yves Pedrazzini,
Hossam Adly, Yafiza Zorro (Eds.)

EPFL Press
Distributed by Routledge

Routledge
Taylor & Francis Group

www.routledge.com/builtenvironment

Taylor & Francis Group Ltd
2 Park Square, Milton Park
Abingdon, Oxford, OX14 4RN, UK

Routledge is an imprint of the Taylor & Francis Group,
An informa business.

Simultaneously published in the USA and Canada by Routledge,
711 Third Avenue, New York, 10017

www.routledge.com

Library of Congress Cataloging-in-Publication Data
A catalog record for this book is available from the Library of Congress

This book is published under the editorial direction of Professor Vincent Kaufmann (EPFL).

ÉCOLE POLYTECHNIQUE
FÉDÉRALE DE LAUSANNE

The authors and publisher express their thanks to the
Ecole polytechnique fédérale de Lausanne (EPFL) for its generous support
towards the publication of this book.

EPFL Press

is an imprint owned by the Presses polytechniques et universitaires romandes,
a Swiss academic publishing company whose main purpose is to publish the teaching
and research works of the Ecole polytechnique fédérale de Lausanne (EPFL).

Presses polytechniques et univeristaires romandes
EPFL – Rolex Learning Center
Post office box 119
CH-1015 Lausanne, Switzerland
E-mail: ppur@epfl.ch

www.epflpress.org

© 2015, First edition, EPFL Press
ISBN 978-2-940222-79-7 (EPFL Press)
ISBN 978-1-13-877539-8 (Routledge)
Printed in Italy

Table of Contents

Introduction

Stéphanie Vincent Geslin, Yves Pedrazzini,
Hossam Adly, Yafiza Zorro

What is a *city*? Does this word describe a contemporary reality, a human invention dating back several thousand years, or the eternal pursuit of a fantasy built space, both just and beautiful? And when we say *city* in Capetown or in Mumbai, *cidade* in Rio de Janeiro, *ciudad* in Medellin, *città* in Naples or *ville* in Lyon, are we talking about the same reality? This is precisely the question. The present book is born of the aspiration of researchers from the Laboratory of Urban Sociology (LASUR), based at the Ecole Polytechnique Fédérale de Lausanne (EPFL/Swiss Federal Institute of Technology Lausanne) to answer these questions and to think, in an interdisciplinary way, about the future of contemporary cities.

This book is also the result of a collaborative process, initially carried out within LASUR then followed by collaboration with international experts in urban research. This two-fold project gave way to an exploratory workshop[1], to which we invitied keynote speakers from India, Canada, Brazil, South Africa and the United Arab Emirates, and where we discussed and

---

[1]   This workshop entitled *Wassup Cities!* took place in Leysin (Switzerland) from November 24–26, 2011, gathering LASUR's researchers and international experts on urban issues.

debated comparative disciplinary approaches, epistemological traditions and empirical examples taken from major urban areas around the world (notably Asia, North America, Latin America, Africa and the Middle East).

The Urban Translation Network, of which this book is a first achievement, emerged on the basis of dialogue accross geographical and academic boundaries – dialogue which gives its particular form to the book. It realizes the necessity for urban researchers to *translate*: from one discipline to another; from one country to another; from theory to experience and, conversely, experience into theory, convinced that the inductive method is productive. This heterogeneity ultimately proved to be an asset when it came to understanding the complexity of contemporary cities. While perspectives on the topic are many, it is the subject itself – the city – that has become diverse and heterogeneous to the point of becoming unqualifiable.

Translating the City thus attempts to reformulate the urban question and express two key questions. Firstly, relative to other research traditions around the world, how do we researchers see contemporary urban reality? Secondly: what can seriously be said about a subject as elusive and shifting as the city?

The quest for urban knowledge

Understanding the contemporary city is a work in progress, a daily workshop in which the knowns and unknowns of known and unknown analytical elements are created and recreated in real time; the knowledge that we believe was gained on Monday proves purely archaic by Sunday. Not a week or a day goes by without a new perspective appearing somewhere in the world, joining forces with those of architects and urban planners – both topical and utopian – who, for at least two-and-a-half centuries the world over, have been considering the modern city and its future, giving it strange names or common ones, so as to perhaps concretize some aspect of it (in general, its form).

This book raises such questions and offers its vision of the contemporary city (in Switzerland, Europe and around the world), as well as a perspective on the dynamics that have developed there in recent years. While it is undeniable that the urban theories to which the editors of this book adhere and have compared with those of the authors (especially those related to issues of social and spatial mobility), the contemporary city remains an enigma to us as it does to any other researcher, professional or inhabitant. This is why we must persist in our efforts to understand the city, all the while establishing – with appropriate reserve – certain principles regarding the study of the urban phenomenon. This likewise involves regularly proposing new names we feel are suitable for describing the rapidly-changing city.

In a certain manner (though others were likewise possible), the authors of this book mark both the end of the building phase of a collective vision of 'the city' – and, consequently, of urban actors that we might call a 'metropolitan' phase of sociology – as well as the beginning of a new phase that we might have called 'global', had this word not long been usurped by proponents of the liberal economy, and which we will instead call 'post-capitalist'. Or alternatively, we might call this the era of a sociology of *emerging* global cities – not London, Tokyo nor New York (at least not since Times Square's Disneyfication), but rather Mexico, Lagos, Karachi or Kuala Lumpur. What is beginning, in these pages as elsewhere, is an era of urban uncertainty, given the chaos of things, forms, flows and desires of the powerful who, long before there were cities, only get involved when and where it behooves them.

Has this task that we have set for ourselves of reducing the scope of the urban enigma by centering our attention, scientific analysis and professional expertise on it – not only for Swiss cities but at the international level as well (in Latin America, Africa and Asia, at the heart of these worlds in transition) – put us in the position to propose *our own* general theory of urbanization? And, if so, should it necessarily be, by the very "nature" of its mission, a *sociological* theory of urbanity? Obviously, the foundations of such a theory (which our laboratory of urban sociology will propose here) should at the very least be developed with some *school* of urban sociology in Chicago, Los Angeles, Frankfurt or Paris. First, in order to continue to introduce novel expertise on urban issues, we must do what we have always done: combine our knowledge and projects with the architects, planners, engineers, economists and geographers with whom we have always looked *for* and *into* the city.

We believe we are capable of reformulating the "urban question" (and attempting to answer it) by including it in the field of contemporary urban studies, as part of a reality augmented by the globalization of practices of metropolitan inhabitants as well as those of confirmed international researchers. Hence, in the real time of globalization, reformulating a hypothesis of the city risks comparing theoretical perspectives forged in the fires of megacities like Rio de Janeiro, Mumbai, Johannesburg, Dubai and Montreal, as well as those of Shanghai, Bogota and Addis Ababa with other urban theories generated, one might naively believe, by the *peace* of cities like Geneva, Lausanne and Paris.

It is in this way that we restated the urban question: what does the city name? The question was asked in the 1970s (following the teachings of Marx), in the 80s (following Richard Sennett and Jane Jacobs), in the 90s (following Francois Ascher), in the 2000s (following – and sometimes preceding – Rem Koolhaas), and finally in the 2010s. The efforts of numerous researchers to define the city has in no way diminished, despite their failure to put a name on this thing we have called 'city' for 3000 years. We obviously have not *ceased* calling it by that name, even though each literary season marks the arrival of new attempts to give it new names. Since its inception, the fundamental research project (that literally founded urban research) is to say what the city names.

To do this, we must gather as many expert opinions as possible and deconstruct what is familiar, especially scientifically. Thus, we must regularly (and obsessively) pose this question, because most everyday realities, of which we believe ourselves to be intimate connoisseurs, are also those that change the fastest. This question has permeated our work well before here and now: What does the city name?

The urban and those who contemplate it

We must resolve a number of elements and constraints in order to guide our work towards transcendence of the historical perspectives of urban sociology. We must reformulate the question of the city and the urbanization of the North and South, but open it up, bring it out of the scope of cooperation and development, remove it from the domain of emergency engineering, keep it close to scientific concerns and an ethics of spatial justice. Take, for example, the notable absence (both in our book's introduction as well as in the different chapters) of the ubiquitous 'state-of-the-art' or 'state-of-the-question', which, per custom, figures early on in the table of contents of any respectable book, regardless of the topic. We felt it was only fair to give our contributing authors the choice to use or refuse such states in their articles, such that they might be responsible themselves for introducing key urban research issues and then exploring them. However, that was not the only reason. Having established the editorial framework, it is within the chapters themselves that the real issues lie.

It was also the general aim of this work – stamped 'made in Switzerland', after all – to offer researchers to whom we are close the opportunity to deliberately go beyond our eternal question, to create a state-of-the-art that plays hide-and-seek with the Chicago School, in particular, as well as some other figureheads of our urban disciplines (primarily French and North American). At the same time, our contributors, from their respective fields of study, presented on a platter the latest developments and histories of science, about which we know nothing and in which we are not included (or are, but without understanding how), due to traces of neo-colonialism inherent to our visions as Northern researchers.

Today, we cannot simply (or conscionably) be satisfied with a recitation of the names of our favorite authors in the urban sciences. We need new states of the art for new times, those of this emerging globalization, whose impact on the development of 'global cities' we regard with suspicion. This is also an opportunity for an urban sociology laboratory (regardless of its interdisciplinary hybridity) to transcend the academic state of the question – the city – and address it based on (and with the help of) other academic disciplines.

Urban everyday life takes forms that are radically different from what we find in a *morro* in Rio, or a slum in Mumbai, or in a bus on the outskirts of Geneva – for good reasons. It is necessary, at the outset of this book, to refute this chaotic vision of the future of major cities in the South – the *Third World*, as we called it in the 20th Century – all too often in the service of 'Northerners' and relayed to Latin American, African and Asian contexts by elites whose power derives from their exclusive control of access to spheres of globalization at the local level. As for the inhabitants of these cities, whose global identity usually only results from a few economic bubbles, they live their precarious, fragmented, hyper-local, ordinary lives, subsisting on what they produce from hopes, projects and collective actions on a daily basis. Thus, while we have not entirely forgotten the often inhumane conditions in which hundreds of millions of inhabitants of inner cities, townships, *favelas* and *villas miserias* are forced to live, we can no longer ignore these people, their knowledge, skills, capacities, trades and self-constructed habitats, the cities they help to build nor the transdisciplinary knowledge they help establish – even in the name of a comprehensive approach.

Thus, in addition to the aforementioned need to assemble the knowledge and practices of sociology, anthropology and other human or technical sciences (history, economy, architecture, urban engineering, etc.) and to create a dialogue in the form of projects and research, one must never exclude knowledge originating from outside of the sciences – that of associations, activists or even citizens who, in one way or another, have always developed their own *state-of-the-art* and edited their own handbook of current cities.

At certain times in the history of sciences, that should be looked at in greater detail, the city was an opportunity to gather knowledge from very different backgrounds to cope with the common confusion born of the apparent elusiveness of the 'big city'. At other times, because of the ways of thinking endemic to the period, this knowledge (i.e. more or less scientific, secular or political) clashed theoretically or empirically, fashioning the city regardless.

Which is why, in this book and broadly in our research, we have always aimed to go beyond specific disciplines and open up the state-of-the-art. In so doing, and because the very act of thinking about the city is a practice, an act, a commitment in the real world, not a mere theoretical exercise, we hope to move forward by crossing and scaling the boundaries of specialization that continue to frame analyses and limit the understanding of what a city is or *could* be.

At first, it seemed that it was the geographical boundaries that needed to be overcome in order to better understand their effects on the making of cities. Thus, we invited researchers to come from their respective countries and cities to literally cross the geographical boundaries that separate us and reflect on urban realities with us (or against us, depending on their point of view). The idea was indeed that, by stepping outside of their academic and geopolitical contexts, they could "address" the concept of city, but also that, once removed from this environment physically and intellectually, they could at the same time question "our" notion of city.

Is the urban setting in Brazil of the same substance – built, human and social – as in Ethiopia? As we will see in the chapters that follow, which aim to present different perspectives on these different realities from "the other urban" by researchers and experts on the city, the answers to this key question vary considerably. But in each case the interest is not only the answers given here and there to this vast question regarding the role of our species in the organization of geographical space, but also the question *itself* – so often asked and so rarely answered. With our Brazilian, Indian, South African, Egyptian and Canadian colleagues – a profession that is quite widespread throughout the world – we take this quest in search of the city one step further.

We then had to attack professional boundaries. We quickly saw that it was easier to get two sociologists or architects from different countries immersed in a subject than two citizens from the same country with different urban professions. Our goal then was to break down this barrier. A new goal thus was born: to attempt to understand the jobs of all those who design and conceive the city today (both theoretically and in practice – in other words, 'applied theoreticians') and to create a more balanced, equitable spatial and social order.

Between theory and practice: foundations for a definition of the profession of urban researcher

These two interdependent components – the object and its subject, the city and those who make it exist, be they sociologists, architects, geographers or engineers – are thus the heart of this book. They are bound by a common goal: the future of urban research itself, as it is true that contemporary forms of urbanity require a constant dialogue between practice and theory. Understanding, describing, planning and building the city today are all part of the same process, the same ambitions that we – researchers in Switzerland – have voiced. One must ask if this process qualifies or should be defined as a profession. Does the profession, 'urban researcher', exist? In our opinion, two ruptures in urban research combine and reinforce one another to justify both asking this question today and looking closely at its answer.

First, it is common for social science departments and research institutes specifically interested in the city to be minority entities within the technical schools and universities geared toward professional practice. This was the first rupture in urban research nearly three decades ago. Until the 1980s and Henri Lefebvre (the author of *Droit à la ville*, 1968, and perhaps the most radical example), the dialogue between urban policies of planning and the social sciences was rather lackluster, with the latter adopting a critical stance regarding functionalist urbanization and the urban transformations which, in the West, characterized the glorious 1930s. At EPFL's LASUR we have always put ourselves in a difficult position with respect to the isolationist position of research, and have advocated for a dialogue between theory and practice. All too often, sociological approaches to the urban attempt to forego a detailed description of the built environment and, conversely, that architects and engineers often find themselves caught up in processes of projection, neglecting the practices and uses of social actors. In light of this, our goal was to serve as an interface between practical knowledge and theoretical knowledge. With the dual mission of contributing to theoretical knowledge in the field of urban research and advising architects and planners, researchers specializing in the city operate in distinct worlds, use different languages and must deal with the compartmentalizing of disciplines and professions.

Thus, the principal dividing line that traverses the genesis of the *Urban Translation* project is the one separating theory from practice. How do sociologists, architects, anthropologists, urban planners, researchers and professionals in general manage to talk about the city together? And are they all talking about the same city? Insofar as the research subjects in the social sciences and architectural projects approach their subjects from very different scales and places, how can the appropriate distance of observation be determined? Is there a vernacular common to these two "worlds" that allows us to both *describe* and *build* the city?

Reconciling these two worlds, striving to build a dialogue between researchers and planners, is dear to our hearts. It is, after all, in meeting places, where the boundaries are more blurred, in contacts with other beings and objects, that cities transform and derive their dynamics. The analysis and description of the city must be as varied and diverse as the city itself, because it is precisely in these borderlands between disciplines that scientific innovation in the urban field is born.

For three decades now, the emergence of user-oriented governance, concomitant with the increase in urban tensions and social inequalities, has created a strong connection between urban theory and practice. One example of this is the contribution of professionals to scientific works (Paquot, 2000), as well as planners' and decision-makers' increasing acceptance of scientific knowledge for correcting certain planning post-war or zoning-related 'mistakes', which most notably led to a redefining of the profession of urban planner (Merlin and Choay, 2007). That is why, for several years now, many of our publications have attempted to develop a dialogue between these two worlds. *Habitat en devenir* sought to 'create solid knowledge on habitat at the frontiers and crossroads of academic disciplines... to reflect on sustainable territorial and urban development' (Pattaroni *et al.*, 2009:2). Prior to this work, *Enjeux de la sociologie urbaine* (Bassand *et al.*, 2007) and some other LASUR books already had aimed to perpetuate the tradition of research applied to the needs of the urban fabric.

The second rupture leading to reflection on the potential profession of urban researcher originates from the circulation of architectural and planning models, forms and norms. Just as it is increasingly difficult to speak of 'culture' (Swiss, French, German, etc.), it seems increasingly outdated to talk about 'architectural cultures'. All North and South cities are linked in one way or another to an urban heritage or past, be it in economic relationships (networks of cities) or dependency. The birth of certain cities saw architecture and urban planning as weapons in the sense of urban colonial strategy, as is the case in Latin America. Effectively, in the latter, this strategy radically altered the built environment, condemning Latin American cities to dependency on the North – and Europe in particular – for their urban development. This dependency was most notably reflected in the call to European architects to visit and plan those future cities during the second half of the 20th century. Today, for instance, it is still hard to cite urban theories that are specifically Latin American, without citing European and North American theoreticians.

Consequently, urban planners, politicians and other developers can no longer overlook the contributions of research, and must adopt a comprehensive view that embraces divergent urban scenarios and seeks out their inherent similarities, continuities and differences. This is the work of urban researchers who, in addition to the two works mentioned above, have made several other notable written contributions in the form of research reports and scientific articles that attempt to provide theoretical support for improving practices. However, these works focus only on the urban context in Switzerland, whereas it is clear that understanding the urban phenomenon – especially if one of the goals is making urban theory applicable – can no longer be limited to localized knowledge of the city. In other words, it no longer seemed possible (or valid) to provide analyses on suburban areas in Switzerland without questioning the reality of suburban spaces in the United States, India or China, and examining their specificities. Today, more than ever, the observation of the city cannot deny its global nature in response to local behaviors.

Contents of this book

The basic idea behind this book therefore stems from this programmatic heritage. We postulate that the work of researchers in urban fields – a compound, heterogeneous field, if ever there were one – lies precisely in this ability to bridge such dividing lines, to adapt to the new interdependencies between research and planning, theory and practice. Differing from the critical stance of the 1960s, urban researchers today are compelled to transcend boundaries –to *translate*. This back and forth between these 'worlds' pushes the urban researcher to translate the language of plans and forecasts into one of social science analysis and vice versa – in other words, to decrypt theoretical knowledge in order to make it useful for urban development.

In order to establish our vision of urban studies as a permanent dialogue between disciplines and scientists across the globe, this book is thematically divided into five chapters. Each chapter presents a dialogue: a proposal by an international urban researcher, which is then discussed, critiqued and put into perspective by authors from LASUR. Each chapter thus offers two responding papers feeding a same thematic by confronting different empirical examples and theroretical analysis. The five discussions found in these chapters are arranged according to their analytical scale – from the most macroscopic (urban form, built morphology, governance, etc.) to the most microscopic (urban counter-cultures, small spaces, etc.).

The discussion in the first chapter of urban segregation in African cities, entitled 'Planning', questions the role of modern urban planning and the different models upon which contemporary cities are designed and built today. Analysis of the social and spatial impact of these planning models thus calls on us to reconsider the tools needed to produce a more just city.

The second chapter, entitled 'Order', continues the reflection on justice in the city through a discussion of urban order, as well as the key issue of mobility in the contemporary city. This chapter puts forward the idea that the city is in transition, giving rise to the need to produce theoretical and empirical tools capable of capturing these changes, particularly by using the knowledge of local researchers.

The third chapter, 'Nature', questions the boundaries between nature and the city, leading to a discussion of what is legitimate in the city and what is not. Using the examples of the Dharavi slum in India and the Grottes neighborhood in Geneva, it makes an appeal to seriously consider practices and expectations of inhabitants now and in the future, to better reflect the diversity of urban lifestyles.

Reflection on this diversity continues in Chapter Four, 'Cultures', through a discussion of specifically urban logics of action, based paradoxically on different post-hero and counter-cultural figures, thereby questioning the very essence of urbanity.

The book concludes with the chapter entitled 'Image', which is oriented toward methodological reflection, supported by an empirical focus on the small urban spaces of Dubaï. As much a methodological proposal as a theoretical one, it reformulates the fundamental goal of this book – that of expressing what the city is by demonstrating that this design is the inevitable result of theoretical and empirical biases.

Then, adding images, cultures, natures, orders and plannings from different parts on earth, we guess our contribution will support other urban "hunters" to pursue the always shifting definition of 'The City'.

References

Ascher, F. (1995) *Métapolis ou l'Avenir des villes*. Odile Jacob, Paris.

Bassand, M., Kaufmann, V. and Joye, D. (eds.) (2007) *Enjeux de la sociologie urbaine* 2ᵉ édition. Presses polytechniques et universitaires romandes, Lausanne.

Jacobs, J. (1961) *The Death and Life of Great American Cities*. Random House, New York.

Koolhaas, R. in Koolhaas, R. *et al.* (2000) Junkspace. *Mutations*. Actar & Arc en Rêve Centre d'Architecture, Barcelona.

Lefebvre, H. (1968) *Le droit à la ville*, Paris: Anthropos.

Lefebvre, H. (1996) [1968] "The Right to the City." In: *Writings on Cities*, London, Blackwell Publishing.

Merlin, P. and Choay, F. (2007) *Dictionnaire de l'urbanisme et de l'aménagement*. PUF, Paris.

Pattaroni, L., Rabinovich, A. and Kaufmann, V. (eds.) (2009) *Habitat en devenir: les enjeux territoriaux, sociaux et politiques du logement en Suisse*. Presses polytechniques et universitaires romandes, Lausanne.

Sennett, R. (1970) *The Uses of Disorder: Personal Identity and City Life*. W.W. Norton, New York.

Meadowlands, Soweto, in the early Apartheid period
Source: 326:331.83, Museum Africa Photographic Library, Johannesburg

Part 1

Planning

This first part explores the relationship between the production of urban space and social interactions, through empirical immersion in the African city. Specifically, it questions the role of modern urban planning in the activation of mechanisms of urban segregation. This reflection raises the fundamental question of urban form – torn between planning and appropriation, models and urban uses. In African cities in particular, this tug-of-war couples with the influence of Western models (frequently legacies of colonialism), which permeate ways of thinking about and making the city, and those of the global city, whose influence is measured by the height of its skyscrapers. This plunge into the African city – South African cities first, followed then by Addis Ababa – offers a comparative view of the effects of planning on cities' social and spatial production. In the first case, segregation seems to result from the superimposing of urban policies at different levels of governance, whereas the second shows the radical, segregative transformations occurring in Addis Ababa under the influence of modern, rapid urbanization.

Through empirical examples that go above and beyond the 'local', these two chapters defend theoretical perspectives about the role of urban planning and its effects. On the one hand, we find faith in the merits of the urban planning process, whose negative effects result only in the simultaneous presence of other logics of governance. On the other hand, we offer the critique of modern urban planning as it seldom, if ever, takes into account local, historical or cultural contexts.

Between these two extremes, however, the reality is rarely at either extreme, but rather falls somewhere in between, surely because cities today – in Africa and elsewhere – rely on a multitude of influences and models in order to exist. The territory, history and culture in which they are rooted shapes a reality that is intrinsically unique and distinct.

Planning, Modernism and the Challenge of Enduring Urban Segregation[1]

Susan Parnell, Owen Crankshaw

Department of Environmental and Geographical Sciences
and Department of Sociology
University of Cape Town, South Africa

The unprecedented growth of cities in the developing world is being followed, somewhat belatedly, by a renaissance in thinking about cities beyond the West and the nature of barriers to their equitable development (Chatterjee, 2006; Robinson, 2006; Roy, 2009). In reframing the enquiry into how cities 'of the South' function and what drives social and economic exclusion in these visibly divided and unequal urban spaces, there has been increasing emphasis on issues of informality. In an effort to come to grips with a dualist urban system that locks individuals into poverty, debate has centered on how to conceive and respond to urban activities that are (depending on one's perspective) illegal, unregulated, unrecognised or under-appreciated (see Mc Farlane, 2012; Roy et AlSayyad, 2004; Roy, 2005; Simone, 2004). In this chapter we will frame the issues of urban inequality somewhat differently, talking instead about how the formal and the informal are interrelated and intersect at the city

[1] An earlier version of this paper was first presented at the LaSUR-funded workshop "Wassup Cities" in November 2011. Its authors would also like to acknowledge the ongoing support of the University of Cape Town and the National Research Foundation. The findings and conclusions of this research are those of the authors, and the NRF does not accept any liability for them.

scale. In other words, we want to study the entire city – not just the part that is excluded or marginalised. More specifically, we are interested in how to identify those mechanisms (legal and otherwise) that divide cities, trapping some residents in inferior conditions and even chronic poverty. Clearly, the rationale for understanding the roots of structural exclusion or segregation is to inform a transformative urban agenda and build better, more inclusive cities.

Cities where there is a division between the formal and informal, rich and poor, legal and illegal, (ex)colonial and indigenous, can all be thought of as 'segregated cities'. In North America, Brazil and South Africa, the various forms of economic and political exclusion correspond, in a certain way, to racial divisions. This palpable, racialized visual expression embodies the dominant lines of an urban rift. Hence, there is a tendency to equate the term *urban segregation* with racial residential segregation. However, cities are segregated in many respects, not only by race. In most cities there is some form of segregation manifest in domains as diverse as access to schooling, healthcare, housing, land, the labour market or the public space. Lines of segregation may be related to race (South Africa), religion (Ireland), caste (India) or language (Canada). In some cases, these divisions are formally codified; in others, they simply function as though they are, or, in certain instances – even more effectively – through unspoken prejudices and practices (see Crankshaw, 2008; Li and Wu, 2008). Whatever the basis or device for spatial and social division, the distribution of urban amenities is never equitable, and some residents are greatly privileged by dualist, unequal allocations and regulations, while others are severely disadvantaged. In order to understand segregation not solely based on overt economic inequalities, we must understand how cities work – including the many technical aspects (i.e. when and in what way services and opportunities were divided historically and how exclusion continues to be perpetuated through similar or new planning interventions) (Beall *et al.*, 2002; Coquery-Vidrovitch, 2005; Freund, 2007; Myers, 2011).

There are a surprisingly large number of cities globally where race, caste, traditional authority control, royalty or even competing political jurisdictions define the rules in such a way that residents cannot move freely across urban systems of housing, land or services (Demissie, 2012). That said, formally or institutionally segregated cities tend to be concentrated in the Global South, where resources are limited, urban inequality is more pronounced and local democracy is less developed. Segregation is so much a part of Africa's urban development that a brutally segregated division of the city – often attributed to colonial legacies – is sometimes seen as its hallmark (O'Connor, 1983; Simon, 1992).

Notwithstanding a half-century of political independence and an overt commitment to ending colonial influences, institutionalised forms of segregated urban development still permeate every aspect of African cities and towns – from macro-financial policy to urban regulation and the lived experiences of citizens (Myers, 2011; Simone, 2004). Similar patterns of structural inequality are increasingly prevalent in the urban form of Chinese and Indian cities, where growing wealth has either compounded or highlighted the underlying inequalities that regulate the lives of illegal or marginal urban dwellers who do not have access to the full range of urban rights (Li and Wu, 2008). The failure to come to terms with the structural basis of urban segregation and why and how it continues in the 21st century lies at the heart of the development impasse, leaving millions of urban inhabitants trapped in poverty while their wealthy counterparts enjoy increasingly comfortable urban lives (UN Habitat, 2001).

In this paper we will only be looking at cities where segregation or partitioning has a recognisable institutional basis (often legal, but not necessarily so) that, at the city scale, defines who has access to and who is excluded from urban services, assets and opportunities. To highlight urban segregation (or structural partition) as a critical development impasse to be overcome in order to guarantee equal urban opportunities, the remainder of the paper is divided into two parts. The first, largely conceptual, explores why the dualist or segregated form of so many cities in the Global South have remained unchallenged for so long. To this end, we underline the uncomfortable relationship many urban planners have with modernism, and in particular with applying modern urban planning in cities in the developing world. Essentially, we suggest that the collective Western embarrassment regarding the oppressive consequences of modernism across the colonial world have essentially made it the sole object of critical reflection, leaving other governmentalites unscrutinised. Having argued that anxieties regarding modernity have dominated and distorted understanding of both the historical evolution of cities outside of Western Europe and North America, we will show that modernism's negative impact on segregatory urban development in the Global South may have been more muted and/or varied than is typically purported. Moreover, we suggest that modernist values such as universalism may have something to offer utopian thinkers with regard to a more egalitarian, less divided urban future. Following the idea that the nature of the relationship between modernism and segregation has been misunderstood, in the second section of the paper, we reflect on how one might approach the enduring legacy of urban segregation using a specific example – that of the thwarted post-apartheid drive to end race-based discrimination – which underscores the necessity of understanding the underlying institutional basis of urban inequality, so as to radically change the way this city is managed.

Imperatives for uncoupling segregation and modernist planning

Planning is not the sole cause of (or cure for) the spatial division of cities – past, present or future. The impression one gets when reading academic planning literature is that elite interests used colonial/modern planning monolithically to create segregation and entrench inequality, making modern planning today an utterly discredited, irredeemable approach to human settlement management (c.f. Healey, 2007; Porter, 2006). However, we wish to suggest that, in the contemporary period, modern urban planning is a maligned, neglected area that may just as easily compound, entrench or erode patterns of segregation in cities, depending on how the instruments are used. In other words, there is no inevitable outcome to the adoption of modernity as a paradigmatic planning approach to building or managing cities. This is not to overburden the expectation of what a (progressive) modern planning agenda might be able to achieve, not least in overcoming the burdens of entrenched colonial inequalities. Prejudice, political configuration, labour markets, national immigration policies and demographic changes are all variables that act independently, or in concert with, modern urban planning to structure or restructure a segregating or desegregating city. The argument here is that it is possible for states and other planning actors to intervene in urban development through the use of instruments such as land use zoning, taxation, building standards, bylaw enforcement, etc. Thus, the impact of planning is not inevitably the oppression of the poor, and modernist reforms can generate universal benefits that are potentially of great value to the most vulnerable. Mindful of the damning critiques of modernism's practical impacts in Africa (c.f. Ferguson, 1994; 1999), acknowledging the possibility of a more ambiguous legacy of modernity brings us back to the utopian promises of modern urban planners, if only to assess the impact of modernist planning relative to the regimes of urban control that currently exist in segregated cities.

There are a number of reasons why there is currently renewed interest in the role of (modern) urban planning, including, most obviously, the general call for greater state involvement in regulating societies in general, in the wake of the global fiscal crisis and threats of global environmental change. Climate changes, disaster risk, urban social protection schemes, demands by major investors and disillusionment due to crime, informality and neo-liberalism also underpin a renewed interest in planning (see UN Habitat, 2009). It would, of course, be naive to utterly discount the controlling aspirations of some states, most startlingly China, who are newly embracing urban master plans, enforcement codes and draconian building bylaws and regulations that, de facto, exclude the poorest and advance the interests of the middle classes (Wu, 2010; Friedman, 2005).

For urbanists, the call to revisit the role of the (local) state presents something of a conundrum as, for decades, planners sought to distance themselves from the government and, by association, from technocratic systems of urban regulation (Healey, 2007; Watson, 2009). Master planning, at least anything seen as top-down or state-centric development controls or spatial planning, fell out of academic and policy fashion for much of the late-twentieth century, especially in the West and the ex-colonial South. In Africa, the compromised credibility of the state as the driver of a legitimate urban planning process was fueled by weak, corrupt local governments that, when they were not invoking colonial planning laws to further their own ends (most notoriously in Zimbabwe, with the massive clearances/evictions in Harare in the 1990s (Potts, 2011), did very little else to promote progressive urban planning of any kind (Myers, 2011). The weakness of universities and the profession in Asia and Africa has meant that, for decades, there was very little critical reflection on how effective planning was in achieving post-independence political objectives, or how it might be done differently (Parnell *et al.*, 2009).

Given the scale of urban problems and the enduring inequalities associated with past regimes, it is not difficult to understand why planning has been discredited, especially in cities in Africa, Asia and Latin America. It is not an overstatement to suggest that, on average, government-led planning processes have either ignored or undermined the poor, or been utterly irrelevant to their lives. Despite this, there are clear, widespread calls for more active involvement by governments in how cities are run (for an overview of the current debate about whether states should engage or eschew a greater role for government and urban planning, see Parnell and Robinson, 2012).

The debate regarding the desirability of increasing the role of government relative to other power bases in cities is not restricted to contemporary development politics. Echoes of the dichotomous positions on government's contribution to urban development appear in the work of urban historians, with key authors such as Mamdani (1996) and Bissell (2010) suggesting that the imperative of a stronger state should be more central to the discussion of the post-colonial transformation, especially at the city scale. They argue that Africa's malaise can be explained by the malformation and failure of the (local) government in Africa and its subsequent inability to exert sufficient power to define modern forms of urban citizenship. These views directly contrast those of equally persuasive urban historians such as Holston (1998) and Sandercock (1998), who point to insensitive, elitist, unworkable urban plans that fail to engage the realities of the urban poor. By this account, the negative impact of modernism on urban management in post-colonial contexts is the foundation of structural inequality and dysfunctionality in the contemporary city.

There are clearly well made points on both sides of these polarized debates. In affirming the need to return to a more active dialogue on the role of modern planning relative to other forms of city organization, we would highlight two points drawn from reflection on the African urban debate. First, the relationship between planning and modernism in the (post-) colonial context has been too narrowly drawn. This is not to contest that planning is a child of modernist thinking, for it obviously is, and modern planning may even have some African roots (Freund, 2007; Parnell, 1993; Wright, 1991). The problem is that urban planning is singled out as a special, negative case of modernism, implying an inappropriate conflation of modern urban land use and colonial conquest. It is true that Europeans used private property as an instrument of colonial subjugation at both the national and continental scale. It is also true that modernism introduced to colonial territories a system of urban land management – i.e. formal land registration under a cadastral system with individual tenure and property rights. This was then overlaid by an urban land use management (zoning and enforcement) and taxation system that impacted land values (the most comprehensive account of the export of colonial planning remains Home, 1997). It is, however, far from clear that conquest is the sole reason modernist urban planning was supported in colonial contexts, or that this is all that modernism achieved; there are numerous examples of urban reforms introduced through colonial housing and welfare policies (see Harris, 2003; Parnell and Mabin, 1995) and other aspects of modernity (e.g. modern science and medicine or engineering innovations such as traffic lights and electricity) that were happily embraced, and their adoption in the colonial context has never been the object of critique in the way that planning has been.

Scholars' tendency to concentrate only on oppressive examples of planning means that modernism is not represented in the same way in historical accounts of cities of the global North and South. In the North, modernism is widely recognized as having both reformist and repressive agendas and outcomes in shaping cities, most famously/notoriously, the unleashing of urban removals from slums while ushering in mass public housing and transportation systems and establishing municipal indigent support. This ambiguity regarding modernity is almost never acknowledged for the cities of the global South, and it may well be the reason that city scale state welfare interventions based on modern assumptions have not been pursued with any vigor (Freund, 2007).

The second reason for revisiting the role of modernism in the unequal and segregationist development of cities in the Global South is that the historical dominance of modernism in the evolution of these cities and their post-independence trajectories may well be overstated. There is a certain irony to identifying statutory planning, development controls and spatial planning as the source of all evil in cities, only to find that the local authority, equipped with its modernist tool bag, is far less powerful than the local chief, than foreign business, than the royal family, than the gangsters, than the church, than organised private business, and so on (Pieterse, 2008). Likewise, it is rarely, if ever, that an urban planner assumes more power within a municipal council than an engineer, finance officer or even medical officer. In sum, it seems that the power of the modern urban planner has been clearly overestimated as the force behind colonial urban inequalities and segregation (Parnell and Mabin, 1995). If this is true, then it is imperative to look beneath the surface and probe what – if not modernism – underpins the persistence of urban segregation and division. Using the case of South Africa, we suggest that the absence of a single, universal system of urban management ensures that segregation cannot be revoked. In other words, it is not modernism *per se* that is the problem, but the co-existence of modernism and alternative rationalities of urban control that are the vice-grip of enduring urban segregation.

Rethinking the legacy of modernity,
given the challenges of post-apartheid segregation

...[I]n many fundamental ways the South African debate has been trapped in an unhelpful tit-for-tat polemical exchange on something crucial to shaping how we respond to our challenges. The flippant dismissal of the weight of the past on our collective present is just as unhelpful as its opposite, a simplistic evocation of that past as an alibi for our own weaknesses. Both have tended to produce shallow explanations for the deep-seated challenges we confront.
(Cronin, 2012)

Understandably, given South Africa's apartheid history, the issue of space is difficult to uncouple from that of 'race,' making planning an obvious object of scrutiny in the search for ways to set the country on an alternative, less divided path (see Lemon, 1991, for an overview of the impact of segregation and its impact on the spatial organisation of South African cities). Almost two decades after the 1994 democratic elections, there is an increasingly urgent imperative to chip away at territorial segregation and advance the vision of 'the rainbow nation.' Within the government, almost every post-1994 policy document (national, provincial and local) highlights the importance of over-coming the spatial legacies of apartheid and, articulated in its place, a vision of racial spatial integration (Berrisford, 2011; Turok, 1994; Harrison *et al.*, 2008). The prominence given to overcoming 'race' in the first decade of democracy is also reflected in academic literature, where debate over the persistence, expansion or erosion of racial residential segregation post- formal apart-heid dominates local urban studies literature (Turok, 2001; Lemanski, 2006; Borel-Saladin and Crankshaw, 2009). Ironically, it may be that the form of the transformation debate that has highlighted the imperative of ending racial segregation has rendered impotent modernist planning efforts, such as the National Spatial Development Perspective (NSDP), which suggest pathways to reconstruction in ways that depart from an instrumentally desegregation-ist imperative (Berrisford, 2011). The NSDP, for example, proposes 'invest-ing in people, not places', thus rejecting a race-based or affirmative action approach to the reconstruction of historically African areas. The contentious policy debate that the passage of the NSDP unleashed in the late 2000s hinged on whether such rational spatial targeting of infrastructure investment could be justified. The argument that deprived ex-homeland areas – now under tra-ditional authority control – should be given preference over all other locations was motivated by a particularly racialised interpretation of the nation's history that (problematically) equated African and rural interests and ignored the fact that South African cities in the 21st century were overwhelmingly African, and in 1996, the census recorded that the majority of Africans in South Africa lived in urban areas (Figures 1 and 2).

The contemporary debate surrounding spatial policy then reproduces an old error. The assumption that South Africa's state policy kept Africans in townships or out of cities misses a fundamental point. Not all Africans were treated the same way, and a complex web of housing, land, job and other regulations shaped the life-course of an individual. Race was not the sole determining factor in how and where one lived in South Africa (Parnell and Mabin, 1995; Hindson, 1985). In the absence of race classification and racist planning laws, many of these divides – although formally repealed – persist.

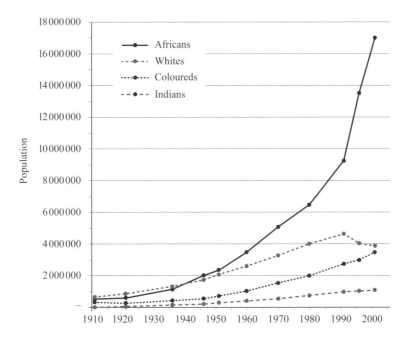

Figure 1   The changing racial composition of the urban population, 1911–2001. Sources: OCS (1922), OCS (1949, Tables 7 & 10), BCS (1955, Table 6), BS (1963, pp. 35, 40), DS (1976, pp. 32, 36 & 38) CSS (1985, pp. 89, 101, 112 & 113), CSS (1986, pp. 109, 111, 119, 120 & 128), CSS (1992, pp. 57, 64, 66, 71, 72, 75) and my own statistical analysis using the Census 1996 and Census 2001 Community Profiles Databases supplied by Statistics South Africa.

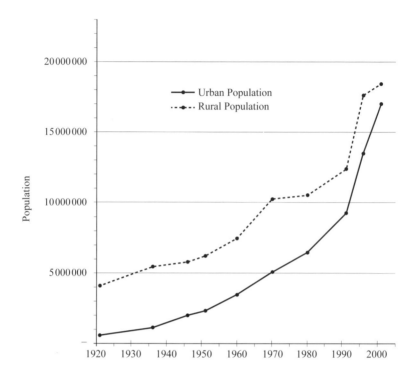

Figure 2   Trends in urban and rural African populations, 1921–2001.
Sources: See Figure 1.

    Colonialism and apartheid did not only separate black and white South Africans; they divided people within their race classifications using territorial manipulation. Table 1 provides an overview of the shifting focus of racial and racialised spatial policy before, during and after apartheid, revealing that the policy frame that underpinned spatial differentiation and partition of the population remains largely intact, especially at the national and intra-urban scale. Exclusionary regional and urban land management policy has not been fully repealed, presumably because it was not expressed in racist language and so has not attracted the attention of activists or Parliament. Space, a keystone of apartheid inequality, thus remains a curiously unreconstructed frontier of South African democracy. What this suggests is that there has been both a conceptual lack of understanding of how the management of space impacts social, political and environmental justice, and/or that there is an apparent absence of political will within government to change the spatial status quo.

Table 1   Spatial policy in South Africa, from pre-union to democracy
(continued on next page).

	Value base of spatial policy	National Scale	City-regional Scale	Intra-urban scale
Pre Union	Unification of Boer and Britton against black majority post Boer War, Cheap labour for mines and towns	Move towards unification of 2 colonies and 2 republics	Milner expanded Joburg boundaries way beyond contiguous settlement to incorporate peri-urban Afrikaners into urban government	Segregated townships emerge in all colonial towns using highly differentiated strategies
Post Union 1910–1939	White supremacy and racial partition between town and countryside and within cities Modernisation of the towns and de facto recognition of urban Africans	4 'white' provinces 1913 land act creates African reserves. The national tier of government has sectoral power (housing, health) over cities but lacks authority to impose residential or transport segregation.	Administrative autonomy of Provinces secured under 1910 constitution Administrative separation of black and white territory	Massive national legislation to keep most Africans out of town or segregate those working in towns, including Natives (Urban Areas) Act of 1923 and Housing Act 1920 Build high quality modern European cities for whites Cities can choose to apply segregationist laws but are obliged to house Africans working in towns
WW@ - early apartheid 1938-1965	White supremacy and racial partition between town and countryside and within cities Modernisation of the towns and commercial agriculture	4 'white' provinces 1913 land act amended, consolidates African reserves SEPC recommends centralisation of planning in national, via provinces to local and also control of housing by a national Planning Dept. Only achieved in diluted form in '64 with Dept. of Planning	SEPC recommends intro of regional planning to drive economic growth, distribute settlement away from main urban centres and introduce rational land use and natural resource planning; The regional plan to frame the town plan, not the other way around	Segregate though Natives Resettlement Act and Group Areas Act of 1950 Build inferior but modern cities for urban blacks Intra racial differentiation of housing standards (Fagan)

Table 1   *(Continued from previous page).*

	Value base of spatial policy	National Scale	City-regional Scale	Intra-urban scale
Late apartheid 1966–1985	Separate development of African and non-African people. Africans impermanent in town Absolute/Total ethnic and racial segregation within towns	African 'independence' of Bantustans Forced evictions from white farms Industrial decentralisation and secondary cities within 'homelands' Provincial Administration Boards dictate and monitor enforcement of segregation by local government	Separate spheres of governance for white and black South Africa persists	Group Areas Act enforcements Ethno linguistic zoning Locations in the sky Bantustan capitals constructed Bantu Administration Boards Regional Service Councils Racially separate municipalities for coloureds and Indians Free Settlement Areas
The transition and early democracy 1986-2004	1996 Constitution	New provinces and back-to-back local government NSDP vs. RIDS etc.	IGR legislation	New non-racial local government. Metropolitan municipalities to create one tax base and foster opportunities for intra-urban redistribution. Urban renewal nodes

Either explanation should raise concern among those wishing to raise the profile of space and the role of cities in national developmental debates.

It may well be that making a case for new regional and urban policy begins with a clearer understanding of how past spatial policies operated, and how remnants of these regimes interact with those that have been overlaid onto them as a result of new political orders. Historically, the state sought to influence the racial character of the spatial economy through the simultaneous manipulation of public investment, land regulation, housing provision and employment incentives by creating barriers and/or incentives at the national scale, the sub-national or city-regional scale and also within cities. In other words, racist tactics extended beyond excluding Africans from well-

resourced, 'modern' urban places and included intra-rural shifts such as evict-
ing farm workers, betterment schemes, and forced removals of villages and
racist intra-urban removals under the Natives (Urban Areas) Act, the Natives
Resettlement Act and Group Areas legislation. This multi-pronged planning
programme operated simultaneously across scales to achieve its ideological
and material objectives.

Table 1 also reveals that, in every phase, the government used a variety
tactics to regulate where and how people lived, based not only on the colour
of their skin, but also where labour was needed and on how much money was
available for housing and services. Some of these provisions have been eliminated – such as the subsidy for homeland capital city establishment and the
Group Areas Act – but others remain, i.e. the general absence of commercial
zoning in once-black residential areas.

The most enduring of the pillars of the segregated spatial economy
is thus a dual urban land use management system (Berrisford, 2011; Turok,
2001; Parnell, 2007). Notwithstanding the extension of local government to
all areas of the country in 1994, parallel land tenure and management systems
have remained in force. This occurs in the old Bantustans (where key aspects
of land tenure remain under the control of chiefs rather than the courts and
land registry) and in the once black townships (which have yet to be incorporated into municipal zoning schemes of the cities). Not only have the early
twentieth century segregation principles established by the 1913 Land Act
and the 1923 Natives (Urban Areas) Act been upheld, despite the repeal of
these laws, but the Development Facilitation Act (DFA) reinforces the notion
of separate development, albeit through the creation of opportunities to fast-
track inferior development for poor areas (Berrisford, 2011; Harrison et al.,
2008). In the post-apartheid period, this secondary circuit of land management
is justified as fast-tracking development in low-income areas, without regard
for what this means for the spatial economy over time (Harrison et al., 2008).

As Table 1 highlights, race-based classification was evident from the
early twentieth century, becoming an increasingly prominent feature of modern territorial policy. But it was not the only form of differentiation used to
designate where people could live. Especially among the African population,
other designations such as ethnicity or work status were used to signify place
of residence (Pirie, 1984). Despite concerted efforts by the post-apartheid
government to overcome these divisions, intra-racial and gender discrimination inequality remains (Beall et al., 2002). In the post-apartheid period,
while formal discrimination has ended, new migrants experience structural

exclusion from state benefits such as housing subsidies and better-paid urban jobs. These traditional cleavages of inequality have been overlain by new marginalisation, as foreign-born residents experience both formal and informal exclusion in urban and rural areas (Seekings and Nattrass, 2005).

Given that formal spatial discrimination ended nearly 20 years ago, one question persists: Why is the distribution of wealth still so physically skewed? Throughout the 1970s and 1980s, radical social scientists believed that apartheid was a quintessentially spatialised and racialised form of public policy that served the wider interests of capital through the structuring of the labour market (for an overview see Crankshaw, 1996). This interpretation was contested by liberal scholars, who highlighted the dysfunctionality and brutality of racist planning over its impact on the cost of the production or reproduction of labour (Lipton, 1984). Curiously, the issue of whose interests the present spatial form and standards of human settlement serves has largely dropped off the academic agenda, with issues of service delivery dominating the call for a more progressive urban developmental agenda.

In revisiting the spatial policies of the twentieth century, we wish to highlight the multiscalar nature of planning interventions and underline the fact that both overtly racial and covertly racialised mechanisms were invoked to craft the spaces that nurtured the country's unequal space economy. There has been inadequate follow-through on this multipronged spatial approach. In the flurry to address obvious housing and service backlogs (experienced largely by African people in old homeland areas), post-apartheid policy makers failed to recognise that inter- and intra-urban economic and infrastructural segregation were integrally connected. Ignoring this and focusing only on the national scale and on the social/infrastructural question led to rural bias post 1994. Thus, in spatial terms, the reconstruction and development years fed the segregationists' myth that Africans were rural people in need, and that cities were underserving affluent centres of 'the white man'. By ignoring the city, regional and intra-urban scales of spatial policy, economic opportunities for developmental intervention were missed. The problems of the rural service focus on national spatial reconstruction (for example, in the calculation of the equitable share) was compounded by the failure to recognise the increasingly African dominance of cities, or the fact that the majority of black South Africans now live in cities (Figures 1 and 2). The assumption that the apartheid space economy was an urban/rural distortion allowed actors like the Fiscal and Finance Commission to argue that apartheid legacies of inequality would be overcome most effectively by addressing rural backlogs. This conflation of urban versus rural and black versus white has clouded the efficacy of spatially targeted, anti-poverty action, potentially trapping people in apartheid poverty traps and undoubtedly stalling the debate on post-apartheid economic reconstruction.

The inability to resolve the imperative for new spatial prioritisation can, in part, be explained by the lack of general awareness of the role of regional and intra-urban policies in creating racialised hierarchies and divisions. By revisiting the different scales of spatial policy, it is possible to demonstrate how national, regional and intra urban territorial divisions were used simultaneously to foster the interests of capitalist development, divide and rule the black population and direct limited resources to the white elite. In other words, colonial/apartheid spatial policy was much more that the erosion of investment in (black) rural/homelands areas in conjunction with a massive investment in (white) cities. It was a sophisticated, differentiated economic policy that used the spatial dimension strategically to advance particular interests *within* as much as *between* urban and rural areas. This means that, even under apartheid, the divisions within race groups were as significant as those between race groups – and since democracy, inter-racial differentiation has become much more pronounced (Leibbrandt, Finn and Woolard, 2012). Overcoming this unequal spatial legacy therefore requires/ a multi-, as opposed to uni-, scale programme to foster shared growth in a manner that will not perpetuate the old distortions of a spatial economy that still favours a largely urban elite, and which has failed to disrupt established or emerging pockets of poverty.

What does a multiscale approach to reconstruction and development actually mean for South Africa's transition? A 2008 proposal by South African Cities Network to manage a National Spatial Economy Programme for the Presidency and the National Department of Provincial and Local Government clearly assumed urban/rural linkages to be important. Arguing that 'on the basis of dialogue with key stakeholders, the revised National Urban Development Framework *has to be rooted in an understanding of the national spatial economy as a whole, and has to recognise the complex pattern of economic, social and ecological connections and inter-relationships between urban, peri-urban and rural areas*'[2]. The interconnectivity of rural places, towns, secondary cities and city-regions was a substantial advance on the earlier

---

[2]   SACN, Proposal by South African Cities Network to manage a National Spatial Economy Programme for the Presidency and dplg, March 2008, (emphasis added).

policy focus of trying to erode white/black separation, but, if applied crudely, has its dangers. The first is that a city-region approach is conflated with the issue of circular migration, negating opportunities for positioning South African cities in their sub-continental and global economic context. In other words, it is an inward – not outward – perspective. The second is that depicting African identity as being somehow bound up in both urban and rural places negates the option of forging an unbridled, assurgent African urbanity (Bass, 2011).

So, in seeking an alternative to a desegregation agenda, urban linkages with the hinterland must be acknowledged. However, the relative importance given to urban-rural linkages and reasons for such an explicit, even dominant, focus must be substantiated and set against spatial dynamics that tie most African South Africans to urban areas. Moreover, if clear urban policy prescription, particularly regarding large cities, gets lost in the debate on circular migration and what to do with the former homelands, it will be a disservice to all those urban dwellers without rural linkages. New ways of thinking about the urban agenda cannot ignore these issues that haunt us from the past, but we cannot replace the ideological reductionism of desegregation with that of African traditionalism.

Conclusion

No one is suggesting that racial segregation is no longer a key moral or political issue for post-apartheid South Africa. Rather, in a temporal extension of the ideas first mooted by Parnell and Mabin (1995), the argument is that racial redress is not necessarily the best – or only – lens through which to address issues of spatial polarisation and inequality. In other words, just as modernist planning provided a non-racial construction for the design of apartheid, in post-apartheid South Africa, racial exclusion may no longer be codified in segregationist law, but the structural determinants of the social and economic fabric of inter- and intra-racial inequality remain embedded in racially 'neutral' or unspecified codes that frame the management of space. Thus, if we are to overturn structural inequality – whether with respect to race, class or gender – we have to, among other things, re-examine the institutions of governance that create and maintain spatial inequality.

Modernism in Emerging Cities: a 'Global-Modern' Concept?

A Theory of the Modern, Postmodern and Global City, and Its Effect on Cities of the Global South

Marie-Paule Thomas, Alexandra Thorer
Laboratory of Urban Sociology
Ecole polytechnique fédérale de Lausanne, Switzerland

We have arrived in history to a point where we can no more refer to any of the classical models – (the American, European or emerging Americanized Asian city models), as examples to guide our future [...] [but rather search] for contextual methods and models for building comprehensive, livable and equitable cities. Zegeye Cherenet, Ethiopian Architect, 2009

Introduction

What is the emerging urban struggle that megacities of the South are facing? In the previous part of this chapter, Susan Parnell and Owen Crankshaw address the issues of racial segregation, inequality and spatial polarization in cities of the Global South. Most notably, they point out the challenges and difficulties occurring in post-Apartheid urban areas – South African cities, which are challenged racially and spatially due to their governance and colonial past. They likewise strongly emphasize the importance of proper urban planning and of raising the awareness of planners in order to get them more involved in the shaping of the city. Parnell and Crankshaw question the role of modern urban planning on urban segregation and show, through the example of South Africa, that segregation is not only due to 'modernism per se [...] but [to] the co-existence of modernism and alternative rationalities of urban control' (*ibid.*:9). In this discussion, we examine the meaning of modernism in the urban context and what it implies in terms of city models. The second part of this chapter looks at the fabrication of the city – and theoretical models used – from an urban planner's point of view. We conclude with the theme of 'modernism' and how it can be understood in an urban context. What is urban modernity? What are the similarities and differences between cities of the 'North' and the 'South'? How does the North influence the South with regard to urban 'modernity'? Finally, we show that Modernity mainly refers to the classic models of the 'modern' and 'postmodern' city and, further, we argue that a new form of 'modernity' called 'global modernism' (a combination of the terms globalization and modernism) is emerging in the Global South.

The evolution of forms and new urban paradigms are indeed strongly linked to social changes and changing value systems. 'At the root of any pro- posed development, behind rationalizations or knowledge that claims to be truth, hide trends and value systems' (Choay, 1965). Society and its social dynamics use and transform the city. As P. Dehan (2006) explains, social pat- terns of the urban space evolve over time, over changes in customs and in society. The shapes of cities, whether specifically designed or more or less the spontaneous result of various dynamics, crystallize and reflect the logic of the societies contained therein'.

According to Comeroff and Comeroff (2012), cities of the Global South may also be referred to as 'post-colonial' cities, as the majority of these coun- tries have been occupied by European powers. The colonial urban policies and planning models implemented have shaped these cities and societies, rais- ing the question of how these urban models were integrated, to what extent they are still valid today and how this has affected the people (and society). However it is not only the colonial past that has influenced and is influencing current changes in urban development; the pace at which African cities are developing today is hard to keep up with. Emerging markets like the BRICS nations are new to the game among the 'traditional' Western players, and play a key role in Africa's urban development by way of economic investments and major construction projects. The situation that cities of the Global South are currently facing is that of the 'global-modern' city, as they are increasingly becoming a part of the global economic network. One of the characteristics underlying these planning models is the relationship between inhabitants' uses and urban and architectural forms. This recurring question of planning actors goes beyond borders and the evolution of cities: must lifestyles adapt to urban models, or should urban models adapt to the lifestyles and uses of inhabitants? Like Genard (2009), we link the evolution of architecture and planning to two key models. On the one hand, the *Modern* city embodied as much in hygienic and functionalist models as in the city-world, which incorporates the precepts of modern urban planning into a global logic. On the other hand, the *postmodern* (or 'authentic') city is inspired by culturalist urban planning and is centered around context, place and use. These figures, or 'city models', exist in both European and American cities and cities of the Global South. We present here these three models and explore their presence in Southern cities, with a special focus on Addis Ababa, as we posit that a certain form of all three models of 'modernisms' are to be found in Ethiopia's capital city.

The modern city

Rationalization, hygiene and colonialization

The first model is that of the Modern City, with a strong focus on hygiene, rationalization, construction and functionalism. The modernization of cities (Dehan, 2006) responds to a collective demand (from the ruling class, most notably) for an orderly, functional city that meets its needs, but also is a reflection of it. Born by the elites, these principles spread throughout European cities and, later through colonialism, to emerging countries. Following the massive rural exodus, the Industrial Revolution was accompanied by a massive increase in the urban population, resulting in overcrowding in popular areas and chaotic development of the city. Due to poor urban sanitation and lack of hygiene, epidemics developed rapidly. In the 18th and 19th centuries, such considerations led to the emergence of hygienic thinking, first in Northern countries and, later, in Southern countries following industrialization. During specific eras in post-industrial cities, such as Paris in the 1850s, Boston in the 1880s, Vienna in the 1900s and Berlin in the 1920s, these cities grew rapidly and were considered synonymous with new and modern ways of life (McKinnon, 2011). This modernity slowly shifted to the rapidly emerging countries, notably in Asia. Today, it is cities such as Shanghai, Hong Kong and New Delhi that are confronted with a new form of modernity, developed through socio-economic and urban growth. However, colonialism in African cities largely contributed to spreading this hygienic utopic vision among colonial elites and subsequently to the indigenous ruling classes that succeeded them. Through the examples of Dakar and Kigali, Benjamin Michelon (2012) shows that, upon their arrival, colonial authorities implemented urban planning documents prescribing segregation. This 'colonial modernity' relied on the establishment of an urban scheduling based on hygienic and militaristic principles specific to the establishment of a city in a landscape still strongly characterized by rurality. Clean, straight streets were mainly home to the infrastructure of the ruling power – in other words, imposing buildings manifesting the presence of colonial power in the making. These developments characterize the technical progress of European industrial society at that time (Michelon, 2012).

The Athens Charter: the urban development of plans and segregation

Following the development of hygienic thinking, architectural and urban-planning modernism emerged, fueled by the precepts of Le Corbusier and the Athens Charter. We find in this urban development model a certain recurrence—the spatial separation of places of work and places of residence. Functionality, strongly influenced by rationalist thinking, was the watchword for the organization of the city. The urban space, as Françoise Choay explains, was divided according to an analysis of human functions. A kind of rigorous classification of distinct places of residence, work, culture and leisure activities developed (Choay, 1965). Modernist urban planners valued the individual, with his universal needs and unique standard of comfort. The old city was banished and bisected by tracks and other equipment to enable more fluid travel. Urban functions were organized rationally: 'A certain rationalism, science [and] technology should help solve the problems of man's relationship with the world and with each other' (Choay, 1965).

Since decolonization, urban development plans in African cities have followed these Modernist precepts by virtue of their realization by Europeans, according to the logic of technology transfer between North and South. Local authorities did not engage in planning approaches specific to African cities until the 2000s. However, these approaches are inspired by planning based on hypotheses and theories from North countries (Harrison, 2006) to respond to the development of slums. According to Michelon (2012), segregative planning leads to the development of a dual city wherein a functionalist view prevails. Housing developments appear to be the mode par excellence of construction for new residential neighborhoods, but they are also a tool for speculation, resulting in the exodus of the poorest inhabitants to undeveloped sites. 'Although the dominant global trend is to evict the poor from city centers, some Third World cities have instead resorted to American-style segregation, with the post-colonial middle classes fleeing from the core to gated suburbs and so-called 'edge-cities" (Davis, 2006). For instance, in Johannesburg, most corporate offices and upscale stores have relocated to the white northern suburbs. The central business district, once considered Africa's financial capital, has become a center for illegal trading and local micro-enterprises, due to the mixture of slum and middle-class apartment complexes (Beall, Crankshaw and Parnell, 2002; Davis, 2006).

These urban models convey some idea of the standards and norms, modeled after an average citizen from a developed country, which is antithetical to the customs and ways of living in local contexts. 'This is part of the global process of imposing regulations to promote a modern city, ignoring the customs and practices of urban residents in these regions' (Michelon, 2012). Parnell and Crankshaw, moreover, point out that 'the scale of urban problems and the enduring inequalities are related to the past regimes', and that 'it is not difficult to understand why planning has been discredited, especially in the Southern cities of Africa, Asia and Latin America (2002:6).

Throughout the history of cities, it has been through modern planning that elites have controlled the development of the informal city. However, the modern city is not the only figure that has guided the evolution of the world cities. A critical theory arose in the latter part of the 20th century in reaction to 'modernism', especially within the academic community.

The postmodern city

The Authentic City/The City of Places/The City of Uses

The second model is the Postmodern City. Starting in the 1960s and 1970s, in parallel with social movements and the shift towards post-Industrial society, a period of 'critique of reason' (Genard, 2009) developed around postmodernism, with a return to old urban forms, according to Genard. This trend was linked to the emergence of values of authenticity, a formalization of the 'authentic' city – widely extolled by Jane Jacobs – and later the sustainable, ecological city, which coincided with the growing number of environmental movements. The return to the 'authentic' city put 'spirit of place' and context at the heart of its argument. In her book *The Death and Life of Great American Cities*, Jane Jacobs (1961) detailed the impact of modernist urban planning ideology, which separates uses of the city and emphasizes free-standing individual buildings, and eventually put an end to urban space and city life, resulting in lifeless cities devoid of people.

In response to the Modern Movement in architecture, anthropological and culturalist considerations with regard to living spaces saw a dramatic increase starting in the 1960s, with active research on neighborhoods and types of housing as cultural areas and communities as a reflection of specific lifestyles. 'These culturalist movements often contrasted with a technocratic vision of the city, taking into account neither its communities nor its history, showing the specificity of certain places and the conditions of appropriation of the city by social groups and their non-material urban needs' (Fijalkow, 2004). Contrary to the modernist movement, this trend showed that humans are not universal and interchangeable, and that the way people use the city is linked to their attitudes and social organization, which evolve based on different social factors. Beyond the most basic requirements (eating, sleeping and shelter from the elements), an individual's needs vary according to culture[3], values and lifestyle (Dehan, 2006). In all of these works (Jacobs, 1961; Lynch, 1960; Alexander *et al.*, 1977; Rapoport and Sayegh, 2003), the human being is at the heart of the spatial analyses. Rapoport and Sayegh (2003), for example, propose exploring the mutual influence of the physical characteristics of the built environment and the characteristics of individuals, thereby making a connection between values, lifestyle and a system of settings. In order to link lifestyles and dwellings, Rapoport conceptualizes lifestyle as an activities system that takes place in a system of settings, and proposes that we observe where and how activities unfold. 'Therefore, the units we should compare are not the two houses, but the systems of settings in which particular systems of

---

[3] "According to Tylor (1871), "culture is a complex ensemble that includes knowledge, beliefs, art, law, morals, customs and all other aptitudes and habits acquired by an individual as a member of society" (quoted by Rapoport and Sayegh, 2003, and Kroeber and Kluckhohn, 1952).

activities take place'. In this urban planning and architectural movement, the emphasis is on architectural and planning proposals that are more respectful of context and 'the identity of places' (i.e. densification, plot size, return to the street, open block, architectural vernacular, quest for sustainability). With the notion of the 'sustainable city' came the social and environmental aspects of development. 'Today, the vision of sustainable development (in Kigali) and the fight against poverty (in Douala) alike are cited as paths to follow in order to reduce disparities and help bridge the gap between the city of places and the city of flows, without necessarily offering a clear or precise definition of these concepts' (Michelon, 2012).

To summarize, the city was influenced by two major developmental phases of architecture and urban planning – the modern city and the postmodern city, both of which were strongly linked to changes in society and value systems. The evolution of the city is consistent with different sociological theoretical positions. Under the influence of the first modernity and determinative rationality, urban theories of hygiene, rationalism and functionalism prevailed. With the shift to postmodernism and the emergence of social movements in developing countries, a new relationship to place was born, giving preference and attention to place, context and the daily practices of inhabitants, and bringing life back into the culturalist movement.

The global-modern city

From Global City to Emerging Global City: a new city concept based on 'global-modernism'?

The concepts of the modern and postmodern city can be placed in a specific timeframe, starting from the beginning of the 20th century until 1970. Today, however, determining what era we are in seems to be a more difficult exercise. Terms such as 'post-post-modernism' (Turner, 1995), 'transmodernism' (Epstein and Genis, 1999) and 'meta-modernism' (Vermeulen and van den Akker, 2010) aim to define new critical theories in art, architecture and philosophy, while attempting to move away from postmodern and modern approaches. Currently, in the reality of the built environment, modernity is embodied in the 'globalized city'. As Manuel Castells points out (2000), we have entered the era of the network society, having shifted from agricultural and industrial society. The network society today, a result of the globalization process, may be defined as the increase and intensification of worldwide economic and social relations. With globalization, the conditions of the economic system and global politics are changing, and territories are being reevaluated and selectively integrated into the international economics network. Hence, specific cities are experiencing a role change relative to the global economy, and no longer function as national or regional centers. Such cities are referred to as *global cities* (Sassen, 2001)[4]. American sociologist Saskia Sassen continued to build on this theory in her book *The Global City* (2001 [1991]). According to Sassen, cities classified as global cities impose a drastic change within the context of their social structure. This structure is shaped by the polarization of income distribution as well as a new form of migration (Sassen, 2001). To quote English geographer David Harvey, whose research examines the link between urbanization and capitalism, 'At this point in history, this has to be a global struggle, predominantly with finance capital, for what is the scale at which urbanization processes now work' (Harvey, 2008).

According to Harvey, global capitalism is the ultimate determinant of urban futures. The transition to network society is characterized by the development of urban marketing and communication architecture (Lacaze, 1995). In terms of urban and architectural form, these models re-examine the achievements of modernism – moving toward global-modernism. It is the 'city of entertainment', the cultural and cosmopolitan city, born with the advent of the culture and entertainment industries. Cities compete for the spotlight, doing frenzied urban marketing, of which iconic, ostentatious architecture (most notably in the form of ever-higher towers) is the symbol.

Yet, there is another form of globalization emerging, as the population in the Global South grows and its cities expand. Unlike the 'global city' concept supported by Friedmann, Sassen and others, cities in the South have developed a unique form of globalization since independence from colonial rule. Exploring inter-ethnic relations in Cairo, Beirut, Istanbul, Bukhara, Lhasa, Delhi, Singapore, Kuala Lumpur and Tokyo, Shail Mayaram (2008) uses the term 'the other global city', looking at the importance of the growing number of emerging cities. It is clear that even developing cities in the Global South are giving rise to a new type of global city, emerging global city, other global city or 'neo-global' city. However, in spite of this phenomenon, these

---

[4]   Based on the 'World-City-Hypothesis' by John Friedmann (1986).

cities do not create their own economic powerhouse (through industrialization, agriculture, etc.). Rather, they cultivate their urbanity based on economic investments from more developed (global) cities, which raises the question of how investment by stronger socioeconomic nations affects local development, social structure, etc., in emerging cities.

The following pictogram illustrates the dynamics among the global cities during the 1990s and their role in the global context today (left) and the influence they exert on the growth of emerging global cities (right).

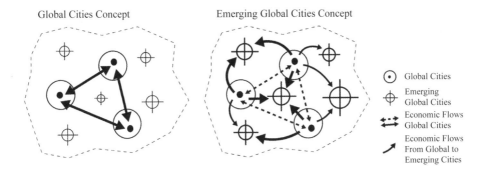

Figure 3   Pictogram concept of Global Cities and Emerging Global Cities.
(Pictogram by A. Thorer, September 2013)

That emerging cities of the Global South are rapidly urbanizing is fact that cannot be ignored. Parnell and Crankshaw begin their article by stating that 'the explosion of growth in cities of the developing world is, somewhat belatedly, being followed by a renaissance in thinking about cities beyond the West and the nature of the barriers to their equitable development' (*ibid.*:1), thus paving the way for what follows.

The term *urbanization* is often directly equated with urban growth as a result of a) natural population increase, b) migration from rural to urban areas and c) urban expansion, such that suburban areas become urban (Cohen, 2006; McKinnon, 2011). Yet today, due to increasing overpopulation, the pace of urbanization is faster than that of urban planning, and cities are faced with the social, economic and environmental consequences in the form of poverty, pollution and insufficient urban infrastructure (water, electricity, etc.). This leaves urban governance with a daunting challenge, as more than half of the world's population is now living in urban settlements. This number will increase to 75% over the next 40 years (UN, 2006; Burdett and Sudjic, 2010), with an exponential growth in the 'underdeveloped' South.

Thus, the urban question becomes a global one – the link between urban forms and urban society, shaped by the homogenizing impact of global flows of capital, people and energy (Castells, 2000).

Due to poor educational systems, economic hardship, political instability and historical struggles, African cities must work together with developed nations to build and modernize to keep pace with growth. The influence on development and investment is strong, and the requisite importing of knowledge from abroad 'de-Africanizes' the urban traditions of the 'African City'[5]. This results in the adoption of non-indigenous building styles, creating a kind of trans-African mono-skyline of high-rises. The city's overall appearance seems modern, as it follows the modern urban structure of homogeneous functional zoning, dominant commercial centers and a steady decline in land value from the urban center to rural suburbia.

> Throughout Africa, especially in the Sudan, Angola and Ethiopia, it is a desire to copy or import an urban model and thereby align with certain economies linked with capital and power. The cut-and-paste-method used in Ethiopia and other parts of Africa implies that buildings designed for one location can be copied and imported to another, regardless of climate, form, or orientation. Existing context becomes irrelevant in the cut-and-paste method, because the buildings are designed for immediate modernization. (Stoll in Angelil and Hebel, 2010)

One wonders whether the implementation of architecture, planning models and governance models can be considered urban 'cut-and-paste'.

In the following section we will discuss the phenomena occurring in the modern city, postmodern City, and global-modern city based on one city – Addis Ababa, Ethiopia's capital – which seems to embody certain aspects of all of these modernisms.

---

[5]   The 'African City' is defined here as a non-(post-)colonial, large African city that was relatively uninfluenced in its urban structure during the colonial occupation.

Urban transition: from postmodernism (via modernism) to global-modernism?

The three pictograms below show the pattern of urban changes in Addis Ababa with respect to the three theoretical models discussed above. We see the city's evolution as it goes from an unplanned settlement (postmodern elements) to a site with modern architecture and urban planning (modern approaches) to what we have today: wide-scale development (global-modern implementations). The three urban modernisms in Addis Ababa are:

II   Postmodern elements: *mixcity*[6], unsegregated, unplanned city

I   Modern approaches: new architecture, urban planning, colonial occupation

III   Global-modern implementations: building boom, foreign/"global" architecture, mega-projects, zoning the city

Traditional pattern/
Post-modern elements

Attempt to modernity/
Modern approches

Segregation/ "Global-Modern"
implementations

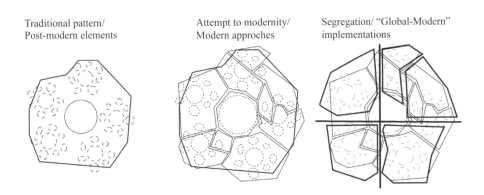

Figure 4   Pattern of urban transition of unplanned, developing cities. An abstract example of Addis Ababa. (Pictogram by A. Thorer, September 2013)

---

6   The term "mixcity," a combination of the words "mixity" and "city" is, for example, used by Ethiopian architect and historian Fasil Gioghis, the ETHZurich (Swiss Federal School of Technology Zurich) and the EiABC (Ethiopian Institute of Architecture, Building Construction and City Development).

Traditional Pattern: 'Mixcity' – city for people

Ethiopia's capital city, Addis Ababa, is unique among large capital cities in Africa. Because of its uncolonialized past and indigenous settlement structure, Addis Ababa is the urban definition of *mixity* or *mixcity* – a city where all functions, economic and social aspects of urbanity are within close proximity. Unlikely for the majority of planned post-colonial cities in the Global South, Addis Ababa's urban pattern has been largely unsegregated. Institutions such as embassies and university departments are scattered throughout the city, literally side by side with informal settlements; the poor live next to the rich, sharing the same space, and social networks, homes and work places lie in proximity. This form of urban diversity is crucial in terms of transportation costs, slumification, etc. (Baumeister and Knebel, 2009). Addis Ababa had never been a city with a fixed structure, but rather an assemblage of villages that amalgamate. In terms of governance, the city is still built on this concept, with its so-called *kebeles*, which are local sub-districts within the city. The more than 17,000 *kebeles* in Ethiopia form the foundation of the structure, where urban services (electricity, water, telecommunications, education, roads, etc.) are addressed.

Attempts to modernism

The postmodern significance of 'a city for people' (Gehl, 2010), however, is steadily vanishing due to Addis Ababa's current rapid growth and the city's master planning. 'Modernization', 'modernity' and 'modern city' are concepts the city aims to follow for its future development.

In the boom-period of the 1960s, the decade during which most African countries gained their independence, Addis Ababa was nominated as Africa's capital city[7]. In order to live up to such a tall order, it was necessary to modernize the city using the newest building materials and construction techniques, as well as to spark an urban 'renaissance'. Traditional Ethiopian architecture is mainly comprised of wood and stone elements, which needed to be adapted in order to be consistent with modern architectural design. A number

---

[7]   The OAU (Organization of African Unity) was established in 1963, with its founding seat in Addis Ababa.

of modern public, governmental and apartment buildings were erected during this era and still stand today, serving the same functions.

Foreign investments + rapid development = 'global-modernism'

Today, the city – in one of the fastest growing economies and urban centers worldwide – is expanding at an irrational rate. Its face has drastically changed, from small, dense, slum-like dwellings to glass-facade high-rises alongside the city's newly expanded road network. With its 5-year master plans and 'clean up the city' program, new architectural and urban infrastructure development focuses on modernizing the city by creating economic spaces to attract local and foreign investors, accommodating new housing and zoning – an urban structure Addis Ababa has never experienced before.

Foreign actors have had a strong impact on Addis Ababa's urban development. Countries, such as China, who are responsible for constructing the majority of Addis Ababa's road and rail networks, as well as developing its telecommunications network. International companies are building high-rises for housing, offices, hotel chains and other businesses. These mega-projects have changed the face of the urban landscape and social environment.

Despite the positive goals the city is achieving, there are a number of challenges it must resolve in order to grow as a sustainable city in Africa. As in other emerging mega-cities, Addis Ababa still faces poverty, water and energy scarcity, pollution and increasing population growth. Due to 'modern' planning and re-zoning of the city this may develop into spatial and perhaps even social segregation.

The move to segregation: a result of 'global-modernism'?

A look at the overall picture shows that the city is gradually being divided. Poor, historical areas with a slum-typology[8] (UN Habitat, 2008) have been more or less eradicated to make room for modern high-rises (shopping malls,

---

[8] The UN defined Addis Ababa as a city consisting of 80% slum-dwellings (2008). It should be noted, however, that this housing typology (mud houses) does not necessarily reflect typical slum characteristics in terms of social status, income or levels of crime.

apartment complexes and luxury hotels). The majority of the inhabitants of these areas have been relocated to the city's outskirts, where extensive residential complexes have been built in recent years to respond to the urgent need for housing. Torn from their social environment, the community has been forced to create a new network within a new environment. Public transportation and road infrastructure in and to these areas have not yet been adequately developed, and schools, hospitals, public spaces and green spaces are lacking. Without proper governance, planning, infrastructure and transportation, such displacements may also slowly lead to exclusion and slumification.

Modern segregation: Housing complexes with thousands of apartment units stretching for kilometers along the newly constructed main road that heads west from Addis Ababa. (Photograph by A. Thorer, March 2013)

Modern segregation: Aerial view of housing complexes on the outskirts of Addis Ababa. (Photograph by A. Thorer, June 2013)

But social relocation is not the only struggle Addis Ababa is likely to be facing in the near future. Infrastructural mega-projects in the road and future urban rail sectors create physical divisions within existing neighborhoods and urban structures. In 1998, the city had Chinese contractors build a ring road[9] to divert traffic around the city, which – in addition to the useful dimension of regulating the increasing traffic due to the ever-growing numbers of vehicles – has divided communities and affected their livelihoods (urban accessibility, commuter traffic and safety, as pedestrians are forced to illegally cross this urban highway).

In recent years, new forms of social and religious segregation have taken shape among the Ethiopian population. Addis Ababa, once a city where religious beliefs and social classes lived side by side in relatively harmony, is experiencing increasing self-segregation by individual groups – though it is as yet unclear whether it is for reasons of religious contention, to create a sense of community belonging, or simply for economic reasons. What is happening in Addis Ababa – as in many unplanned cities in the Global South – is that the urban landscape is changing from a 'mixcity' (postmodern city) to a planned 'modern city' through functional inner-city zoning. Historical buildings and spaces are being destroyed to make room for the development of new high-rises, road networks and rail systems – primarily built by foreign contractors ('global-modern' city).

The desire to preserve Addis Ababa – or at least its essence – likewise reflects the desire to preserve its distinctive diversity, to return to the original village-like structure and promote *mixcity* – 'the fact that, in most districts, people of different social classes live side by side as neighbors'[10].

One could even claim that Addis Ababa's former socio-urban patterns reflect Jane Jacobs' (1961) stance of the need for urban diversity, human scales and proximity of functions in cities. The well being of our cities lies in a comprehensive understanding of the relationship between the built environment (housing, buildings, transport, infrastructure, streets and public space) and the social, economic and political processes that give rise to them.

---

[9]   Completed by Chinese contractors in 2003, conceptual plans for a ring road around the city were first developed during the time of the Emperor, in the 1950s.

[10] Interview with Fasil Giorghis in *Perpectives* # 3.12, p. 11.

Conclusion

What would the most effective planning process be for emerging cities in the Global South?

On the one hand, in the example of post-apartheid South Africa, 'modernist planning provided a non-racial construction for the design of apartheid', as Parnell and Crankshaw conclude their paper, after arguing 'that Modernism's negative impact on segregationist city development in the Global South may have been more muted and or varied than typically depicted... using the notion that the nature of the relationship between modernism and segregation has been misunderstood' (*ibid.*:4). The strong arguments for this unusual approach are insightful, and simultaneously give rise to a new perspective with regard to the relationship between modernist planning and (urban) segregation.

For this article we attempted to follow Parnell and Crankshaw's recommendation with regard to imagining a 'more egalitarian and less divided urban future' (*ibid.*:4), attempting to 'define' the three directions of modernity from an urban planning perspective, whereas the global-modernity neologism is more in keeping with an observation of what is going on in terms of globalization as a whole (i.e. segregation, urban development and socio-economic ties).

The example of Addis Ababa was solely chosen to broach Parnell and Crankshaw's notion. However, like the two authors, we conclude that what is important is a sustainable urban future.

In general, to remain in keeping with Parnell and Crankshaw's position, it is important to avoid top-down governance, using a variety of models and development approaches aimed at 'good development' – from in-depth ethnological and ethnographical work to large-scale surveys. With regard to post-apartheid South African cities, the issue of segregation, as mentioned in the first part of this chapter, is a key concern for urban governance and urban planning. Crankshaw and Parnell conclude that 'institutions of governance that create and maintain spatial inequality' need to be re-examined (*ibid.*:18).

As segregation is not exclusively spatial or racial, the focus needs to be on developing education, infrastructure, the economy and the environment, to avoid its perpetuation in these areas. This interconnectivity was likewise addressed in the South African Cities Network Proposal of 2008. As Crankshaw and Parnell observe (*ibid.*:16), in order to understand the 'national spatial economy as a whole [one] has to recognize the complex pattern of economic, social and ecological connections and inter-relationships between urban, peri-urban and rural areas'. On the urban planning level, urban planners need to create a new form of planning for cities in the Global South. Classic modern master planning does not provide a platform for people to develop their environment but operates around a small group of decision-makers determining urban form and progress. One approach may be to rethink zoning schemes and replace master planning with strategic planning. This includes clarifying which urban model is anticipated, integrating the public with the private sector, adapting to new circumstances and improving citizens' living conditions.

Clearly, modernization is important for the development process of rapidly emerging cities where basic infrastructures are not yet fully developed. But what *is* modernization? 'Modernizing' a city is not necessarily synonymous with creating a 'modern city'[11], but in many (African) eyes, modernization means development, which essentially consists of the construction of buildings, road and rail, and thereby a 'modern city' or 'global-modern city'.

We wish to clarify that we are not *against* 'global-modern' development or the 'modernization' of cities, but feel it is necessary to raise the awareness of the importance of postmodern elements within urban development to build a 'city of uses' – a true 'city for people' (Gehl, 2010).

What emerging cities of the Global South urgently need – be it Addis Ababa or South African cities – is to utilize the opportunities afforded by local development, economic growth, increasing political stability and the positive outcomes of globalization, in order to develop into sustainable, intelligent, functional, ecological, diverse cities: cities that can shape the people of the future and vice versa. The 'global-modern' cities that seem to be emerging in the Global South undoubtedly need to develop planning tools and specific forms of governance in order to design and build cities with more social and spatial equality. Above and beyond questions relative to the segregative mechanisms of modern planning, we should consider the emergence of new forms of urban modernity that call for specific planning tools more oriented toward the investigation of uses and lifestyles.

---

[11] Discussion "Addis Modern: Re-discovering the 1960s Architecture" Presentation at Goethe-Institut Addis Ababa, May 21st, 2013.

48   Planning

References

Alexander, C., Jacobson, M., Ishikawa, S. and Silverstein, M. (1977) *A Pattern Language: Towns, Buildings, Construction*. Oxford University Press, New York.

Angelil, M. and Hebel, D. (ed.) (2010) *Cities of Change Addis Ababa: Transformation Strategies for Urban Territories in the 21st Century*. Birkhäuser, Basel.

Bass, O. (2011) Palimpsest African Urbanity: Connecting Precolonial and Postapartheid Urban Narratives in Durban. *Social Dynamics* 37, 125–147.

Baumeister, J., and Knebel, N. (2009) The Indigenous Urban Tissue of Addis Ababa – A City Model for the Future Growth of African Metropolis. *Proceedings of African Perspectives*, 157–160.

BCS. (1955). *Population census 8th May 1951, Vol.1: Geographical distribution of the population of the Union of South Africa*. South African Bureau of Census and Statistics, Pretoria.

Beall, J., Crankshaw, O., and Parnell, S. (2002) *Uniting a Divided City: Governance and Social Exclusion in Johannesburg*. Earthscan, London.

Berrisford, S. (2011) Apartheid spatial planning legislation in South Africa. *Urban Forum* 22, 247–263.

Bissel, W. (2010) *Urban Design, Chaos and Colonial Power in Zanzibar*. Indiana University Press, Bloomington.

Borel Saladin, J. and Crankshaw, O. (2009) Social Polarisation or Professionalisation? Another Look at Theory and Evidence on Deindustrialisation and the Rise of the Service Sector. *Urban Studies* 46, 645–664.

BS (1963) *Population census 6th September, 1960, Volume 1: Geographical distribution of the population*. Bureau of Statistics, Pretoria.

Burdett, R. and Sudjic, D. (2010) *The Endless City*. Phaidon, Berlin.

Castells, M. (2000) *The Rise of the Network Society* 1. Blackwell Publishers, Oxford.

Chatterjee, P. (2006) *The Politics of the Governed: Reflections on Popular Politics in Most of the World*. Columbia University Press, New York.

Cherenet, Z. (2009) The Next Urban Explosion in Ethiopia. *Construction Ahead* Sept.–Dec., 16–17.

Choay, F. (ed.) (1965) *L'urbanisme: utopies et réalités: une anthologie*. Seuil, Paris.

Cohen, B. (January 2006) Urbanization in Developing Countries: Current Trends, Future Projections, and Key Challenges for Sustainability. *Technology in Society* 28, 1–2, 63–80.

Comaroff, J. and Comaroff, J. L. (2012) Theory from the South: Or, How Euro-America is Evolving Toward Africa. *Anthropological Forum* 22, 113–131.

Coquery-Vidrovitch, C. (2005) *The History of African Cities South of the Sahara: From the Origins to Colonization.* Marcus Wiener, Princeton.

Crankshaw, O. (1996) *Race, Class, and the Changing Division of Labour Under Apartheid.* Routledge, London.

Crankshaw, O. (2008) Race, Space and the Post-Fordist Spatial Order of Johannesburg". *Urban Studies* 45, 1692–1711.

CSS. (1985) *Population census 1980: Geographical distribution of the population with a review for 1951-1980, Report no. 02-80-13 (1980).* Central Statistical Service, Pretoria.

CSS. (1986) *Population census 1985: Geographical distribution of the population, Report No. 02-85-01.* Pretoria: Central Statistical Service, Pretoria.

CSS. (1992) *Population Census 1991: Geographical distribution of the population with a review for 1970-1991, Report no. 03-01-02 (1991).* Central Statistical Service, Pretoria.

Davis, M. (2006) *Planet of Slums.* Verso.

Dehan, P. (2006) *Introduction à l'urbanisme. Notes de cours.* Université de Technologie de Compiègne.

Demissie, F. (ed.) (2012) *Colonial Architecture and Urbanism in Africa: Intertwined and Contested Histories.* Ashgate, London.

DS 1976: *Population census 1970: Geographical distribution of the population, Report no. 02-05-10.* Department of Statistics, Pretoria.

Epstein, M. and Genis, A. (1999) *Russian Postmodernism: New Perspectives on Post-Soviet Culture.* Berghahn Books.

Ferguson, J. (1994) *The Anti-Politics Machine: Development, Depoliticization, and Bureaucratic Power in Lesotho.* University Of Minnesota Press, Minneapolis.

Ferguson, J. (1999) *Expectations of Modernity: Myths and Meanings of Urban Life on the Zambian Copperbelt.* University of California Press, Berkeley.

Fijalkow, Y. (ed.) (2004) *Sociologie de la ville.* La Découverte, Paris.

Freund, W. (2007) *The African City: A History.* Cambridge University Press, Cambridge.

Friedmann, J. (2005) *China's Urban Transition.* University of Minnesota Press, Minneapolis.

Friedmann, J. (1986) World-City-Hypothesis. *Development & Change* 17.1, 69–83.

Gehl, J. (2010) *Cities for People.* Island Press, Washington, D.C.

Genard, J.-L. (2009) *Architecture et réflexivité*. Les cahiers de la Cambre.

Harris, R. (2003) A Mixed Message: The Agents and Forms of International Housing Policy, 1945–1973. *Habitat International*, 167–191.

Harrison, P., Todes, A. and Watson, V. (2008) *Planning and Transformation: Learning from the Post Apartheid Experience.* Routledge, London.

Harrison, P. (2006) On the Edge of Reason: Planning and Urban Futures in Africa. *Urban Studies* 43, n° 2, 319–335.

Harvey, D. (2008) The Right to the City. *New Left Review* 53, 23–40.

Healey, P. (2007) *Urban Complexity and Spatial Strategies: Towards a relational planning for our times*. Routledge, London.

Hindson, E. (1985) South Africa: a Personal Observation. *Fundamentalist Journal* 4.7, 60–72.

Holson, J. (1998) *Insurgent Citizenship: Disjunctions of Modernity and Democracy in Brazil*. Princeton University Press, Princeton.

Home, R. (1997) *Of Planting and Planning: The Making of British Colonial Cities*. E and FN Spon/Chapman Hill, London.

Jacobs, J. (1961) *The Death and Life of Great American Cities*. Random House, New York.

Lacaze, J.-P. (ed.) (1995) *La ville et l'urbanisme*. Collection Dominos 78. Flammarion, Paris.

Leibbrandt, M., Finn, A. and Woolard, I. (2012) Describing and decomposing post-apartheid income inequality in South Africa. *Development Southern Africa* 29.1, 19–34.

Lemanski, C. (2006) Desegregation and Integration as Linked or Distinct? Evidence from a Previously 'White' Suburb in Post-apartheid Cape Town. *International Journal of Urban and Regional Research* 30, 564–86.

Lemon, A. (1991) *Homes Apart: South Africa's Segregated Cities.* Paul Chapman, London.

Lipton, M. (1984) *Capitalism and Apartheid: South Africa, 1910–1986*. New Africa Books.

Lynch, K. (1960) *The Image of the City*. The Technology Press. Harvard University Press, Cambridge.

Mamdani, M. (1996) *Citizen and Subject: Contemporary Africa and the Legacy of Late Colonialism.* Princeton University Press, Princeton.

Mayaram, S. (ed.) (2008) *The Other Global City*. Routledge, London.

McFarlane, C. (2012) Rethinking Informality: Politics, Crisis, and the City. *Planning Theory & Practice* 13, 89–108.

McKinnon, M. (2011) Asian Cities: Globalization, Urbanization and Nation-Building. *NIAS Monograph Series* 120. Nias Press, Copenhagen.

Michelon, B. (2012) Planification urbaine et usages des quartiers précaires en Afrique: étude de cas à Douala et à Kigali. Ecole polytechnique fédérale de Lausanne, Lausanne.

Myers, G. (2011) *African Cities: Alternative Visions of Urban Theory and Practice.* Zed Press, London.

O'Connor, A. (1983) *The African City.* Taylor and Francis, London.

OCS. (1922) *Third census of the population of the Union of South Africa - Enumerated 3rd May 1921: Population, organisation and enumeration, number, sex, and distribution (all races). Part 1, U.G. 15–23.* Office of Census and Statistics, Pretoria.

OCS. (1949) *Population census 7th May, 1946, Volume 1: Geographical distribution of the population of the Union of South Africa, UG51–1949.* Office of Census and Statistics, Pretoria.

Parnell, S. in Cox, K., Louw, M. and Robinson, J. (eds.) (2007) Urban Governance in the South: the Politics of Rights and Development. *A Handbook of Political Geography.* Sage, London. 595–608.

Parnell, S. (1993) Creating Racial Privilege: the Origins of South African Public Health and Town Planning Legislation. *Journal of Southern African Studies* 19, 1–18.

Parnell, S. and Mabin, A. (1995) Rethinking Urban South Africa. *Journal of Southern African Studies* 21, 39–63.

Parnell, S. and Robinson, J. (2012) (Re) theorising Cities from the Global South: Looking Beyond Neoliberalism. *Urban Geography*, in press.

Parnell, S., Pieterse, E. and Watson, V. (2009) Planning for Cities in the Global South: a Research Agenda for Sustainable Human Settlements. *Progress in Planning* 72, 232–240.

Pieterse E. (2008) *City Futures: Confronting the Crisis of Urban Development.* Zed, London.

Pirie, G. (1984) Ethno-Linguistic Zoning in South African Black Townships. *Area* 16, 291–298.

Porter, L. (2006) Planning in (Post)Colonial Settings: Challenges for Theory and Practice. *Planning Theory & Practice* 7, 383–396.

Potts, D. (2011) Making a Livelihood in (and Beyond) the African City: The Experience of Zimbabwe. *Africa: The Journal of the International African Institute* 81.4, 588–605.

Rapoport, A. and Sayegh, S. El (eds.) (2003) *Culture, architecture et design.* Collection Archigraphy, Témoignages, InFolio Editions, Gollion.

Robinson, J. (2006) *Ordinary Cities: Between Modernity and Development*. Routledge, London.

Roy, A. (2005) Urban Informality. *Journal of the American Planning Association*, 71.2.

Roy, A. (2009) The 21st Century Metropolis: New Geographies of Theory. *Regional Studies* 43.6, 819–830.

Roy, A. and AlSayyad, N. (eds.) (2004) *Urban Informality: Transnational Perspectives from the Middle East, Latin America, and South Asia*. Lexington Books, Lanham.

Sandercock, L. (ed) (1998) *Making the Invisible Visible: A Multicultural Planning History*. University of California Press, Berkeley.

Sassen, S. (2001) [1991] *The Global City: New York, London, Tokyo*. Princeton University Press, Princeton.

Seekings, J. and Nattrass, N. (2005) *Class Race and Inequality*. Yale University Press, New Haven.

Simon, D. (1992) *Cities, Capital and Development: African Cities in the World Economy*. Belhaven, London.

Simone, A. (2004) *For the City Yet to Come: Changing African Life in Four Cities*. Duke University Press, Durham.

Turner, T. (1995) *City as Landscape: A Post Post-modern View of Design and Planning*. Taylor & Francis, London.

Turok, I. (1994) Urban Planning in the Transition from Apartheid. *Town Planning Review* 65, 242–258.

Turok, I. (2001) "Persistent Polarisation Post-apartheid? Progress Towards Urban Integration in Cape Town", *Urban Studies* 38.13, 2349–2377.

Tylor, E.B. (1871) *Primitive Culture: Researches into the Development of Mythology, Philosophy, Religion, Art, and Custom* II. John Murray, London.

UN Habitat. (2008) *Ethiopia: Addis Ababa Urban Profile*. UNON Publishing Services Section, Nairobi.

UN-Habitat (United Nations Human Settlements Programme) (2001): *Cities in a Globalizing World. Global Report on Human Settlements 2001*. Earthscan, London.

UN-HABITAT (2009) *Global Report on Human Settlements: Planning*. UN-HABITAT, Nairobi.

UN, Centre for Human Settlements (Nairobi) (2006) Cities in a Globalizing World. *Global Report on Human Settlements 2001*. Earthscan, London.

Vermeulen, T. and van den Akker, R. (2010) Notes on Metamodernism. *Journal of Aesthetics and Culture*. http://aestheticsandculture.net/index.php/jac/article/view/5677/6304, (consulted April 2014).

Watson, V. (2009) Seeing from the South: Refocusing Urban Planning on the Globe's Central Urban Issues. *Urban Studies* 46.11, 2259–2275.

Wright, G. (1991) *The Politics of Design in French Colonial Urbanism.* University of Chicago Press, Chicago.

Wu, F. (2010) How Neoliberal is China's Reform? The Origins of Change During Transition. *Eurasian Geography and Economics* 51.5, 619–631.

Favela Santa Marta, Rio de Janeiro, R. Coutinho Marques da Silva

Part 2

Order

Continuing with thoughts regarding the contemporary city's modes of production and their effects, this chapter reflects on the phenomena of violence associated with urban segregation. Using two examples from Latin America – Rio de Janeiro and Medellin – this chapter analyzes the relationships between spatial segregation, social exclusion, mobility and violence that is both physical and symbolic.

While architect Rachel Coutinho's article shows that violence is a consequence of the segregation of populations who have been abandoned by the state and, in a certain sense, left to their own devices, the response of Maksim *et al.* demonstrates that mobility is likewise a (if not *the*) key issue when it comes to understanding the effects of urban segregation and the violence often associated with it.

The premise of this chapter is that two contemporary urban realities – realities which, at times, converge and, at times, clash (structures vs. dynamics, fixity vs. movement, modernity vs. postmodernity) – are, in fact, superposed here.

The contemporary city seems to be in a period of transition, revealing the incompatibility between structures, institutional functioning and political decision-making, and the cosmopolitan dynamics of a postmodern world whose emergence seems forever delayed. However, it is this incompatibility that allows us to understand the sources of urban disorder, as well as the gap between law enforcement strategies (the urban capitalist ones of the past, in particular) and the expectations of citizens who are ready for the strategies and order of the future.

A Radical Strategy to Deal with Slum Upgrading in the City of Rio de Janeiro

Rachel Coutinho Marques da Silva

Graduate Program in Urbanism, School of Architecture and Urbanism
Federal University of Rio de Janeiro, Brazil (PROURB/FAU/UFRJ)

Conflict and violence in the city of Rio de Janeiro: a historical overview

Conceptualization of the contemporary city can go in different directions and include various approaches. My research deals with favelas, conflict and violence, and my main observatory is the city of Rio de Janeiro. It also deals with spatial segregation and social exclusion, and its ultimate goal is to propose strategies for inclusion and integration. It is important to have specific methodological tools to understand the social and political dynamics of informal settlements in Rio in order to be able to design upgrading schemes and plans that will be effective in solving the many problems confronting the population that inhabits the favelas.

As the capital of Brazil until 1960, Rio de Janeiro was the stage for many political conflicts, some of them due to social inequalities and popular riots. The transfer of the national capital to Brasilia had a profound impact on the urban economy based on the public sector. The city lost its prominent position as an industrial center to São Paulo in the 1940s. During the 1970s, Rio was still losing other important economic sectors to São Paulo, such as the financial one. Thus, the transfer of the national capital affected the city's economy strongly. Nevertheless, an internal migration flux from the northeastern states was intense in the 1970s. As a result of the economic boom (known as the 'Brazilian economic miracle'), the civil construction sector expanded, due to the National Housing Bank's policies regarding middle-class housing. Migrants from the northeastern regions came to Rio to work mainly in the civil construction sector (men) and as domestic servants (women). The 1970s saw an increase in the number of favelas and also in urban violence.

The economic and fiscal crisis of the 1980s was followed by neo-liberal policies of the 1990s, which increased unemployment rates and deepened income concentration and poverty. These factors had an enormous influence on the growth of criminality in Rio. Since the 1980s the city itself had been experiencing a decline in industry and finance. The euphoria of the first years of the re-democratization period had passed, and the harsh social reality demanded more investments than the city's public treasury was able to support. This coincided with the expansion of drug trade in Rio, when the city became an important distribution port for drugs coming from the Medellin cartel towards the U.S.A. and Europe. Local armed drug dealers grouped themselves into local cartels associated with important international cartels and took control of strategic points in the city of Rio. Due to their social, political and institutional reality, favelas were a favorite location for drug cartels (the so-called *comandos*) – especially those located on the hills. Violence and armed conflict between drug dealers and the police escalated after the 1990s. A vicious circle was formed, in which poverty and social exclusion associated with spatial segregation fueled conflict and violence. In the years since the 1980s, life in Rio de Janeiro became risky and dangerous. Discourses on violence and crime increasingly began to infiltrate the media. At the same time, new businesses such as private security firms (formal or informal, such as the militias), the media, politicians and the real estate market flourished from the increasing fear of the population.

At that same time, favelas were also increasing in number and size. Between 1980 and 2010 the population living in favelas grew considerably: 40% from 1980 to 1991; 16% from 1991 to 2000; 19% from 2000 to 2010. In the decade preceding 1980, population in favelas had grown at a rate of roughly 11%. In 2010 the inhabitants of favelas represented 23% of the total population of the city (between 2000 and 2010, the total population of Rio rose from 5,857,994 to 6,320,446 – a growth of 8%). While the growth rate of the population in favelas was 19% in the 2000–2010 period, the growth rate of population living in formal areas was a mere 5%. Today approximately two million people live in 968 squatter settlements in the city of Rio de Janeiro. Some favelas in Rio already have more than 50,000 inhabitants (Complexo da Maré and Favela da Rocinha). Among the six largest squatter settlements in Brazil with more than 50,000 inhabitants, two of those are located in Rio (Rocinha with 69,161 inhabitants and Rio das Pedras with 54,793 inhabitants). If one includes the so-called *complexos*[1], then Rio has the three largest favelas in Brazil: Complexo da Maré (pop. 129,770) and Complexo do Alemão (pop. 69,143), besides the already mentioned Favela da Rocinha. Currently, favelas in Rio are experiencing the phenomenon of vertical growth, due to the lack of space to expand outwards. A typical form of vertical expansion is the informal selling of the concrete slab rooftop (*laje*)[2]. The rise of violence in the city coincides with the growth of favelas, thus making it an easy correlation, as though the favelas were responsible for the urban violence in Rio[3].

Given the context above, it is important to consider possible theoretical approaches to understand the real causes of violence. One has to avoid the easy path that considers violence as a consequence of the physical space of favelas, whose remedy would be to eradicate them and to plan an orderly and segregated city, where the poorest would live far away from the upper classes.

Conflict and violence in a risk society: a theoretical approach

Giddens, Beck and Lash propose a new approach to understanding contemporary society, for them only a transitional period from modern to post-industrial

---

[1]   A group of adjoining continuous favelas forms a Complexo. In Rio de Janeiro, there is the Complexo do Alemão, a group of 13 favelas, with a population of 69,143 inhabitants (2010) and 21,272 housing units (2010) and the Complexo da Maré, a group of 16 favelas, with a population of 129,770 (2010) and 43,038 housing units (2010).

[2]   A "*laje*" is being sold at a market price of R$30,000.00 in the most valued favelas.

[3]   The city of Rio de Janeiro presented for two decades (1980 and 1990) extremely high homicides rates; if one considers homicides rates due to firearms related deaths (mainly due to drug gangs warfare and shootings with the police), then the city showed the highest rate in Brazil in the 1990s, circa 90% of the registered homicides (Waiselfisz, 2008). In 1980, there were 59 deaths (homicides) per 100,000 inhabitants; in 2000, there were 56.6 deaths, mainly men between 15 and 19 years old living in shantytowns; in 2010, the homicide rate decreased to 24.3 deaths per 100,000 inhabitants (Waiselfizs, 2011). It is important to point out that, depending on the source, data on homicides and crimes differs considerably (Zdun, 2011:188–199).

society. Rejecting the term *postmodernity*, instead they propose the concept of *reflexive modernization* to be applied to the current processes (Giddens *et al.*, 1997). This process implies the obsolescence of the industrial society and the emergence of the risk society, as defined by Beck. He argues that in this phase, traditional institutions lose control of social, political, economic and individual risks, and two stages emerge: one where the 'effects and self-threats are systematically produced, and became public issues or the center of political conflicts' and another when 'the institutions of industrial society start to produce and legitimize the threats that they cannot control' (Giddens *et al.*, 1997:15–16).

Thus, modern state institutions cannot control risks produced (i.e., ecological risks). Hence, in order to avoid new dangers, a defensive strategy is set in motion (this applies also to terrorism, rebellions and other threats). In this stage, some social and political aspects become problematic. Society still makes decisions and acts according to old patterns, while interests groups and the judicial and the political system become immobilized by the conflicts born within the risk society. Beck argues that, with the advent of the risk society, the conflicts over the distribution of benefits (income, employment and social security), which were the essential conflict of the traditional industrial society and that shaped state institutional policies, are now disguised by the conflicts over the distribution of costs and its negative effects (Giddens *et al.*, 1997). In other words, in the risk society one observes the return of uncertainty, which means that the worst social conflicts are seen as risks. The author identifies changes in three areas arising from the concept of risk society. First, there is the relationship of modern industrial society in which the resources of nature and culture changed traditional lifestyles. Furthermore, there is the relationship of society with threats and problems produced within it, which does not fit into the traditional concepts of social safety. Finally, the concept of individualization acquires a very different meaning from that of the early 20th century. Individuals no longer have confidence in the industrial society; they now face the turbulence of the global risk society. Thus, Beck points out that social conflicts and urban violence are part of reflexive modernization – a phase that will be superseded subsequent to the environmental crisis, when society frames the ecological question as 'a providential gift for a universal self-reform' (Giddens *et al.*, 1997:67).

Giddens follows up on Beck's argument and introduces another concept – that of post-traditional society (versus postmodern society). In this phase, traditional institutions and tradition itself become unreliable and no longer serve the needs of contemporary society. This phase is characterized by reflexive modernity, which means a period of self-confrontation. This process entails a progressive disengagement from tradition and from old social forms. Aspects such as fixed gender roles and trust in state institutions are questioned, forcing people to make their own decisions and be responsible for their own existence. A process of individualization follows, in which decisions are increasingly taken on an individual basis. This growing engagement with the self and with the body is an important characteristic of risk society. Individuals face their own history set in a context of risks, dangers and hazards. Knowledge about health risks prompted many people to change their lifestyles. At the same time, excessive knowledge of the potential risks and dangers that surround us increases the feeling of insecurity. Out of the disenchantment and lack of trust in the efficacy of state institutions, one sees the emergence of a different form of political action, which Beck calls *sub-politics*, coordinated by interested groups or citizens. Sub-politics can take several forms, and Beck explores the emergence of NGOs as one characteristic form. How can we connect the above concepts and notions proposed by Giddens and Beck and apply them to favelas? Is this a helpful concept for our purpose?

Looking at the specific case of Brazil, and more particularly the case of Rio's squatter settlements, one can observe certain characteristics of risk society, as defined by Beck, and also some features of reflexive modernization, as described by Giddens. As a country that never fully achieved the status of an industrial society (as it overlaps with a traditional agrarian society), paradoxically the nation nevertheless had modern state institutions. However, within the modern state apparatus, old patron-client practices co-existed that were inherited from the agrarian society, despite many attempts to reform or abolish these practices. State institutions responsible for public safety, such as the police and military forces, were given almost unlimited power to maintain order and to crush opposition to the regime during the military dictatorship period (1964–1985). Both the judicial system and legislative power were significantly weakened. Having banned the majority of political parties, the military regime instated a controlled two-party system. Outcast political groups began to operate, some of which used the tactics similar to those of armed guerrillas groups. In effect, the military regime produced the political threats necessary to legitimize its power. Torture was used to eliminate any group that opposed its goal of turning Brazil into a developed capitalist society. The social and political consequences of the military dictatorship period in Brazil were many, most of which were negative. It increased income concentration and the gap between poor and rich classes, consequently increasing social inequality. It failed to implement a sound social housing policy, thereby encouraging the growth of squatting and informal settlements. It failed to modernize state institutions and, worse, it contributed to increasing client-patron relationships within the state bureaucratic apparatus. Concerning public safety, it instilled an authoritarian police that was above the law and whose actions were not subjected to the civil judiciary system. The final decade of the military system corresponded to the most significant expansion of favelas in many cities (in population and in the number of favelas), particularly in Rio de Janeiro.[4] It also corresponds to the infiltration, dissemination and expansion of drugs and drug dealers into the territory of favelas. From this time on, violence in the favelas increased, with poverty, inequality and lack of citizenship as its fuel and its form of domination, breeding new values and symbols – not to mention a perverse culture.

Another factor influenced the scenario of increasing violence and the state's failure to provide public safety. The 1980s and part of 1990s saw the dismantling of the welfare state in the context of globalization. In southern hemisphere countries such as Brazil, this was combined with a substantial economic and fiscal crisis, further increasing social inequalities. The provision of collective consumption goods, such as social housing – which was already problematic – became even more difficult. The socially disadvantaged became progressively excluded and marginalized, because they could not individually enter the formal real estate market or provide their own means of security. In Brazil, the new world order of reflexive modernization meant that those excluded from the formal markets would be subjected to different forms of domination and power structures.

Violence and the risks produced within society and disseminated by state institutions spiraled out of control. As in Beck's argument, a defensive strategy was put in motion. The judicial and political systems became immobilized by violence. Trust in state institutions, particularly in the police, diminished. Individualization of risk followed, resulting in the privatization of public safety by the wealthy, by the firms (private security) and by the poor (militias).

---

[4]   Beck considers sub politics as a progressive form of public involvement. Several NGOs, such as Amnesty International and Greenpeace, are becoming popular and powerful because they are succeeding in pressuring state officials. The situation of the Secretary of Public Safety in Rio from November 1998 to March 2000 demonstrates the complex situation of the police department in Rio de Janeiro and the intricate and immoral relationship between the state institutions, politicians and the drug dealers (Soares, 2000).

If we consider the issue of sub-politics, as cited by Beck, we can observe that a different type of sub-politics emerges in favelas, either in the form of neighborhood associations (which perform typical state functions, such as property registering, resolving conflicts between neighbors, postal services, etc.) or in the form of drug dealers and militias, which control the territory (also performing typical state functions, such as police protection, social assistance, etc.). Actually, Beck´s conceptual framework about the individualization of society and of risks fails to account for the asymmetrical class relations that exist in many countries, especially in Latin America. He sees sub-politics as a progressive force in society but does not consider that many countries contain a marginalized society that is socially excluded from mainstream institutions, also known as *second-class citizenship.*[5]

The concept of the individualization of risk fits in the case of favelas. Risks – and here I specifically refer to the risks of violence – are produced collectively, but managed individually; they no longer belong to the sphere of the state (because of the lack of trust in state institutions) and become a matter of private responsibility. Associated with the individualization of risks is the commodification of risk, to which Beck gives little attention. With regard to violence, firms selling protection or safety devices have proliferated in recent decades – the new so-called industries of security and safety. Their products range from burglar alarms to private personal insurance. Evidence of this is very much visible in the many gated communities, in segregation, marginalization and society's fear of favelas (perceived as a threat), as well as in safety apparatuses installed in cars, buildings and even in public spaces.

In the next section I will examine the issue of order and disorder, which gained new momentum with Rio's increase in conflict and violence.

Order and disorder in the urban space

In the contemporary unequal Brazilian city, which fluctuates between the logic of order and chaos, the concepts of order and disorder and their impact on the

---

[5]   José Murillo de Carvalho coined this term. In his study about the city of São Paulo, Holston identifies a new form of citizenship in the city's periphery, which he terms *insurgent citizenship.* It is a form of second-class citizenship that, together with systems of inequality (social, economic, spatial), feeds violence in these areas. This insurgent citizenship gave rise to new forms of exploitation and violence (Holston, 2008).

urban structure must be examined. Several social practices of non-compliance to norms and rules exist, especially among the marginal groups and the poorest social segments. Real estate firms and developers want more flexible land use controls, and some use illegal means to bypass the law. Some wealthy and affluent individuals likewise do not comply with norms and rules. The end result is a fragmented urban space.

Different authors from diverse fields have discussed the theme of urban order. Urban designers and planners searched for a utopian controlled and ordered urban space. The notion of urban order often pertains to the idea of public order, which usually refers to empty urban spaces. This notion was important to the ideology of suburbs, which developed in opposition to the apparent disorder of downtown areas. The perception of city centers as disordered spaces also shaped policies of urban renewal and slum clearance.

In 19th century Paris, the perception of the old urban fabric as being chaotic and disorganized, useful for urban riots and unsuitable for the development of a modern city, prompted Baron Haussmann to undertake massive urban reforms. The alleged disordered districts were inhabited by the poorest, who lived in unhealthy tenement housing. The Parisian urban reform set an example to be followed by other towns. This positivistic view purported that urban order would bring economic development and human progress to towns (Coutinho M. da Silva, 1984). 19th century urban planners focused on the issue of ordering the city and on the best way to achieve that goal. Medieval street design was a barrier to modern urban design. Heterogeneity was perceived as disorder and homogeneity as order. To impose spatial order on the city, planners used urban legislation in the form of zoning and building codes.

As much as 19th century planners, Brazilian professionals today still consider the issue of order and disorder in urban space, which is a major topic on the planning agenda of local governments in Brazil and elsewhere. Different types of demonstrations (social, political, environmental and physical) in several cities attest the relevance of the theme. London, Paris, Rio de Janeiro and New York, among others, have experienced recent tensions that may be viewed as expressions of collective disorder. However, daily tensions are subtle; their material signs can be seen in the gated and ghetto communities and exclusive spaces that are only accessible to a few residents. The social and spatial segregation that exists in most metropolitan areas can be attributed to different historical and cultural processes. In Rio de Janeiro, social exclusion is connected to spatial segregation, which is in turn related to processes of corruption in the social, political and bureaucratic spheres. Thus, segregated urban forms and informal spaces must also be analyzed in the framework of the law, economics and politics[6].

In a capitalist society, the concept of order is linked to the logic of industrial production, while the concept of disorder is related to the domain of power (Coutinho M. da Silva, 2006). In the contemporary city, rules and norms are created to produce a pseudo-order and to exert control and power.[7] Norms acquire a mediatory role between economics and politics (i.e. they assume monetary and legal forms). Since the urban space is also the space for acquiring power and wealth, norms become crucial in this political economic arena.

Urban order and the industrial city

It was in the midst of modern urban planning that norms and land use controls became standardized. They followed the demands of industrial society based on Fordism. The main instrument for ordering the city was the functional zoning, in which each land use should be placed in a pre-defined space. This type of zoning (that I have defined in another article as *Fordist zoning*) was created to conform the industrial city to the Fordist mode of production.[8] The failure of this type of regulatory planning and its land use control mechanisms is visible in most Brazilian cities, not only in the informal areas that do not comply with the urban legislation but also in the formal areas of the city.

In Rio de Janeiro the search for an orderly urban environment did not achieve its objectives. On the contrary, it has contributed to disorganized spaces, because it did not take into account historical processes and cultural traditions. A culture of disorder has resulted from the utopian search for an impossible urban order. Based on the principles of modernism, it advocated

---

6   In another article I have analyzed how non-compliance with urban legislation in the city of Rio de Janeiro contributed to form an urban space that is seen by planners and part of the population as chaotic and non-ordered. Thus, public officials push forward an agenda of urban programs and projects in Rio which seeks to reorganize and give order to urban spaces.

7   An important aspect of norms and rules in the urban space is the urban land use controls or, more generally, urban legislation. Land use controls assume an exchange value, where those who have the power to control the legislation exchange favors with those who have the money to pay for the non-compliance with the legal norms.

8   The Fordist production system is characterized by chain production and by the productivity of labor power, both organized through rational work methods.

segregation and separate land uses through mono-functional zones and created legislation that only suits the interests of the real-estate market and the
upper classes. Rather than promoting a better social environment, this modernist concept of the city only contributed to isolating the poor in informal
areas, thereby promoting spatial and social segregation.

The city of Rio de Janeiro inherited a positivist tradition in cultural mat-
ters, and urban planning was no exception. The idea of 'order and progress'
became an ideology that pervaded urban models and legislation throughout
the 20th century. Urban plans often used the gridiron street pattern to impose
order on public spaces, while land use controls and building codes imposed
order on private spaces. Unwanted uses and misbehavior should be eliminated from the city by means of urban renewal plans and police repression.
While modernist planners endorse the rational approach, other urban scholars
argue that the social and physical environment should be democratic and promote encounters between different individuals and social groups. The public
space should be a place where different people could find the uncontrolled, the
unpredictable and the spontaneous. This is the notion of the 'right to the city'
(Sennett, 1970; Jacobs, 1961; Lefebvre, 1968; Harvey, 2008).

The idea of order in urban history came with human's necessity to build
shelter and organize daily life in society. There are many explanations for
humankind's quest for order in the built environment – from Darwin, who
considered it innate to human nature to search for order and perfection in
a physical world separated from the natural world, to Kant's view that the
search for order in our world is a means of ensuring survival in an uncontrolled environment[9]. Others, such as Lefebvre, argued that order is merely
an expression of a consumer-driven society, and of the needs of capitalism to
generate and circulate surplus value (Lefebvre, 1968).

He presents another view on the debate on urban order. He argues that
the models used by modern urbanism were the result of seeing the urban phenomenon as a sub-product of industrialization. For Lefebvre, that thinking
reduced the urban to factory logic, i.e., urban reality was reduced to industrial
rationality. This prompted planners to submit social requirements to the laws
that govern the social division of labor in the industrial world. He criticizes
modern planners and modern urbanism for being unable to see the intrinsic
logic of urban society. He explains the obsession for urban order and the pro-

---

9   This argument is developed by Norman Crowe, who based his argument on notions from the field
    of perception psychology as well as in historical examples (Crowe, 1997).

cedures created by modern planners as a failure to understand urban reality, on behalf of reason, law, authority, technique, the state and the hegemonic class. Everything serves to legitimate and enthrone a general order, which corresponds to the logic of consumer society and its world, realized at a truly global scale by capitalism and the bourgeoisie.

Lefebvre's discussion of order and disorder comes from a much broader one. He uses the term *urban society* to refer to the post-industrial society that, after a long process, followed the industrialization period, after which old urban forms inherited from the discontinuous transformation 'exploded'. An important theoretical aspect for the author is locating this process of discontinuity in association with continuity and vice-versa. He proposes the hypothesis of *complete urbanization*. This is the key to understand *urban reality,* in order to propose an *urban praxis* (Lefebvre, 1968:15–32). Finally, he defines the term *urban revolution*, meaning the set of transformations taking place in contemporary society leading to a new period, in which the urban question would prevail against all others.

He also argues that urbanism, as it was practiced until that period, had an institutional and ideological character, which justified the neo-liberal and free-market discourse from the right as well as a utopian approach, detached from the real.

Lefebvre proposes three levels to approach the confused discourses about the city and the urban: the global level, the mixed level and the private level (Lefebvre, 2003:77–86). The global level 'accommodates the most general and abstract, although essential relations, such as capital markets and the politics of space' (Lefebvre, 2003:79). It embodies the institutional space and it is the domain of institutional urbanism. The mixed level is the specifically urban level (the site, streets, squares, city halls, schools, churches, etc.) (Lefebvre, 2003). It is the ground level as well as that of social relations. The private level, where the built environment prevails (mainly housing and private homes of all kinds) is where the daily life occurs. Lefebvre also proposes that one should start with the private level, proceeding to the mixed level, and then analyze the global level.

The realm of power

Taking a different approach, Foucault argues that urban order is a means to exert power and control. The need to organize urban space occurs because power needs to be used. He developed the concept of *disciplinary power*. Discipline is a method of organizing people in space; it is a technique that distributes individuals in a hierarchical and categorized space. It is a procedure to control time and to compel individuals to produce with maximum efficiency. Vigilance is another important instrument to exercise control. It has to be permanent and continuous. Thus, in Foucault's view, an orderly, hierarchical and visible space is the best to exert vigilance, discipline and therefore power. He acknowledges other forms of power that are employed in different ways by the state, which are fundamental to its maintenance and efficient actions. He introduces the notion of the network of power associated with the state bureaucracy that lacks any source of responsibility (Machado, 1979). Power, hence, assumes regional tangible forms, penetrating state institutions and reproducing itself with domination techniques.

Based on Foucault's notions, we can understand the role of power within informal urban spaces in the contemporary city. First, there is a network of power articulated to some state administrative spheres. Second, there are groups who have a vested interest in maintaining the current situation of informal areas in order to dominate these spaces. Finally, state bureaucracy also wants to exert power over the formal space, so as to maintain order and to guarantee property rights.

In this sphere of social relationships established by the network of power, one observes the constitution of peripheral powers that are not confiscated or absorbed by the state. In favelas, some sectors of the state establish a complex network of power, connected to the drug dealers. In exchange for letting drug dealers exert power and domination in favelas, segments of the state extort huge sums of money from dealers. Thus, order and disorder assume a dual role: they are expressions of power in practice and power relations in the social structure[10].

An important Brazilian scholar, Carlos Nelson F. dos Santos, influenced by Foucault, addressed the issue of space and power in the late 1970s. Santos points out that the spatial ordering of the city is itself a discourse with a specific syntax. He claims that the arrangements of populations and land uses

---

[10]   Foucault examines the issue of disciplinary power and its many aspects.

in space is a result of the availability of good infrastructure, distance to work and urban services, and as such reveals the structure of power in urban areas and the subtle mechanism of segregation. He argues that spatial segregation is essential to the exercise of power. The market arranges space hierarchically according to income, and thus produces segregation (Santos, 1979).

Therefore, not only segregation but also exclusion is produced, as there are groups who cannot afford even the less-valued locations. Segregation and exclusion are also related to land use controls, which increase or decrease land values.[11] Under capitalism, land markets produce 'disordered spaces', in which civil disobedience and the non-acceptance of hegemonic principles can occur. To counteract this tendency toward spatial 'disorder', the official urbanism seeks an ideal ordered space, which ultimately will only be favorable to those who wield power. In the case of Rio de Janeiro, these pseudo-disordered spaces are the favelas and irregular subdivisions. Most 20th century policies and legislation aimed at removing or relocating these 'disordered' settlements. When order is emphasized in a context of unequal land market relations, it produces exclusion and segregation, considered by many to be disorder.

Paulo Freire's pedagogy of the oppressed

Another important concept to be examined in this paper is that of oppression. The notable Brazilian scholar Paulo Freire has intensely studied this condition. He proposes a new relationship between teachers, students, and society; his philosophy is based on a dialectic concept of oppression and on Marxian class analysis (Freire, 2007). The true educator must work in such a way as to bring the consciousness of oppression into the oppressed, so that the latter recognizes his knowledge and participates in the process of creation and liberation. Freedom is achieved through a balance between theory and practice, and the educator also must acknowledge his role as a mediator and be willing to accept knowledge from pupils. Freire's key methodological proposition,

---

[11] The relationship between land use regulation and exclusion has also been observed for major U.S. cities. Pendall has analyzed five land use controls in 25 of the largest U.S. metropolitan areas and connected it with racial composition. The study showed that low-density-only zoning, which restricts residential densities to fewer than eight dwelling units per acre, consistently reduced available rental housing and limited access for Black and Hispanic residents (Pendall, 2000:125–142).

which can be employed by those who work in favelas, is *dialogics*, an instrument to liberate the oppressed (the colonized), by means of cooperation, unity, organization and cultural synthesis. *Dialogics* is opposed to *antidialogics*, which uses manipulation and cultural domination as its educational method. He not only rejects traditional education, but also populist education, as both support the *status quo*. His critical pedagogy proposes to connect knowledge and power, to bring *conscientization* (a term he uses) to the excluded, so that constructive action can be taken. For the purposes of developing a methodological approach to work in favelas, three elements are important here. The first step of his praxis is to bring consciousness to the oppressed so they can take action against their condition. Then, Freire insists that dialogue should involve respect. Here the planner or designer should cooperate with the community and should strive to build social capital. Finally, dialogue and consciousness should be based on the lived experience of people in the community. Thus, the professional must search for words that have the potential to transform the lives of the oppressed.

A methodological proposition

Working with favelas requires an understanding of their social, economic and political dynamics. Based on the authors discussed above, I propose a methodological approach that highlights the aspects of conflict, risk and vulnerability as they relate to order, disorder, power and oppression.

Giddens' concept of reflexive modernization and Beck's notion of risk society give a broad framework in which to understand the transitional period confronting contemporary global society. Two levels of analysis are fundamental: socio-spatial relations and power structure. Their characteristic elements are superimposed on favelas' social, economic and spatial reality, in order to achieve a local expression. An important characteristic of reflexive modernization in Brazil is that of socio-economic exclusion associated with different forms of domination and power structures. As a consequence, social conflicts and violence increased. The state lost its control over risks (which were produced by means of erroneous institutional practices). Trust in state institutions diminished, particularly regarding the security apparatus. The state put forward defensive policies while individualization of risk spread into different social segments. As a result, public safety left the sphere of the state and became a private matter. This explains the increase in private security (for the upper classes) and in the militias (for the lower classes).

The proposition is also based on the notion of *the right to the city* which, in turn, must be understood regarding its practical possibilities.[12] Lefebvre also proposes to understand the urban space as a force field that expresses itself in forms that contain the contradictions of urban reality. Both Lefebvre's and Foucault's analysis of order and disorder are useful to deal with spatial segregation, social exclusion, urban violence and conflicts in favelas (Coutinho M. da Silva, 2006:89–102).

How, then, should an urban planner approach a low-income community? Initially, one must examine the social relationships and the spatial configuration of the favela and its surroundings according to the levels and dimensions proposed by Lefebvre. The private level is considered essential in the analysis of the morphological, social and economic elements, since it is from this level that one may propose policies aimed at integrating the formal and informal areas. The global level is used to examine the community's power structures as well as institutional policies and plans for favelas.[13] The intermediate level focuses on the public spaces and the urban form of favelas.

The next step is the analysis of power structures and the network of power present in these areas. At this phase, the research should identify the main interest groups and institutions (private and public; formal and informal) that are operative in the favela. In doing so, the most prevalent conflicts should emerge, as well as the degree of violence, the perception of risk and fear, and the degree of urban deterioration of the shantytowns. Looking carefully at the network of power within favelas, one can grasp how power is exercised in these areas (and its connection with the state apparatus), how it subjects inhabitants to control and how domination techniques are used. One must investigate the reflection of control and domination over the favela space and its internal workings. It is necessary to identify the invisible frontiers that prevent individuals from exercising the basic right to freely move in such

---

[12] Harvey commented on that notion: "The right to the city is far more than the individual liberty to access urban resources: it is a right to change ourselves by changing the city. It is, moreover, a common rather than an individual right since this transformation inevitably depends upon the exercise of a collective power to reshape the processes of urbanization. The freedom to make and remake our cities and ourselves is, I want to argue, one of the most precious yet most neglected of our human rights" (Harvey, 2008:23–40).

[13] Examples of recent programs to be examined are the Morar Carioca and the Pacifying Police Units (UPPs).

areas and that contributes to the deterioration of public spaces. Understanding these aspects may result in plans and designs that enable the exercise of fundamental civil rights.

The next step is to identify the cultural potential present in the favelas, mapping existing cultural activities, initiatives and groups. The aim is to work with the transformative potential of these spaces into places of social and cultural interaction. Here one must also observe the urban practices of social groups. Conflict should be introduced in the social logic, so that disputes should evolve into demands. The ultimate goal is to acknowledge the existent points of vulnerability and conflict, and instead of eradicating them, to use them creatively to build resilience and adaptation. The whole planning and designing process in a particular favela necessarily requires the participation of the community. This involvement should bring awareness of their precarious living conditions. Proposals should be cooperatively created and based on inhabitants' experiences.

The purpose of the method is to foster a radical urban strategy away from ideological urbanism, one that encourages invention and promotes liberation, that recognizes plurality and difference, conflict and harmony. This radical urban strategy should arise from the people involved and include them in the planning process.

A Theoretical Proposal to Reconsider the Contemporary City as Violent, Segregated and Mobile

Hanja Maksim, Xavier Oreiller,
Emmanuel Ravalet, Yafiza Zorro
Laboratory of Urban Sociology
Ecole polytechnique fédérale de Lausanne, Switzerland

Introduction

Under the impact of globalization, cities have been the venue for important morphological and social changes. As such, efforts to describe and theorize the contemporary city in order to address and understand the issues that those who 'create and inhabit' the city encounter are both timely and crucial. By observing that each city – despite being part of an overall global dynamic – has its own specific local characteristics, Rachel Coutinho defends the importance of new methods of analysis for understanding the contemporary city.

The context from which Coutinho observes and reflects on the city is that of the *favelas* of Rio de Janeiro. While not a field of analysis per se, they serve as a basis for her thinking. However, to address the issues she feels *favelas* raise, Coutinho builds on writings and theories from Western contexts.

The questions raised by the Carioca reality and *favelas* in particular have prompted Coutinho to treat the city as inherently segregated and violent. These two striking characteristics can, of course, be readily observed in Rio, as well as in other Latin American cities, and in most cities around the world in varying degrees. They likewise contribute to linking built spaces and social spaces, one of the author's key ambitions. The city is thus described in terms of Anthony Giddens' work on modern post-industrial society and Ulrich Beck's work on risk society. She also adheres to the notion of reflexive modernization conceptualized by these two authors, wherein urban violence is presented as being central.

Coutinho's effort to theorize aims to find a new way of thinking about Brazilian society based on inclusion and integration processes. The increase in the number of *favelas* coincides with the rise in violence, linking the two phenomena by a relationship of cause and effect, but without taking into account the impact of broader economic and planning policy decisions. Today, inhabitants of *favelas* are held liable for all manner of violence, without understanding – as Coutinho mentions – the vicious circle formed by poverty, social exclusion and spatial segregation.

In a reverse perspective, Coutinho attempts to understand Rio as a society of risk, in which trust in classic public institutions has been undermined. The population concerned must focus on itself in order to protect itself, which in turn favors the emergence of a different kind of political action, which Beck calls *sub-politics*. These can take different forms, including NGOs and neighborhood associations. In addition, Coutinho notes that the asymmetry of Latin-American society produces counter-forms for these sub-politics, such as militias or groups of drug traffickers who control urban areas. Given this situation, Coutinho questions the concepts of order and disorder based on the works of Foucault, for whom urban order is a means of gaining control and exercising power over a society. Following this same logic, order would imply moving slums and informal settlements from the city center, where the price of land does not have high economic value. Finally, Coutinho proposes acting in the territory using the levels of action recommended by Lefebvre. The first is the private level, for which the needs and dynamics are the most visible. The idea would then be to operate on the global level and to conclude with the intermediate level – that of the city.

In this contribution, we do not seek to question Coutinho's proposed approach to contemporary urbanity through the lens of segregation and violence, but rather to incorporate a third dimension – that of mobility – which we feel is the missing link to better understand issues of urban segregation and violence. Moreover, mobility is already quite present in Coutinho's contribution, is at the heart of the approaches of the key authors to whom she refers (namely Beck, Giddens, Lefebvre and Foucault) and is likewise a fundamental concept in much of the literature on the contemporary city.

We will begin by returning to modern and postmodern theories of the city to highlight the importance of mobility in explaining urban violence and segregation. We will then demonstrate the validity of our theoretical approach using the example of the *communas* of Medellin, an urban reality both similar to, yet distinct from, the *favelas* of Rio.

Re-thinking the city through violence, segregation and mobility

Violence and segregation are relevant entry points for linking theories on the city. However, in order to truly understand contemporary phenomena of urban exclusion and violence, we have placed mobility at the center of the debate, as this link appears to be missing from Coutinho's proposal. We will defend this position throughout the article.

Like Coutinho, we too rely on an approach for understanding the intricate, complex relationship between physical space and social space. In fact, mobility is much more than just movement in physical space; it also includes movement in social space and, hence, social mobility, which raises the issues of inequality and segregation. Research on mobility and the attention given to it by sociology has increased exponentially, leaving us with the impression that the contemporary world is a world in motion (Sheller and Urry, 2006). Hence, a gradual shift can be observed from theories of mobility linked to places, rootedness and a certain spatial order, to those of mobility based on the concepts of flow and dynamics (Creswell, 2006). Nevertheless, both continue to exist – sometimes in parallel, sometimes distinctly. Thus, mobility has become a key concept for describing modern societies and, by extension, the urban phenomenon. 'The priority given in mobility in contemporary societies is deeply embedded in the process of capitalist development, where the concept of time as a value is increasingly relevant,' (Vasconcellos, 2001:54).

Being able to move physically or virtually can be a source of empowerment, improved social status or the expression of the right to mobility, which should not be separated from the right to the city evoked by Coutinho. For her, this right to the city implies a democratization of the social and physical environments to stimulate encounters between individuals. In this sense, the right to move freely in a democratic space is strongly linked to the right to mobility.

However, while mobility has been valued to the point of being considered a right, it has, consequently, gradually become a norm. And, as Le Breton (2005) stresses, norms may produce deviants. By extension, the author argues that *immobility* in physical space is equivalent to *immobility* in social space. In this respect, and to echo the importance of segregation in the Carioca context, it would be useful to better address the issue of mobility in *favelas*, and thus continue the work of B. Motte-Baumvol and C. Nassi (2012). More broadly, it would be useful to further address the potential links between residential segregation and daily mobility behaviors for all urban contexts (Ravalet, 2009).

In recent decades, the changes associated with increases in speeds and the emergence of intensive mobility have gradually forced us to use mobility potentials as a resource in choosing our residential location (Holmes, 2004), relocating and for organizing complex activities schedules. This makes mobility a vector of social inequality because it does not affect everyone in the same way (Le Breton, 2008). Some people are very mobile and have access to numerous amenities scattered over the territory, while others do not have the means to get around and must settle for local resources.

Moreover, the potential receptiveness of specific areas is determined by the type of link between a given space and mobility: thus, each territory offers a specific scope of possibilities when it comes to accommodating the projects of individual and collective actors (Kaufmann, 2008; Maksim, 2011). They consist of various ingredients, in a wide range of possible combinations.

–   available networks, their development, their performance and their conditions of accessibility (i.e. road, highway and rail networks, airports, regional telecommunications facilities),
–   the space itself and its configurations (including functional centralities, institutional territories, etc.),
–   the job market (including employment/training opportunities and the unemployment rate),
–   the institutions and laws regulating human activities are, in one way or another, part of a territory's potential receptiveness (i.e. family policies, property and housing assistance, immigration policy, etc.)

Thus, each region has a specific quality and combination of these elements. If these elements do not meet the needs and expectations of those they serve, then the latter will undoubtedly be frustrated in their efforts to bring their projects to fruition. Social inequalities therefore stem from the possibility of realizing projects (or not) based on the combined features of a given territory.

In other words, an area's 'potential receptiveness' refers to the ensemble of social relations and models of success proposed by a given society (Pattaroni *et al.*, 2010). However, when institutions fail to provide sufficient alternatives in terms of mobilities and activities, initiatives emanate from local communities.

The example of the development of an informal transportation service in Rio shows the central role that citizens and residents can play in the development of an area's potential receptiveness. Thus, among the many modes of transportation available to Rio residents are minibuses, which are responsible for approximately 10% of urban trips daily. These minibuses – called *kombis*, in reference to the type of vehicle – can carry 12–15 people and provide service to areas that are little served by urban bus and subway networks. Created based on individual initiatives, they respond directly and specifically to a demand for mobility to which the authorities could not. The vehicles, whose number was estimated at 10,000 in 2007, are the property of the drivers or transportation cooperatives, but are not registered with the municipality and do not pay taxes[14]. This example of an informal economic sector (as opposed to those networks recognized by the prefecture) illustrates the challenge of contemporary urban planning, torn between top-down planning and support for bottom-up initiatives. A formalization of this mode of transportation at the citywide level by the introduction of various taxes, authorizations and regulations (in other words, formal appropriation by the public authorities) would be detrimental to the qualities developed in a self-management milieu.

The relationship between regional planning and mobility has been a key and recurrent theme in public policy in European cities in recent years. The aforementioned example and theoretical elements call for a more in-depth analysis of this relationship. Understanding the links between geographical spaces, mobility and socio-spatial segregation indeed implies focusing on the particularities of the local context, the institutional architecture, the relationships between the actors and the doctrines and policies of the past (Palier and Surel, 2005; Gallez and Maksim, 2007).

Latin American literature is teeming with examples of analyses of this link between social inequalities, mobility and territories, with the recurring overlapping of the issue of residential segregation (Jirón, 2008; Ducci and

---

[14] http://www.alerj.rj.gov.br/common/noticia_corpo.asp?num=16353

Soler, 2004). The impact of context is strong, and is reflected in the spatial distribution of social inequalities at different scales, from the national level to the neighborhood level. The qualities of each territory likewise vary: functional qualities refer to accessibility and services, sensitive qualities to urban and architectural morphology, and social qualities to socio-spatial distribution and segregation (Thomas, 2011). Based on these characteristics, the environment has potential receptiveness that is more or less suited to the lifestyles of residents. If this potential receptiveness clashes with the lifestyles of its residents, the impacts in terms of segregation are particularly marked.

This segregation therefore results from unequal urbanization and undemocratic conditions, as conceptualized by Y. Pedrazzini (2005) with the concept of the violence of urbanization. This violence has repercussions from a more global scale (the violence of globalization) to a more local one, through social violence or 'the violence of the poor'. In this respect, the latter is the result of the complex socioeconomic processes that have traversed the various social and geographical scales, with social violence resulting from the frustration of economic differences, the lack of social and urban policies and even racism.

'It is…'differential' security policies that divide the city, separating those with access to it from those accused of threatening it. However, it is not the violence that divides the city; on the contrary, the city is 'unified' by violence that, paradoxically, has succeeded – where democracy has failed – in uniting fragmented territories within the same urban project' (Pedrazzini, 2005:73)[15].

Mobile risk society

Mobility theories address the dynamics between order and disorder, which Coutinho discusses most notably in reference to Foucault and Lefebvre. The approach of the Chicago School, for instance, shows that mobility can be thought of as a disruptive factor or as out of balance (Gallez and Kaufmann, 2009), and thereby establishes a link between mobility and social and urban disorder. In the same vein, R. Putnam (2000) sees in the increased mobility of Americans and the breakup of certain geographical spaces – as one con-

---

[15]   Translated by the authors.

sequence, but not the only – an explanation for their civic, community and political disengagement.

These reflections on the link between mobility and urban disorder lead us to the issues raised by risk society, which are set out in Coutinho's contribution and which we propose complementing from the perspective of *mobile risk society*. Resulting from a paradigm shift in German sociology, the concept of risk society was concretized in particular with the publication of Ulrich Beck's *Society of Risk* (2001). This marked a transition from the sociology of industrial society to the sociology of risk society, raising the question of the modernization of modernity, or *reflexive modernity*. Risk society also has its origins in the debate on the end of the nation-state, which was characterized by the 'fixity' of modern societies. Global risk society makes sense particularly in light of the terrorist risks and illegal networks that are increasingly present on a global scale. Among the many ideas dear to Beck with regard to risk society, we will focus on cosmopolitanism and globalization.

The cosmopolitan approach he proposes precludes what he calls 'national'. For instance, the image of the community is no longer based on a defined area but is broader, and depends more on the shared interests and emotions of its population. The consideration of a cosmopolitan context, in his opinion, allows us to better understand social phenomena and to grasp how globalization has abolished and reconfigured classic distinctions. This can be understood through a logic of 'inclusive distinction' (Beck, 2006); in other words, we are no longer looking at an exclusive, 'either-or' perspective, but rather an inclusive, cumulative, 'and-and' perspective. Differences remain while interdependencies increase, with borders becoming transparent and no longer closed. As a result, the 'inside-outside' distinction is replaced by a comprehensive perspective that includes both inside and outside. Moreover, mobility can be used to manage risk, which can be reduced using various strategies. Hence, long-distance trips and telecommunications help make the realms of daily life more permeable (Kesselring, 2006).

In terms of mobile risk society, many modern sociological concepts have become what 6,349 deaths by violence Beck calls 'zombie' categories because they are no longer able to account for changes and are derived from a sociology of industrial society. In this sense, his idea echoes Lefebvre's in its desire to break free from industrial logic to understand contemporary urban phenomena. However, Beck considers that no theoretical alternative as yet allows us to dismiss these zombie categories. Considering the number of authors who make this critique, then illustrating it with examples from specific Latin American contexts, Coutinho's reflections contribute to the possibility of finding new alternatives to old concepts. For Beck, it is this task that future theoretical developments must tackle.

But are these issues echoed in the field? Firstly, these theoretical approaches include an infinite variety of contemporary urban realities but do not directly address contexts similar to that of the favelas of Rio. They offer an approach to globalization that does not provide the necessary tools for appreciating people's daily lives in a direct way. They highlight the issues of diversity, cultural opportunities and *sub-politics* in authors like Beck, but do not allow us to sufficiently grasp this dimension dear to Coutinho. Also, though rapidly changing, the Rio context is still characterized by old, inherited political, economic and urban structures onto which new dynamics – and most notably mobility – have been added. This complex overlapping then justifies not dismissing outright the categories of classic sociology, which must continue to co-exist with more recent ones, in order to allow for an analysis that reflects the reality of a given context as accurately as possible. Taking this idea one step further, the national perspectives in Brazil and Europe alike surely have a stake in social analysis, as the porosity of borders seems more like an ongoing process than an established fact – and one that may never be fully realized. Old theoretical concepts are not necessarily obsolete, and neither should new ones replace nor eliminate them.

In our view, the conflict between old concepts and recent ones largely echoes the conflict between modern and postmodern theories, which we consider here, as they nurture reflection on issues of socio-spatial segregation. In reference to approaches to modernity, Z. Bauman (2000) speaks of 'heavy modernity', which he associates with the era of territorial conquest, as opposed to so-called 'liquid' modernity. The latter corresponds to a phase of domination of space by time (to literally erase distance) by means of transportation, telecommunications and information. The modern world is subdivided into distinct places and societies, and the nation-state is a typical form of modernity. Differences found within the national space or between nation-states have often been considered temporal, corresponding to different stages of the same linear development. The social origin – rooted in space – is therefore a source of inequality and segregation.

The postmodern approach considers the phase that follows classic modernity; this time, the solutions to the problems of inequality, space and mobility are manifold. It suggests that spatial dimensions have lost their pertinence relative to social dimensions. This is what Bauman (2000) calls 'liquid

modernity', which most notably is characterized by technological development that aims to accelerate movement, leading to the annihilation of space
by time. Finally, it takes stock of more differentiated spaces and places. More
broadly, mobility is the main factor of social success.

However, it behooves us not to see these developments as a series of
phases (heavy modernity, liquid modernity) that replace and succeed one
another. Instead, we support the idea that the problem of socio-spatial segregation – especially in the Rio context – is fueled by both approaches. If
contemporary urban planning makes sense in a 'liquid modernity' in which
the spatial dimension has been annihilated by time, then both the social institutional organizations of heavy modernity (i.e. nation-states, provinces, cities,
etc.) and their urban planning decisions must be adaptable. The urban riots
Coutinho discusses in her text are, as such, directed against institutions, their
spatial forms and social organization, deemed defective and unable to meet
the expectations of the people. Such destruction challenges organizational
principles, calling for new types of solutions based on truly democratic urban
planning.

Thus, mobility – which is fundamental for understanding phenomena
of exclusion and the violence associated with it – appears to be the missing
link in Coutinho's analysis. What is more, the centrality of this concept in the
theoretical approaches of the authors on which Coutinho builds her argument
further reinforce the central role of mobility as a building block for the advent
of a postmodern society based more on flows and movement than on structures (although the latter have not disappeared). Mobility is therefore a value,
a high expectation and a right to participate fully in contemporary urban life
within the paradigm of reflexive modernity.

Medellin: a violent, segregated, mobile city?

Coutinho's theoretical efforts – as well as ours – deserve to be put to the test
in an urban terrain, which we propose doing presently. Coutinho's purpose
was to provide a broader, more comprehensive framework for interpreting
and understanding the issue of favelas in Rio. But to what extent are these
theoretical efforts – and their methodological scope – suited to grasping urban
and social fragmentation and the inequality associated with it?

To outline some of the answers to this question, we propose to describe and analyze an urban reality that is both similar to and dissimilar from that of favelas, namely that of the *comunas* of Medellin. Our goal here is to identify and understand the factors and actors at work here, and how they interact.

In recent years, Medellin has experienced important changes, both planning-wise and socially, and dealing with the mobility issue has played a key role. This example gives the chance to explore the issue of mobility in the designing and planning of the contemporary city. The favelas of Medellin, which are home to the city's most disadvantaged populations, are known as the *comunas* of urban agglomerations. Inhabitants of these areas live in difficult social conditions, where violence has played a key role in recent years.

Hence, it is possible to draw a parallel between the Carioca reality as presented by Coutinho, and that of Medellin – not only because segregation there is obviously apparent, but because this city has likewise undergone a number of important transformations in the past decade. Many of these urban interventions have focused on the disadvantaged through urban integration projects.

Medellin has gone through periods of particular hardship that have deeply scarred the city, leaving behind a society stigmatized by a negative image it is trying to shed. During the 1980s and 1990s, it was considered the most dangerous city in the world: in 1991, the city reported 6,349 deaths by violence[16], mostly due the war between drug traffickers and the state. This period saw the development of illegal activities, especially in Cali and Medellin, two of the three largest cities in the country, and Columbia was labelled as the world's top drug producer.

This period was also characterized by the weakening of the state and various institutions. Thus, power was seized and re-seized by different groups (guerilla forces, drug traffickers and even the state), making it impossible to implement the necessary reforms. It was within this context that clientelism and corruption fomented a country of privileges reserved for a small minority, at the expense of the majority. For example, the education sector was largely neglected by public investment, leaving entire generations with scant cultural capital. Yet, in this era of globalization, these generations are confronted with profound technological changes that they cannot fully enjoy. The poor are thus

---

[16]   Project Agreement 017: Development: "Medellín un hogar para la vida" 2012–2015, Aníbal Gaviria Correa.

deprived of the means to deal with these changes, and are faced with symbolic violence (Pedrazzini, 2005).

Increasing inequalities, exclusion and social segregation – in other words, strong social fragmentation – thus awakened the need for alternatives, other opportunities and loopholes. This need is notably reflected in the emergence of marginal groups that establish their own rules, often in opposition to society. The emergence of such groups – as Coutinho mentions, citing Beck's theory – results from lack of trust in public institutions. 'Aspects such as fixed gender roles and trust in state institutions are being questioned, forcing people to make their own decisions and take care of their own existence' (this volume, 61).

In this way, the city of Medellin became the country's primary breeding ground for political and social demands. It was the epicenter of conflicts involving armed organizations, guerillas, paramilitaries, drug traffickers and soldiers. The seizing of various territories by these groups fostered a climate of threats and extortion. In search of territorial domination, these groups have created imaginary boundaries that separate residents of the same *comunas*, further reinforcing the division and breakdown of the social fabric, ultimately paralyzing the society and rendering it unproductive (Medellin, 2011).

From this point of view, the *comunas* of Medellin are the spatial representation of the social fragmentation of the city: detached from the rest of the agglomeration and isolated from opportunities the city might otherwise have to offer. We therefore wonder if a specific field of possibilities for *comuna* inhabitants that includes the projects of individual and collective actors exists or can be developed. In recent years, the city's administration has worked to expand this range of possibilities.

The implementation of the changes mentioned above is thus born of an initiative to develop projects and strategies designed to integrate the population without losing the overall vision of the city. These communities obviously have little access to the rest of the city. In this regard, the entire city has benefitted from the creation of the new 'metro' system. More recently, the administration finally understood that the first step to integrating the *comunas* was to involve *comuna* residents in renovation projects and stop excluding them from development, despite the challenges these measures raised (including the feeling of exclusion of the populations concerned and the topography).

Medellin was thus the first city to use 'Metrocable' cable cars (which are more common in the tourist sector) as a means of collective transportation. The system's first line opened in 2004, thus offering a connection to the

Comunas Nororientales. The interesting outcome of this approach was that it not only provided a transportation system for residents, but it also pushed a much more ambitious strategy of intervention – one that claimed to make neighborhoods in this area of the city a part of a larger project of urban integration. The aim was to improve living, working and environmental conditions for these communities. As such, these transportation projects were accompanied by the building of facilities (libraries and schools), public spaces of high architectural quality and infrastructures at the local level (Dávila, 2012).

These physical changes were accompanied by various measures to overcome the vote-catching approaches of traditional policies, followed by concrete changes in the policies (Dávila, 2012). The 'participatory' aspect was at the heart of the 1991 reform of the national constitution, which resulted, above all, in the implementation of two approaches: participatory planning and the participatory budget[17]. The objective of these two measures was to establish a transparent system between the State and society, based on communication regarding its policy programs and greater transparency as regards public expenditure (Brand *et al.*, 2012). The aim was to renew trust between the state and its citizens by providing more detailed information about government projects and by encouraging the participation of those communities concerned[18]. While public demand has invited itself to the political debate in recent years, it is a way for the state and various institutions to pay a debt to these communities so long forgotten (Coupé, 2012). This proved to be a demonstration of the great potential of local initiatives.

In recent years, Medellin has attempted to create a new identity for itself. In this urbanization process, we observe the relationship between the global level (meaning the state and its shift toward policies of participation) and the private level (meaning daily life, habitat and the community). These links were framed by a new approach that aims to insert the city into a social context redefined through 'social urbanism'. This term refers to all the physical and social changes that have reshaped the territory – not only that of

---

[17] The participatory budget (*presupuesto participativo*) gives the community an opportunity to access and use 5%–10% of the budget scheduled by the administration. This decision-making power given directly to the communities helped strengthen and enhance local power. The first investments were allocated to development (by the strengthening of social and community organizations) (Brand, P. *et al.*, 2012).

[18] The Sergio Fajardo administration's 2004–2007 Development Plan "Medellín, compromiso de toda la ciudadanía," and Mayor Alonso Salazar Jaramillo's "Medellín es solidaria y competitiva" 2008–2011 Development Plan.

Library in one of the Comunas of Medellin, Photo Yafiza Zorro.

Metrocable Medellin, Photo Yafiza Zorro.

comunas but also throughout the city. This was first employed by architect Karl Brunner in 1952, who likewise greatly influenced planning in Latin American cities such as Santiago de Chile, Bogota and Panama City in the 1930s and 1940s (Brand and Dávila, 2012). This proposed development now creates a link between local and global levels through participatory policies which materialize at an intermediate level – that of space, through public spaces and architectural projects.

While providing better access to urban residents is important in the name of the right to mobility, regional planning must nonetheless go beyond mobility alone. In this mobile risk society, mobility has become the norm. But does this norm clash with the preferences and lifestyles of the people, who show a strong sense of belonging to their areas of residence? Because of their 'immobile' character, these populations are called upon to develop other strategies for success, especially through the appropriation of cultural and economic identities. For example, at the cultural level, this manifested in strong associative dynamics, hip-hop groups, etc. In the latter, the music's lyrics – often political – attest to a violent reality and lack of opportunities. Other expressions of this type are reflected in graffiti and, in a more typically Colombian way, in football, with sports fields often becoming popular meeting places in these neighborhoods. In the economic sphere, many micro-enterprises have been created or supported by local economic development programs, such as the opening of the Cedezo business development center (Coupé, 2012). This economic program was also made possible by an offer of credit from 'the bank of opportunity' (Coupé and Cardona, 2012). Meanwhile, a large number of informal businesses have likewise been set up.

Obviously, the potential offered at the local level allows us to reflect on the urban reality and its management in another way. It is true that developing economic and cultural dynamics at the local scale (in other words, through local roots) goes against the idea that mobility is essential. But we must undoubtedly aim for a balance between flow dynamics and place dynamics.

Conclusion

This chapter provided an opportunity for us to consider how to link various theoretical contributions to contemporary urban reality to better shed light on the urban condition in all its diversity. Segregation, violence and mobility can be found in all contexts in varying forms and to varying degrees, and are closely related. Their interactions – for better or for worse – show us the city in its extremes and require that the government renew its role in order to remain capable of taking action.

In her text, Coutinho stresses the link between social space and built space in a contemporary urban environment marked by segregation and violence. As a counterpoint to her theoretical research, we introduced the idea of spatial and social mobility. As spatial mobility has become a norm today, lack of access to it is a vector of inequality. In order to understand violence and urban segregation, it is crucial to consider inhabitants' residential locations in the city, their daily mobility and how these two elements interact. The encounter between territory and mobility defines the city's potential receptiveness (networks, places, economic/political activities, etc.), bolstering or thwarting inhabitants' projects. In this sense, social inequality arises from this variable potential and how it fits with inhabitants' expectations. This mobility potential is not the exclusive domain of institutions; it also depends on the people themselves, which directly questions how urban space is produced. Only a detailed study of each local context would help us understand the mechanisms of segregation and violence, of the frustration generated by the undemocratic, fragmented development of the capitalist city of which Coutinho speaks, and by the violence of urbanization – or symbolic violence – evoked by Pedrazzini (2005).

A mobility-based approach allowed us to address issues of urban order and disorder, extended by the concept of mobile risk society. The social, political and economic categories that hitherto prevailed in industrial society now must give way to a non-exclusive overlapping of the same. In this relative cosmopolitanism, mobility is a strategy for managing the environment that manifests itself in a host of practices. Mobility refers not only to this new liquid modernity, but also clings to a heavy modernity characterized by the prevalence of spatial dimensions. Thus, in order to grasp a fragmented reality and its social consequences (urban riots), it is necessary to place these events in a dialectic between these two forms of modernity.

The example of the city of Medellin ultimately allowed us to discuss a form of urban management that combines global planning and local participation. By extending the urban transportation network beyond the too often impermeable borders of the slums, Medellin has improved the potential receptiveness of these places. This kind of social urban development, in our view, illustrates the involvement of intermediary levels of which Coutinho speaks, at the crossroads between the dynamics of flows and localized strategies.

The shift from heavy modernity to liquid modernity, which tends towards widespread mobility and territorial specialization, ultimately raises the question of the roles of institutions and of planning. Can they adapt and are they relevant – or necessary – for civic action and urban production? Meanwhile, the practice of urban professions should undoubtedly focus more directly on achieving urban functions (Bourdin, 2010), which includes 'urban amenities, uses of the city, management and organization'. This means that 'the interaction between actors takes place in the right conditions, and that the knowledge and common references that allow them to understand one another either already exist or are being built (through collective learning)' (Bourdin, 2010:97).

References

Bauman, Z. (2000) *Liquid Modernity*. Polity Press, Cambridge.

Beck, U. (2001) *La société du risque*. Flammarion, Paris.

Beck, U. (2006) *Qu'est-ce que le cosmopolitisme?* Flammarion, Paris.

Bourdin, A. (2010) *L'urbanisme d'après crise*. Editions de L'Aube.

Brand, P., Coupé, F. and Dávila, J. (2012) *Medellín: contexto institucional y cambio de paradigma urbano. Movilidad urbana y pobreza: Aprendizajes de Medellín y Soacha*. U. d. C. d. Medellín.

Brand, P. and Dávila, J. (2012) *Los Metrocables y el 'urbanismo social': dos estrategias complemetarias. Movilidad urbana y pobreza: Aprendizajes de Medellín y Soacha*. U. d. C. d. Medellín.

Coupé, F. (2012) *Los Metrocables: riesgo, pobreza e inclusión. Movilidad urbana y pobreza: Aprendizajes de Medellín y Soacha*. U. d. C. d. Medellín.

Coupé, F. and Cardona, J. (2012) *Impacto del Metrocable en la economía local. Movilidad urbana y pobreza: Aprendizajes de Medellín y Soacha*. U. d. C. d. Medellín.

Coutinho Marques da Silva Carvalho, R. (1984) Urban Planning in Rio de Janeiro: A Study of the Urban Redevelopment Plan During Passos Administration (1902–1906), Master's Thesis. Cornell University.

Coutinho Marques da Silva, R. in Pinheiro Machado, D. (2006) Ordem e irregularidade no espaço urbano: uma perspectiva regulatória e urbanística. *Sobre Urbanismo*. Viana & Mosley/PROURB, Rio de Janeiro, 89–102.

Cresswell, T. (2006) *On the Move. Mobility in the Modern Western World.* Routledge, New York.

Crowe, N. (1997) *Nature and the Idea of a Man-Made World: An Investigation into the Evolutionary Roots of Form and Order in the Built Environment.* The MIT Press, Cambridge.

Dávila, J. (2012) *Introducción. Movilidad urbana y pobreza: Aprendizajes de Medellín y Soacha.* U. d. C. d. Medellín.

Ducci, M. E. and Soler, F. in De Mattos, C. and al. (eds) (2004) Santiago: de un proceso acelerado de crecimiento a uno de transformaciones. *Santiago en la Globalización, ¿una nueva ciudad?* SUR-EURE, Santiago.

Freire, P. (2007) *Pedagogy of the Oppressed.* Continuum, New York.

Gallez, C. and Maksim, H. (2007) À quoi sert la planification urbaine? Regards croisés sur la planification urbanisme-transport à Strasbourg et à Genève. *Flux* 69, 49–62.

Gallez, C., and Kaufmann, V. in Flonneau, M. and Guigueno, V. (2009). Aux racines de la mobilité en sciences sociales: contribution au cadre d'analyse socio-historique de la mobilité urbaine. *De l'histoire des transports à l'histoire de la mobilité?* PUR, Rennes.

Giddens, A., Beck, U. and Lash, S. (1997) *Modernização Reflexiva: política, tradição e estética na ordem social moderna,* Editora da UNESP, São Paulo.

Harvey, D. (2008) The Right to the City. *New Left Review* 53.

Holmes, M. (2004) An Equal Distance? Individualisation, Gender and Intimacy in Distance Relationships. *Sociological Review* 52.2, 180–200.

Holston, J. (2008) *Insurgent Citizenship: Disjunctions of Democracy and Modernity in Brazil.* Princeton University Press, Princeton.

Jacobs, J. (1961) *The Life and Death of Great American Cities.* Random House, New York.

Jiron, P. (2008) Unravelling invisible inequalities in the city through urban daily mobility. The case of Santiago, Chile. *Swiss Journal of Sociology* 33.1, 45–68.

Kaufmann, V. (2008) *Les paradoxes de la mobilité: bouger, s'enraciner.* Presses polytechniques et universitaires romandes, Lausanne.

Kesselring, S. (2006) Pioneering mobilities: new patterns of movement and motility in a mobile world. *Environment and Planning* 38.2, 269–279.

Le Breton, E. (2005) *Bouger pour s'en sortir. Mobilité quotidienne et intégration sociale.* Armand Colin, Paris.

Le Breton, E. (2008) *Domicile-travail: les salariés à bout de souffle.* Les carnets de l'info, Paris.

Lefebvre, H. (1968) *Le droit à la ville.* Anthropos, Paris.

Machado, R. (1979) *Por uma genealogia do poder, Foucault Michel, Microfísica do Poder.* Ediçoes Graal, Rio de Janeiro.

Maksim, H. (2011) Potentiels de mobilité et inégalités sociales, la matérialisation des politiques publiques dans quatre agglomérations en Suisse et en France. Master's Thesis. Ecole Polytechnique Fédérale de Lausanne, Lausanne.

Medellín, A. d. (2011) *Medellín: Una ciudad que se piensa y que se transforma*. Medellín.

Motte-Baumvol, B. and Nassi C.D. (2012) Immobility in Rio de Janeiro, beyond poverty. *Journal of Transport Geography* 24, 67–76.

Nelson Ferreira dos Santos, C. (1979) Espaço e Poder. *Cadernos do IBAM*, 46–52.

Palier, B. and Surel Y. (2005) Les «trois i» et l'analyse de l'État en action. *Revue Française de Science Politique* 55.1, 7–32.

Pattaroni, L., Kaufmann, V. and Rabinovich, A. (éds.) (2010) *Habitat en devenir*. Presses polytechniques et universitaires romandes, Lausanne.

Pedrazzini, Y. (2005) *La violence des Villes*. Collection Enjeux Planète Le livre équitable. Editions de l'Atelier, Paris.

Pendall, R. (2000) Local Land Use Regulation and the Chain of Exclusion. *Journal of the American Planning Association* 66.2, 125–142.

Putnam, R. (2000) *Bowling Alone: The Collapse and Revival of American Community*. New York: Simon & Schuster.

Ravalet, E. (2009) Ségrégation urbaine et mobilité quotidienne, une perspective internationale. Etudes de cas à Niamey, Puebla, Lyon et Montréal. PhD ès Etudes Urbaines, I.N.R.S.-U.C.S., Montréal, Doctorat en Economie des Transports, Université de Lyon.

Sheller, M. and Urry, J. (2006) The New Mobilities Paradigm. *Environment and Planning* 38, 207–226.

Sennett, R. (1970) *The Uses of Disorder*. Knopf, New York.

Soares, L. E. (2000) *Meu Casado de General: quinhentos dias no front de segurança pública do Rio de Janeiro*. Companhia das Letras, São Paulo.

Thomas, M.-P. (2011) En quête d'habitat: choix résidentiels et différenciation des modes de vie familiaux en Suisse. Ecole Polytechnique Fédérale de Lausanne, Lausanne.

Vasconcellos, E.A. (2001) *Urban Transport, Environment and Equity: The Case for Developing Countries*. Earthcan, London.

Waiselfisz, J. (2011) *Mapa da Violência 2012: os novos padrões da vioência homicida no Brasil*. Instituto Sangari, São Paulo.

Waiselfisz, J. (2008) *Mapa da violencia dos municipios brasileiros*. UNESCO, Brasilia.

Zdun, S. (2011) Difficulties Measuring and Controlling Homicide in Rio de Janeiro. *International Journal of Conflict and Violence* 5.1, 188–199.

Dharavi. Source: URBZ.

Part 3

Nature

Beyond the phenomena of segregation, violence and mobility in the city lies the question of urban order and disorder. This third chapter continues the discussion by looking at the roles of nature and slums. As urban planning and the modern city are founded on a clear physical and theoretical separation between nature and the city (or *civilization*, we should say), slums only appear illegitimate as regards neo-liberal urban order, due in particular to their functional diversity.

As such, this third chapter invites us to go beyond the notion of domesticated nature and illegitimate – even illegal – slums in the contemporary city by analyzing the historical, theoretical and epistemological assumptions that underpin the notion of urban order. In so doing, the two contributions in this chapter, in their own way, propose a different methodological and epistemological approach that accounts for urban diversity and breaks with an inevitably negative, degraded view of slums.

From the toolhouses of Dharavi to the squats of Geneva, the authors invite readers to go beyond the spatial and economic functionalism conferred by Modern urban planning to reflect on the social and political conditions that make urban equality and diversity possible and, finally, to imagine and design cities that are more receptive and open to the diversity of contemporary urban lifestyles.

The Elusive Slum and Uneven Spatial Trajectories, Focus on Dharavi, Mumbai, India

Rahul Srivastava, Matias Echanove

Institute of Urbanology, Dharavi, India

This essay is based on our discursive engagement with urban issues as well as our role as urban practitioners in the field of planning, architecture and design. We tend to work in habitats that are popularly called 'slums', because they are integral to dominant urbanization processes in a global context.

These habitats bring together our own engagement with practice and discourse while existing along several fault lines. In this essay we examine some of these fault lines, which can be understood as follows. First, mapping territories that are urban, rural and forested as discrete categories tends to create fixed aggregative habitats like villages, cities and wild habitats. Any anachronism becomes an issue to be resolved. Second, such mapping of territories feeds back into each of those habitats as discrete functions, which are seen to be appropriate, either to one or the other. This mostly translates into activities being classified as appropriate or inappropriate. For example, farming or cattle rearing cannot take place in cities, while manufacturing activities are not seen to function as efficiently in rural areas. Cities are perceived as taking over rural areas and forests are seen to be threatened by the existence of all human presence. Thirdly, this further expresses itself at a micro-level in the smallest unit of occupying space, which mostly becomes about zoning.

So a family can ideally only live in occupied or owned space but has to work elsewhere. Work and livelihood have to be separated as much as possible. Eventually, entire cities are created by distancing residential and economic functions from each other. (Of course, new urban practices mark a departure from some of these assumptions, but the dominant tendency in many parts of the world, especially India, is much more segregative in a traditional way.)

Our work has shown us that Dharavi, in Mumbai, India's most celebrated 'slum' (a nomenclature we resist as will become evident in this essay), is called as such not only because of the objective attributes – such as lack of civic infrastructure – but also because it encompasses all these fault lines within itself.

It is dominated by the tool-house, where residential and working functions collapse. It is predominantly a space where manufacturing, processing and recycling happen, but its typology, layout and cultural attributes are reflective of rural life. Besides, even though it is allegedly one of the densest human settlements in the world, it exists next to a small preserved nature park and is part of a highly populated metropolis, Mumbai, which encloses within it a large tropical forest with active wildlife.

It is our contention that by linking the story of Dharavi and its micro-units to the larger story of urbanization and the uneven, fluid spatial trajectories that exist in its context, we will be able to liberate concepts that concern habitats in the contemporary world. This will eventually evolve more effective policies with regard to urban issues as a whole.

As this happens, it will also become obvious that the concept of the 'slum' as a definitive category loses its use and value. Cities like Mumbai will become more accepting of its diverse habitats[1] and will eventually form landscapes that may not look like a modern high-rise city but will be equally distant from the slum narrative.

This paper begins with the general description of the contexts we have outlined above. It delves into specifics by looking at Dharavi and, more closely, examining the tool-house as its main organizing principle. Even though the shifts in scale that we make in our analysis are large and sudden, we feel it is necessary to present the arguments in this way to become actively conscious of the way in which conceptual categories tend to map onto lived experiences in very concrete ways.

---

[1] There are officially more than 150 urban villages in Mumbai. The population of residents living in these villages is estimated to be around one million residents.

India's uneven urbanization?

Our engagement with Dharavi has deepened our understanding of the relativity of space, perceptions about spatial use, and the unexpected ways in which categories of space emerge[2]. What is considered to be dense, empty, an open field or a crowded street? What is considered entrenched in functionality or simply useless is often a matter of perception, practicality and interest.

While Mumbai has one of the most densely populated habitats in the world in Dharavi[3], what is barely known about the city is that within its urban limits it also has about 104 square kilometers of bio-diverse tropical forests (part of the western Sayadhari mountain range). This is locally known as the Borivili National Park, (or officially the Sanjay Gandhi National Park) which is fairly regulated and controlled (notwithstanding real estate encroachments now and then). Similarly, next to Dharavi's 400 acres of intense habitation, survives the 37-acre Maharshtra Nature Park (Bapat, 2005).

These spaces of protected nature were part of a nationwide move by the state, initiated in the early 1970s, to protect forests from commercial exploitation. For a couple of decades it replayed a colonial drama of pushing out indigenous communities from the forests, accusing them of being integral to the destruction process (Padmanabhan, 2011).

Their official criminalization was accompanied by the entry of organized players who created another kind of economy of use. They exploited forests for timber and minerals. In recent years the government has restored rights to previously criminalized tribal communities, and it has launched partnerships between local state agencies and them to be custodians of the forests together.

We introduce the landscape of the city's forests to complicate the narrative of density that typically associated with Mumbai. While, on one hand, images of Mumbai's high-rises juxtaposed against its shanties constantly circulate around the global media, what is not reported are the several cases of leopard attacks on human settlements around its forest edges (sometimes less than 30–40 km from the city center), according to the *Afternoon Despatch and Courier* (2013). The Borivili National Park curves in an out of the city,

---

[2]   www.urbz.net, www.airoots.org

[3]   Most accounts, including Sharma's definitive work on the neighbourhood (2000) indicate that this is so, even though no reliable figures for measuring this density exists.

making it a sudden backdrop to high-rise residential apartments, sharing walls with forests with predatory animals like panthers and leopards.

Mumbai's unpredictable use of space, its folding into and firewalling off forests from dense settlements, its ability to allow varied land-use patterns (the presence of cows and buffaloes grazing from trashcans is not just a rare exotic vestige, but part of active milk-producing local economies that can enclose a stable or a farm in a highly populated neighbourhood) (Lewis, 2008), its highly skilled habitats such as Dharavi, which can produce space from multiple uses (Nijman, 2009), intelligent temporal organization of work and a million other activities can co-exist with relatively vacant lands still being transacted in the real-estate market, as well as forested areas that surround the northern frontiers of the city.

This essay contends that these distinctive spatial uses, coexistence of a wide variety of habitats, and the city's very problematic official attitude towards housing and land management needs to be understood in terms of wider inter-referential categories, such as urban, rural and the natural forest. Segregating these concepts tends to harden fundamental assumptions of the city, the village, the slums and the forest, making them increasingly discrete and distinct from each other. Larger urban policies are anchored to these categories and notions of urbanization, and its accompanying processes are overlaid on realities that are essentially more cross-referential. The fact that urban histories and structures can encompass a wide variety of spatial uses and habitats is not adequately appreciated, leading to faulty policies related to housing, especially in the context of the issue of housing shortages and the presence of slums.

The level of urbanization in the country (which technically means the number of people living in habitats of a minimum population of 5000 with at least 75% of male workers engaged in non-agricultural pursuits and a density of at least 400 persons per sq km), is still less than 30% of the total population of over one billion. Even with such a wide definition of what constitutes 'urban', India's urbanization levels are low, notwithstanding its three or four mega-cities with a 10 million plus population (Census, 2001). Rural-urban migration has also slowed down further since the 1980s (Darshini et al., 2010).

The most recent census from the government points out that household industrial units in villages and the growing dependence on non-agrarian incomes have gained in importance. According to the 2001 Census, 986,629 houses are used as factories and workshops in urban areas alike but as many as 1,224,283 such sites exist in rural India (Census, 2001). Thus, in the words of urban sociologist Dipankar Gupta, 'in economic terms at least, the village is not exactly textbook fashion rural any more' (Gupta, 2011). The same Census study also points out that the share of urban population in the million plus cities in 2001 stood at 68.7%, but by 2011 this came down to 42.6% – a decline of roughly 26%. Whatever urban growth is happening is not taking place in the big cities but in small towns all over the country. These small towns are deeply integrated into their rural hinterlands with people commuting everyday, up and down and across, creating urban systems over vast territories. India's other tough truth is that the rural population remains very high and has probably increased by a slight margin since the last census. The most recent figures show that 72.2% of the population continues to live in India's 641,000 villages (Census, 2001).

Male migration from village to village, both intrastate (41.6%) and interstate (20.7%), remains significant. A migrant's destination in India need not always be a city, even though that is mostly the case. The rural net domestic product is as high as 45.5%. This means that nearly half the village economy is no longer agricultural, with many more workshops and household industries in its fold. People are staying in the village but not necessarily working on land, at least not for a lot of their time. This rise in commerce in rural India is a symptom of how urban areas in the vicinity of the villages are also changing (Census, 2001).

Our own research reveals that a substantial number of migrant communities in Mumbai invest in building or rebuilding homes in their native towns – sometimes more than a 1000 kilometres away – with which they keep connections intact (Echanove and Srivastava, 2013). Familial structures ensure multiple sources of income, act as social security in times of crisis and help with credit to start new ventures. Each family can have members spread across the country. They use the country's vast and inexpensive train network to sustain this lifestyle. A dramatic example of this state of affairs is outlined in historian Raj Chandavarkar's book on Bombay's working classes (Chandavarkar, 1994). He points out that around half of the city's textile mill workers in the early 20th century came from one district on the west coast of India: Ratnagiri. They commuted seasonally using a ferry service, to inevitably participate in seasonal agricultural activities back home every year. Their industrial income and agricultural income complemented each other. As members of Mumbai's celebrated working class, this example is particularly poignant.

Our ongoing engagement with and research on Mumbai also affirms that migrant communities from cities such as Mumbai and Delhi invest in both non-agricultural activities in their villages and real-estate projects. Their affiliation with at least two (sometimes more) locations, through their family structures and constant travel via railways (and these connections have been facilitated further by cheap mobile phones) create all kinds of spatial dynamics that do not easily fit into a vision of urbanization as a one-way street, with people flocking to cities with no resources.

The simplistic models urban planners and national agencies use (predicated on the idea of urbanization as a permanent singular moment) do not do justice to realities – at least on the Indian sub-continent.

The main concern we have is that such simplistic models create distorted and apocalyptic notions of urban futures and present the issue of housing (and the presence of so-called slums in many cities around the world) as the main cause of urban problems. Mike Davis's work, *Planet of Slums* also succumbs to this vision even though it attacks neo-liberal policies more specifically as the cause of the housing crisis (Davis, 2006). However, by not looking at the larger issue of uneven urbanization trends in countries such as India or ignoring the internal dynamics of habitats in terms of categories and nomenclatures (many of Mumbai's slums share typlogical, functional and historical characteristics with villages within its urban framework), the notion of slums, as he uses it, becomes a simplistic category that only partially addresses pertinent issues.

Shifty concepts: slums and other habitats

Expressing dissatisfaction with the use of the word *slums* to describe and label such habitats has been a recurrent theme in our arguments (Echanove and Srivastava, 2008). What is or is not a slum is often unclear. Villages, working class settlements, settled habitats that are not easily assimilated in a growing urban sprawl, sometimes even middle-class but shabbily constructed buildings, are all lumped together under this category.

The term *slum*, if used loosely, tends to be ideologically co-opted, especially when it absorbs these diverse built forms under its label. Such an ideological intention often plays itself out in the speculative financial world of real estate construction. Real estate lobbies are well known for their hunger for new territories in a world of finite land resources. They find creative ways of reinventing needs for spatial use; the redevelopment of older habitats is a very common mode of doing so. By labeling a habitat as one that needs redevelopment, it also receives the support of administrative agencies. In this way, the word *slum* develops an ideological resonance and the discursive space surrounding it becomes strategic.

The more we engage with the reality of construction industries as they play themselves out in a contemporary urban context such as Mumbai, the more evident it becomes that slum redevelopment projects here are less concerned with the life of their inhabitants than with generating new construction sites for building companies who are servicing a speculative economy. Today, thanks to the Slum rehabilitation Scheme in Mumbai, most rehabilitation of slum dwellers is subsidized by release of land for constructing apartments to be sold in the market (Patel *et al.*, 2009). As mentioned earlier, Mike Davis uses a large canvas to talk about the future of housing and the rise of slums at the global level. His analysis works brilliantly in analyzing the rise of inequality in terms of a force-feeding of liberal economic policies to developing countries. However, if we accept Davis's vision of slums as being manifestations of certain kinds of economic relations, then we are forced to view slums as an integral rural phenomenon as well. After all, just because the huts of landless and poor peasants are not historically seen as slums does not mean that they have never functioned as such. Davis traps himself in a tautology by zeroing in on economic principles as the defining moment for housing and ignoring the larger discussion of typologies and forms. If his argument is pushed ahead, the whole world has always been predominantly a planet of slums. Peasant homes, tribal hamlets and residences of slaves in a pre-modern context were all functions of economic relations besides being dependent on – and exploited by – dominant classes.

In this observation alone, our thesis contradicts Davis's overall argument. The planet is not set to witness an increased presence of slums for the first time in its history. It is simply re-arranging resources to suit an economy that is now openly acknowledging the fact that the indicators of development are almost singularly indicators of a certain kind of urban growth. It is not just that the poor migrants are moving to cities and creating slums; they are also bringing in their histories with them. Slums from rural areas are being transplanted in urban contexts. In countries such as India, urban contexts are treating the urban poor exactly as older feudal agrarian economies treated their rural poor.

Conversely, as Jan Breman points out in his review of Davis, modern slums are emerging in villages as well and are being referred to as such, complicating the process of urbanization in countries such as India (Breman, 2006). In fact, it is becoming particularly difficult to distinguish slums from villages in many parts of the peri-urban areas of the country.

If one adds to this explanation the special case of Mumbai, then slums are not only a question of developing a critique of the economic policies that the world is choosing for itself but also about the idea of the city. Many studies demonstrate how the city produces more pockets of urban poverty by converting its land-use patterns into real estate development zones that push the poor to its peripheries. These real estate development zones subscribe to a certain kind of appropriate built-form – the high-rise – to validate its imposition. In cities such as Mumbai, this form itself helps in escalating costs and pushes the poor further into infrastructure-deprived regions.

As Linda Clarke and David Harvey demonstrate (Clarke, 1992; Harvey, 2012), capitalism has always operated best within the context of the city. It has not only responded to the rise of the modern city after industrialization but has also actively propagated it as the most appropriate human habitat for modern living. Besides, this propagation has a material basis – the construction industry – that benefits most from this process and is constantly looking for new land and new ways of appropriating old modes of land use.

The construction industry, along with its baggage of architects, engineers and urban planners, have an historical advantage in that they have been perceived as playing an ideologically neutral role in the process of economic transformations. For long, we were under the impression that they service a foregone economic choice: the logic that industrialization follows urbanization. However, as Davis himself demonstrates, they may also lead the process. While doing so, they evoke ideological justifications (as do all economic interests) and use the notion of the city – a specific kind of city – as their ideological anchor. They transform the city from a site where different ideologies play themselves out to becoming an ideology itself.

While theoretically, the high-rise apartment block has been used in Mumbai as a possible solution to the city's problems of density, in reality it has only produced more slums. This happens because the high-rise apartment block comes hand-in-hand with increased costs of building and a new economy of land use, one that depends significantly on wider roads, more parking spaces and, in the final order of things, fewer occupants per square foot.

In Mumbai, the earlier colonial mode of monopolistic land use was substituted, in independent India, by an enormously corrupt administration that protected large land-holdings and worked in tandem with corrupt builders. What it used to justify this state of affairs was the argument that land in Mumbai was scarce and people too many. Besides, the image of the city as a modern city meant funneling all resources to the production of appropriate habitats.

This process was recently evident most clearly when the city's industrial history was re-written. Old defunct mills, with acres and acres of land in them, were released into the market even as housing activists cried themselves hoarse saying that a proportion of the land be used for housing the poor. Not only did the authorities not respond to the demand, even the use of land for open space and parks was rejected. Old chawls in the area were then rapidly pulled down to make room for shopping malls and high-rise apartment blocks.

Looking at the story of slums across the world, one is struck by the relativity of the term. In one context it appears as impoverished living in the most basic sense – without water and toilets – while in another it could denote a full-fledged middle class housing complex that is a slum only in relation to the larger story in which it is embedded.

If one builds on this cross-cultural understanding of slums and locates the one common variable that cuts across contexts, we suspect it is that the slum is simply an inappropriate habitat in contrast to the larger aspiration of the economy in which it is embedded. One is not de-contextualizing the impoverished slum from the story. The impoverished and the inappropriate habitat are collapsed into one for the overall push in a specific direction: the one to which the construction industry aspires. It is this idealized notion of the high-rise city that is used by builders and urban planners in cities like Mumbai to push forth a land-use pattern that produces more slums.

Thus far, the city's poor have responded to the crisis by highlighting their impoverishment – a move that is picked up by Davis to indicate that the problem lies mainly in questions of economic transformation. However, the issues of homelessness and slums also need to address issues of inappropriate habitats as well. This can require some well-constructed arguments such as those by Charles Correa in his work *The New Landscape*, mentioned earlier (Correa, 2010). According to Correa, the high-density low-rise form that much of Mumbai historically demonstrated is widespread in urban areas not only in India but also throughout much of Asia. In concrete terms, it is the relinquishing of this habitat ideal – in favour of the high-rise apartment complex – that most benefits the builder and urban planning lobby and contributes to the increasing presence of slums all around the world.

According to Correa, in the Mumbai of the late 19th and early 20th centuries, the relationship of dwellers to architects, builders and living space was more interactive. Dwellers had more control over the process of building homes, and learned building skills played a vital role in the development of these spaces. Villages, clusters of small buildings and colonies of bungalows were built through these negotiations. Even though major architectural and engineering companies shaped the docks, government offices and public buildings, the inhabitants in most of the native city had a greater say in building their own homes. In many cases, and definitely until the early twentieth century, much of the native spaces were surprisingly 'rural'. Orchards and paddy fields accompanied the docks and industries as backdrops for a newly emerging city.

Interestingly, the poor in Mumbai still follow a similar pattern of building habitats. They find cost-effective ways of building them that incorporate a multitude of skills. What causes them to become slums is that the land on which they reside is part of a competitive market. This renders their built-forms illegal and squeezes them into a zone of non-citizenship that traps them further in a spiral of oppression. Almost all their income is eaten up by this status, and they become victims of the informal apparatus of the state, which exploits their position and earns massive illegal revenues from these transactions. This creates a context in which their growth and the threat of their annihilation is a constant presence.

This story is well known in Mumbai. However, even as this knowledge fuels an activist zeal amongst everyone – the non-corrupt dimension of the state, voluntary groups and the media – it often translates itself into a desire to build homes for the poor, mirroring the construction industry. This involves planners, builders, engineers and architects. The mathematics is worked out to allow for a particular kind of built-form to dominate the city's landscape – most certainly vertical and definitely out of the control of the dwellers. Almost immediately, the question of costs rises and advocates for an acceptable compromise that lets in for-profit builders and allows them to subsidize the homes of the poor. The homes for the poor become shadowy and shaky versions of the real thing – built in the image of the modern city – but not only are they never numerically enough to absorb the impoverished millions, there is no guarantee that they will outlive even one generation of the intended inhabitants.

The ineffectiveness of this method is becoming clearer as slums continue to dominate the landscape, and vast tracts of precious (hitherto unavailable) land is used to create massive, expensive apartments. Defying all logic, Mumbai sees more tall buildings appearing with fewer people utilizing the floor space index. Where verticality is supposed to absorb more populations, space is manipulated to produce expensive habitats, and of course these approximate the aspirational habitats that one finds all over the world – with swimming pools, enormous personal spaces, multi-storied car-parks and lush gardens. However, in poorer economies like India, their horizons are always darkened by the presence of the poor and their shabby habitats.

According to Leeds (1994), we cannot view urban and rural spaces solely in terms of their geographical and occupational distinctions. He points out that throughout human history, although most people have lived in rural habitats, these habitats have been shaped and ruled directly or indirectly by the relatively smaller populated urban centers. Agricultural practices have often evolved to produce certain kinds of grains for taxation, and farming systems have been linked – through feudal structures – to important urban centers. Thus, the world had been urbanized for a very long time (even if most people did not physically live in cities), and the industrial revolution only marked a quantitative shift of populations into urban spaces. Most importantly, the narratives accompanying modernity, progress and urbanization have been used and re-used in different ways. The ideology of urbanism as presented above is very much part of this narrative and needs to be analytically isolated, especially in contexts such as India, with its long history of (urbanized) rural habitats. There are remarkable similarities between urban slums in Mumbai and the rural habitats its inhabitants have left behind. How should cities look like in an increasingly unequal world?

Dharavi: tool-house city

Mumbai is India's financial capital and has always attracted immigrants from all over the sub-continent. The neighbourhood of Dharavi is a living testimony to that history, with populations coming from all parts of the country. The city's authorities, unable to cope with the its rapid growth, which only accelerated after India gained independence in 1947, have left newcomers to develop their own habitats, which have now become fully integrated into the city's economic and political life. From a small fisherman's village at the mouth of the Mithi River, Dharavi has grown into a hyper dense settlement and hub for all kinds of cottage industries ranging from recycling to leather-work, embroidery to food processing.

Often described as a large slum, Dharavi is in fact a highly upward-ly-mobile neighbourhood that generations of local masons and residents have built over the years. We refer to it as a neighbourhood 'in formation', because it never ceases to improve and reorganize itself. The malleability of its built form has led to the emergence of particular architectural typologies and patterns of movement. One of the most distinctive aspects of its urban fabric is the presence of what we call the 'tool-house', a space that is used both for living and for income generation. The tool-house emerges in response to the need to optimize space in a context of scarcity, but it is also embedded in a cultural mould, where community ties are strong and permeate both personal and professional spaces.

One of the most enduring artefacts of pre-industrial society in contemporary times is the tool-house; the habitat of the artisan where work and residence co-exist amicably. Conceptually located between Le Corbusier's machine for living and Ivan Illich's convivial tool, the tool-house is an apparatus fulfilling economic and sheltering purposes. It is a dominant architectural typology in many parts of Mumbai that have never been planned or zoned, including Dharavi. The tool-house integrates functions that are usually segregated in planned neighbourhoods. The aspect of the tool-house that is most relevant to this study is that it combines many functions within a restricted space. These functions can be superimposed, with the same space being used in different ways throughout the day. Or they can be juxtaposed, allowing different activities to be performed simultaneously. Sometimes, functions are merged, producing new opportunities.

The principles at work in the spatial organization of the tool-house can be extended to the entire neighbourhood of Dharavi, and thus help understand the relationship of such unplanned neighbourhoods to the rest of the city. In the past, production practices took place mostly in the artisanal homes of rural areas, while cities were political and trading centres (Echanove and Srivastava, 2008). Today, in a post-industrial hyper-urbanized era, versions of the tool-house can be found in an artist's loft, a web-designer's den, a hidden restaurant in an immigrant enclave or in an up-market artisanal shopfront behind which an old family continues to perform a traditional occupation.

Several of Mumbai's unplanned settlements are shaped by the contours of the tool-house. Every wall, nook and corner becomes an extension of the tools of the trade of its inhabitants, where the furnace and the cooking hearth exchange roles and sleeping competes with warehouse space, with eventually a cluster of tool-houses making for a thriving workshop-neighbourhood. The form is intimately linked to the larger economic context of decentralized production and the subsidizing of costs by the complex and layered use of space. It is organically connected to the units of the family, the community and the persistence of the village form in the modern metropolis. The relativity of space and time are evident in a place like Dharavi through the form of the tool-house, where space and distance expand and contract in flexible ways.

Without moving an inch special spatial arrangements can transform a static entity such as a home into a dynamic economic vehicle of mobility. This happens by ensuring that it functions efficiently as a tool-house and only moves goods and people when needed. It sometimes uses multiple versions of itself all along the intended route of transport to relay information, goods and people without anything more advanced than individual physical energy. At other times, it does this by delivering goods to its borders on time, so that they can be plugged into a courier system to the airport and then to another part of the country and world via the most advanced technological modes of transport.

There are several kinds of tool-houses. They can be a small room or rooms owned or rented by a family or by co-workers. They can be attached to a restaurant or another commercial establishment or someone else's home. A tool-house can be an elaborate structure or a corner of a room being used in multiple ways. It can be a dormitory-workshop, a family home-workshop or simply a home with a shopfront. Even if people from other areas in the city commuted to Dharavi, their place of work typically would not be a commercial establishment but a residential-work site combination where other workers lived.

Functional optimization of living spaces is a feature of many high-density cities throughout the world, but it is nowhere as prevalent as in Asia. Tokyo, Hong Kong, Bangkok and Mumbai have often fascinated visitors for this reason. We have seen countless photo-documentaries showing tightly organized interior spaces in Asia, with the bicycle hung on the wall or the bed slotting into the wall at the push of a button. We have seen futuristic visions of metabolic buildings made of 8 sq m residential capsules being built and destroyed in Tokyo. But no other city has pushed the integration of functions as much as Mumbai.

In Mumbai domestic spaces often incorporate productive or commercial activities, such as cottage industries or retailing. This extreme exploitation of space is often seen as a consequence of poverty; in a context where space is scarce and expensive, its value must be leveraged. Yet, relation to space – and those who occupy it – is also eminently social and cannot be reduced to economic factors alone. Throughout South Asia, even in contexts that are not space-deprived, the 'home' is not necessarily a 'personal' space, and easily accommodates visitors and multiple functions.

Throughout India, social structures such as families, community and castes play an important role in income generation and space formation. It is fairly typical to see children or grandparents helping at the counter of a shop, while the parents are busy elsewhere. Intergenerational transmission of crafting skills and goodwill are also very much alive. Community ties facilitate business transactions, as it is easier to trust people who come from the same village or go to the same temple. Thus the house is often open to an extended family that includes people from one's neighbourhood or place of origin. Having distant relatives sharing sleeping space on the floor for a few weeks is not unusual, even in middle-class families. In that way, village ties, caste membership and culture play an important role in the (re)configuration of living and working spaces in the city.

Unfortunately, this entire intricate habitat is blanketed under the word *slum*, and Dharavi has been declared an unfit area for habitation and in dire need of redevelopment.

Uneven cities

Urbanization, says Debord (1996), breaks local barriers and autonomy only to separate people and communities along functional lines. Shifting residents from their houses to high-rise buildings in Dharavi means disconnecting them from their tools of production and the street economy. What has rooted Dharavi in the city is its own breakup into over eighty *nagars*, each with its own sense of independence, local identity, set of productive practices and regional ties. These industrious neighbourhoods, with their rural roots, small-enterprises and communitarian ethos, are urban avatars of Gandhi's idealized vision of the village.

Dharavi's cosmopolitism and urbanity lives in its infinite number of streets and gullies that serve as public and market spaces. This is where the multitudes come together. This basic freedom to interact, trade and strive for a better life is what Dharavi has offered to generations of migrants. The planned redevelopment of Dharavi ignores these dimensions, making it destructive.

The impulse to demolish in order to reconstruct is not new, nor is there anything inherently wrong with it. However, it ought to incorporate a trajectory of preservation and creation. In the context of Dharavi, what needs to be preserved are not individual houses but the ability of residents to improve them. This know-how is embedded in the way people relate to their environment. Any forced eviction and destruction would be a crime against people and their history. Demolition without preservation, especially when it is institutionalized and normalized through state machinery and entrenched social prejudice, can create destructive bitterness and resentment.

Fifteenth century architectural theoretician Leon Battista Alberti condemned demolition as an act of extraordinary violence, which he called a crime and violation of fundamental rights. He says that the actual reason for most demolitions is the incapacity of architects to build without eliminating everything that already occupies the site. According to Alberti, the reasons to avoid demolishing are economy, respect for previous human generations and the preservation of a heritage that has foundational values for the identity of a place. The preservation of the built environment permits the collective development of a humane world.

In an important essay on demolition in architecture, anthropologist Françoise Choay gives the example of Japan where Shintosit temples are rebuilt every twenty years (2006). The reconstruction is an opportunity to evolve, perfect and pass on a tradition to future generations. It brings new innovations each time. Ancient construction crafts and techniques have been not only preserved in Japan, they have also spread beyond sacred spaces into the city. For instance, masons with ancestral knowledge are still building millions of small homes in Tokyo. Rather than preventing growth, this practice contributes to becoming the most populated and advanced city in the world.

Choay echoes poet and linguist A.K. Ramanujan (1990) when she points out that the form of preservation through recreation is similar to the transmission of myths. Myths have historically been oral retellings with the imprint of a new voice and personality each time. This plasticity of form and its impermanence is what allows for creative architectural practices as well as powerful myths to emerge and endure. When neighbourhoods like Dharavi are disempowered, erased and ultimately substituted for totally different urban forms and spatial organization, it is the whole city that is cut off from its evolutionary process. This is why we can say that the redevelopment of Dharavi gravely imperils its development, the development of its people and the future of Mumbai. It would produce a convenient location for exclusive and privileged real estate development on the graveyard of one of the most open, inclusive and upwardly-mobile parts of the city. The impressively dynamic industrial base of Dharavi and its evolving urban morphology would disappear, and a majority of its dwellers would be pushed back to the city's edge, forced to restart from zero. Instead of clearing a slum, the redevelopment project would actually create new slums and poverty.

The urbanization process as it is unfolding in Mumbai will not give Dharavi residents more legitimacy, money or independence. The redevelopment of Dharavi is aimed at creating more value around the land and eventually creating a new speculative economy for residential and commercial buildings. Current residents will either have to integrate into the new economy as service providers or leave.

Urbanization produces more pockets of urban poverty by converting its land-use patterns into real estate development zones. These zones eventually push erstwhile slum dweller to its peripheries, which then are seen to be dark horizons again waiting to be developed. These real estate development zones subscribe to a certain kind of appropriate built form – the non-slum structure, which is usually a commodity meant for a speculative market. In cities like Mumbai this process itself escalates costs and pushes the poor further into new corners. What we are seeing in Dharavi today is not a slum development project but the same process of new slum generation along with the exploitation of valuable land that wants to convert a living neighbourhood into a past-tense.

It is understood that the construction industry in the city is in cahoots with the state government and bureaucracy, which are in a hurry to see this process unfold as soon as possible. What they are pushing is the high-rise apartment block as a quick fix for all problems of density and alleged homelessness. What is simply happening is that the high-rise block comes with increased costs of building and a new economy of land use, which eventually out-prices most erstwhile slum dwellers even if they have been initially 'rehabilitated' on site. Thus, the ex-slum dwellers are squeezed into tiny housing blocks neighbouring high-end flats, built on the land released by the slum redevelopment project. Eventually the ex-slum dweller moves, since it is not economically sustainable to stay. The released space goes back into the market.

The ineffectiveness of slum redevelopment projects in the mode of proposed master-plans for Dharavi is increasingly evident. As so-called slums continue to dominate, the city tracts of precious (hitherto unavailable) land are used to create habitats for the real estate market. Defying all logical use of space, Mumbai sees more of these complexes appearing which absorb less of the population and witnessing spiraling costs. Where fresh construction is supposed to absorb more populations, in reality the space is manipulated to produce habitats based on speculative needs – with swimming pools, enormous personal spaces, multi-storied parking lots and lush gardens. Paradoxically, the more space released into the market, the scarcer it becomes, as it is instantly gobbled up by the construction industry selling homes to speculators or high-end users. Many flats sold in the city remain vacant, newer flats take longer to be sold and prices continue to soar.

Debord claims that social emancipation is not only about appropriating the means of production but also about the appropriation of our own history. The ongoing process of urbanization in Mumbai and the world at large is one that erases as much as it builds. What is at stake in Dharavi is not only the sheltering of hundreds of thousands of people and their economic independence, but also their social history, which – far from being celebrated by the authorities – is dismissed and deemed unworthy of a future. The process of urbanization that Debord describes negates the city because it deprives neighbourhoods of the chance to reproduce and reinvent themselves.

What master planners and developers propose would interrupt an ongoing process of development. The idea that development follows a linear trajectory from the village to the slum and the slum to the 'modern city' is plainly wrong, particularly if that indicates a specific form of urbanization characterized by high-rise buildings and large motorways. This 'modern city' is, in fact, urbanization without a city. What makes the city is the people that inhabit it and the way they interact with their environment, making it their own, constantly balancing between their history, present needs and aspirations, both individually and collectively. The city is reproduced everyday through millions of social and commercial interactions. The city should therefore not be understood as a counterpoint to the village, or the place that ends where farmland starts. These are enmeshed at many levels in the city's economy, fabric and ethos. The city ends when its inhabitants can no longer communicate with each other and interact with the world around them.

Conclusion

This lack of communication is as much a function of weak concepts as it is conflicting purposes and a confusion of visions. In this essay we have only touched the tip of a huge conceptual iceberg. There is much more to explore and explain. Our engagement with Dharavi and other such settlements in Mumbai and elsewhere leads us to a larger understanding of habitats and connecting concepts including that of forests, villages and wilderness, which we see as invisible but influential categories through which the idea of 'urban' operates.

We conclude with a fascinating story told by anthropologist Suresh Sharma in *Tribal Identity and the Modern World* (1994). The Agaria tribes of the forests in Central India were adept at smelting iron and had a rich legacy of crafts involving ironwork. They responded with enthusiasm to the coming of the iron and steel world of the railways but were confronted with an administrative gaze that could not see them as anything more than savage forest-dwellers. Instead of harnessing their enthusiasm, their presence in the forests (where they used to shallow-mine iron in an ecologically sound way) was criminalized. The forests then were either mined and destroyed or zoned as a Nature Preserve.

This compulsion for categorization and zoning runs deep. A village in a city is eventually considered to be anachronistic and must either be gentrified or lose its identity as a village. In Mumbai, several of the biggest slums, including Dharavi, have a nucleus that once was a recognizable village. It is easy for a village – which should not exist in the city in the first place according to the laws of demarcation – to slowly be downgraded into a slum, especially when rural refugees start crowding the city and need to be housed.

A place like Dharavi, which is almost all about industry, is illegal for another reason. It violates another zoning taboo whereby residences and work places must never overlap. This taboo makes no sense in Dharavi where the main built form is the tool-house, a multi-use space that defies categorization and zoning. Yet, the laws continue to cite disputable and excessive reasoning – at every level.

We work at both levels: on the ground by examining, working and subverting administrative logic about such habitats in Mumbai while simultaneously being engaged with the theoretical concerns and assumptions about urban life and forms. Therefore, it was necessary for us to contemplate the points of convergence between these realms.

As Max Weber has famously said, the concept is a useful fiction but one that is very real in its impact on the world. That point of impact is the site of convergence. Dharavi as a subversion of the concept of *slum* is at the heart of such a convergence in the context of Mumbai. Dharavi challenges some fundamental concepts with which we work – the house, workplace, density, space, village, city, urban, rural, wilderness. These challenges are the starting point for our engagement.

Urbanization Regimes of the Ordinary City

Luca Pattaroni, Tobias Baitsch

Laboratory of Urban Sociology

Ecole Polytechnique Federale de Lausanne, Switzerland

It is becoming increasingly clear that the current concepts used to analyse, build and govern contemporary cities throughout the world are inadequate, as they do not reflect the diverse realities of habitats and ways of life and fail to provide what is needed to invent a shared urban world.

In the search for alternatives to our urban future, the work of intellectuals such as Rahul Srivastava and Matias Echanove, who work at the crossroads of academic research and urban innovation, can serve as an invaluable guide. Engaged on a daily basis in the contested reality of urban development in Mumbai, they use *action research* to question the enforcement of radical and destructive urban projects, arguing that overarching and reductive theories (most notably, the contemporary separation of nature and urban civilization), still determine urban development in cities around the globe. This division is manifest in the self-reinforcing, clear-cut distinctions between concepts such as *city*, *village* and *forest*, which do not correspond to the reality of the intricate habitats and ways of life of today. Such reductionist perspectives are not only a matter of abstract debate; they also play an active role in a normative model of city development that tends to reduce the expression of key differences and opens the door to neoliberal urban projects that enhance the city's exchange value.

Faced with these epistemological and practical challenges, Srivastava and Echanove therefore propose reversing our understanding of urban development, taking the intricate habitat that is the slums as the paragon of an incremental development of a city more hospitable to urban differences. By calling for a reassessment of the fundamental concepts of our notion of urban planning, Srivastava and Echanove belong to the ever-growing tradition of subaltern urbanism literature which criticizes the primacy of western ideology and calls for more cosmopolitan urban studies (Robinson, 2006; Roy, 2011). As we will suggest here, such debates could gain a great deal from opening up to larger theoretical and empirical attempts to tackle the pluralism of contemporary societies, such as French 'pragmatic sociology' (Boltanski and Thévenot, 2006) and, to a certain extent, the Actor Network Theory (ANT) (Latour, 2005).

In this chapter we will discuss Srivastava's and Echanove's arguments, along with inputs from various scholars engaged in conceptual work that seeks to overcome the limiting epistemological frame of modernity and reinvent urban studies. This discussion will summarize broader reflections on the study of urban order. We defend a pragmatist approach of urban order, focusing on the way cities handle difference – accepting, transforming or negating it – while building a common world. The last part of the article creates a dialogue between the alternative model of incremental development in Mumbai's slums and our recent work on the question of urban difference in Geneva. The hope is to foster a more systematic, comparative approach that will allow us to identify the main elements at play in the ordering of 'ordinary cities' (Robinson, 2006) throughout the world.

1. The city and its other: an alternative path to urban development

As suggested in the introduction, the contribution of Srivastava and Echanove can be interpreted as an effusive counter-narrative to the dominant developmentalist[4] discourse that underpins Mumbai's contemporary urban projects. In

---

[4]   We refer here to the concept developed by Jennifer Robinson (2006).

this dominant perspective, one of the major problems facing the city are large 'slums' that are seen by the local government and major urban developers as providing poor living conditions to urban dwellers, even presenting a danger to the city itself (as breeding grounds for disease and criminality). In their opinion, these slums must undergo massive redevelopment, which generally is synonymous with their destruction.

In reaction to this negative image of slums – which primarily serve financial speculation (as symbolized by high-rise buildings) – the authors invite us instead to reconsider the conceptual tools that underlie it. In the tradition of post-colonial studies, they question the disjunctive categories of the Western, modernist tradition of urban planning and defend the idea that using exclusive categories such as city, village or forest fosters an impoverished way of considering and handling urban development.

Their argument builds on examples of uneven spatial trajectories in the urban development of the city of Mumbai and India in general, which historically grew through the absorption of villages, forests and mangroves. The outcome of this 'incremental development' is a city of 'uneven urbanization', where one finds a whole range of various urban fabrics, including high-rise buildings, but also a low-rise and very dense, intricate habitat and inhabited forests. This evolutionary process of incremental development was disrupted by industrialization and the importation of a modernist conception of urban ordering through colonization, which separated human life into 'objectified' functional activities and assigned distinct places for their execution. This urban order, based on the valuation of formal efficiency and strict spatial and social divisions in opposition to mixed and porous use of space, has resulted in the de-legitimization/criminalization of hybrid territorial and social compositions. Consequently, the contemporary diversity of spatial and social forms – which account, according to them, for Mumbai's vitality – is blanketed, and often negated, under restrictive categories such as 'slum' or 'protected forest'.

The paths to a meta-critique of the neoliberal urban order

Opposed intellectually and politically to this reductive approach to difference in the city, Srivastava and Echanove open the way to an in-depth critique of

the situation, further denouncing neoliberal speculative interests by considering the anthropological roots and formal dimensions of the dominant mode
of urbanization that underlies them. This is meta-critical in that it allows one
to question a reality as defined by dominant institutions, and to make heard
what was, until now, inaudible (Boltanski, 2011). This move away from a
basic critique of neoliberal interests requires two complementary approaches
– methodological and conceptual – to reveal the normative apparatus that
underpins contemporary speculative operations in Mumbai.

1) The methodological approach uses ethnographic and historical methods to fully grasp the social and spatial complexity and intricate characteristics of the urban fabric. The rich description of the incremental development
of the slums allows the authors to consider not only its economic dimensions
but also its spatial and social ones. As the authors point out, critics of neoliberal urban development such as Mike Davis (2006) tend to reduce slums as
the sole manifestation of a 'certain kind of economic relations', neglecting the
urban and historic specificity of slums (This volume: 101). On the contrary, to
fully grasp what is at play in and around contemporary spaces labelled *slums*,
they link economic arguments with a detailed discussion of 'typologies and
forms' and their ideological background.

2) The second approach, which goes hand-in-hand with the first, is
theoretical and conceptual. In order to analyze the reductionist dimension of
the concepts used to describe and regulate urban development, Srivastava
and Echanove invite us to question some of the most fundamental disjunctive
categories upon urbanization. This kind of archeological quest (Foucault,
2002 [1969]) allows them, with the help of the work of fiction writer Amitav
Gosh, to trace the modernist disjunctive tradition back to the way 'nature' has
been opposed to 'urban civilization'.

In our opinion, this is the most profound and stimulating aspect of
their argument. Indeed, it can be argued that one of the distinctive features of
modern Western thinking is the radical division between nature and culture, in
other words, a classification based on the distinction between entities obeying
the 'law of matter' and those obeying the 'hazards of convention' (Descola,
2005). According to French anthropologist Philippe Descola (2005), such
a clear-cut distinction has no equivalent in other historical or geographical
traditions, which, to the contrary, are based on models of classification that
stipulate continuity between the various entities of the world, as is, for example, the case in Japan (Berque, 1997) or India (Descola, 2005). Consequently,
other ways of representing the world have, in this tradition, been considered

'primitive' and fundamentally detrimental to the development of civilization (Descola, 2005:122).

In the realm of urban studies, as demonstrated by Jennifer Robinson (2006), this modern tradition resulted in a normative division between the way of life in the modern city and other, more 'primitive' lifestyles, such as those that were allegedly characteristics of rural areas and villages. Therefore, the same urban ideology or concept of the 'good' urban order explains the desire to eradicate slums and, at the same time, preserve forest areas as pristine spaces.

Policing urban order

As the various examples in the text illustrate, there is no such thing as a 'pristine' forest or a purely rural village. Forests were and are inhabited and are even home to industries; contemporary villages offer more than rural occupations. Urban habitats like Dharavi, with its tool-houses that escape all functional assignment, are both living and working spaces. Faced with these conflicting entities, authorities work to transform or eliminate them, in order to reaffirm a disjunctive modernist urban order. Srivastava's and Echanove's work give us two key examples of the *police*'s[5] work maintaining urban order: the disentangling of inhabited forests and the negation of slums.

The disjunctive principles of modern urban planning play an important role in the way that natural settings, such as the forests and mangroves, have been policed in order to be integrated into Mumbai's urban order, based on a strict separation between nature and city and, more specifically, protected areas and cultivated land. Nevertheless, confronted with unfit realities such as leopard assaults in nearby neighborhoods, the local government is constantly obliged to reinforce or negotiate the borders of the urban order they attempt to enforce. One telling example is that indigenous populations were finally

---

[5]   We use the term 'police' in the sense of Jacques Rancière, meaning the various material, conventional and institutional systems created to enforce on a daily basis a specific ordering of the society. Such policing is what turns ideology – political models of the ideal society – into a concrete 'distribution of the sensitive', or, in other words, a practical division of the world that allows one to physically sense and experience the place of each being – and their eventual exclusion from the established order (Rancière, 2004).

allowed to live in the national parks (but without any proper infrastructure, showing their weak political importance, regardless of their received legal rights). Slums, on the other hand, do not even benefit from the legitimacy conferred by ecological principles, and typically exist only through negation.

Just as inhabited forests contradict the notion of pristine nature, slums question the urban order. As a place where living and working are intimately tied, they contradict the modernist zoning paradigm of functional segregation, as well as its more contemporary manifestation of the 'warranted city' (see below). What is and was possible to do with nature – spatial separation of functions – is not so easily applied when it comes to slums; although the aim of creating order by separating functions remains the same, the means – eradication and replacement, in this case – are different. Rooted in the modernist tradition, rehabilitation projects for 'slum' dwellers in Mumbai have but one purpose – that of living, thus destroying the synergies of space, time and activities that slums' urban fabric allow.

The quest for another urban order

After showing at length the shortcomings of the modernist 'idea of the city' behind Mumbai's urban development, Srivastava and Echanove call for a new form of urban development that is more respectful of diversity. The starting point for this alternative path should not be the contemporary, dystopian vision of high-rise buildings, but, on the contrary, the intricate fabric of the slum itself, as the key to re-imagining both urban and forest.

With the concepts of 'neighbourhood in formation' and the 'toolhouse', the authors propose categories that go well beyond clear-cut functional delimitations to consider the actual procedural character, which better describes a multifaceted reality and does greater justice to the diverse habitats of today's cities. What is more, they are not only fit for the reality(ies) in India, but potentially for cities around the globe. Behind this question is a larger one relative to the nature of this alternative urban order: is it specific to Mumbai's 'neighbourhoods in formation', or is it a local expression of a more fundamental alternative that has manifested itself in various ways throughout the world?

2. Opening up urban futures

Srivastava and Echanove's text is part of a larger academic critique of the primacy of Western and modern concepts in urban studies, which attempts to explore an urban future based on a pluralistic approach to urban development. One of the fundamental analytical operations of those critiques is that of 'symmetrization', allowing one to approach objects that are considered (in the modernist tradition) ontologically distinct (urban vs. rural, city vs. village) within the same analytical framework.

The end of disjunctive thinking: the challenge of symmetrization

Symmetrization strategies have been central to many of the innovative theoretical turns in recent decades, most notably in the work of Bruno Latour and Michel Callon, in the development of the social studies of science (Callon, 1986; Latour, 1988) and also in French pragmatic sociology (Boltanski and Thévenot, 2006; Thévenot, 2006). The idea behind symmetrization is that we need to return to a careful description of the world before applying preconceived categories, which often tend to mute the dynamic of complex realities. It is, above all, a call to return to descriptive work and use methodological tools that specifically allow one to follow the world in the making (Latour, 2006): to document how people, objects and conventions interact to produce a common world (Thévenot, 2006, 2014; Pattaroni, 2007, 2014; Cogato Lanza *et al.*, 2013). Using this methodological principle, we can move beyond preconceived ideas about rural or urban life, and start identifying their similarities as well as their differences. Preconceived distinctions aren't de facto relevant to describe contemporary realities, as Srivastava and Echanove illustrate in their description of 'urban villages,' 'industrial forests' and those elaborate habitats known as 'slums'.

However, the symmetrization of contrasting realities also requires a careful look at concepts in order to build a vocabulary both broad and general enough to grasp the roots of the phenomena being described and, at the same time, to allow for comparisons between various compositions. Such is the case in the aforementioned book by Descola, *Par-delà nature et culture* (Descola, 2005). In this groundbreaking book, he symmetrically considers the modern division between nature and culture – what he calls 'modern natural-ism' – alongside other classification models. For this, he develops a 'new ana-lytical field in which modern naturalism, far from being a benchmark for the appraisal of other cultures distant in time or space, would be only one of many possible expressions of more general schemes governing the objectification of the world and 'the other" (Descola, 2005:13, our translation). As Descola suggests, there are only four major types of ontologies, or 'systems of prop-erties of existing things': animism, totemism, naturalism and analogism (Descola, 2005:176). Naturalism is specific to modern Western thinking, asso-ciating us to nonhuman beings through material continuities and dissociating us from them through our cultural aptitudes (where, for example, *animism* attributes to nonhuman beings the interiority of human beings while differ-entiating us from them through the body). One of the essential aspects of this analytical frame is that these four modes should no longer be associated with only one cultural region but instead must be understood as different modalities of the contemporary re-compositions of the fabric of human societies.

Similarly, any attempt to symmetrize South and North cities requires the creation of such an analytical frame, enabling not only the description of intricate entities or 'urban assemblages' (Robinson, 2006) but, more funda-mentally, the distinction between various regimes of composition and their political implications – that is, of the various *modes of ordering* that compete in cities throughout the world.

Symmetrizing urban studies

To a certain extent such a perspective is akin to recent developments in urban studies under the influence of post-colonial studies, as exemplified in the works of Ananya Roy and Jennifer Robinson. They both try to develop analyt-ical frameworks that enable a more symmetrical consideration of cities around the world (Robinson, 2006) and also different paths of urbanization, be they 'formal' or 'informal' (Roy, 2011). Their work converges with and highlights some of the arguments central to Srivastava and Echanove's article. However, they also have shortcomings, which we will attempt to address in the last part of the chapter.

The quest for ordinary cities

Anchored in post-colonial studies, the aim of Robinson's work is to go beyond the various categorizations of cities throughout the world – for example 'Western, Third World, developed, developing, world or global' – to consider all of them symmetrically as 'ordinary cities' (Robinson, 2006:1). One of her major arguments for doing so is the fact that most of these categories are rooted in an exclusive understanding of urban modernity inherited from the West. Central concepts such as *modernity* and *development* work together 'to limit both cultural imagination of city life and the practice of city planning'. In the Chicago School tradition in particular, the (Western) city is the paragon of *modern* society – rational and individualistic – as opposed to more traditional 'primitive', 'irrational' modes of organization and ways of life. The problem, as stated by Robinson, is that this 'fantasy of urban modernity' became the major benchmark for evaluating urban development. In order to go beyond this dominant 'fantasy', she calls for truly 'cosmopolitan' urban studies that will approach all cities as 'ordinary cities': 'Ordinary cities, then, exist in a world of cities [...] in which cities everywhere operate both to assemble diverse activities and to create new kinds of practice' (Robinson, 2006:65).

Although she does not refer to it specifically, this is very close to the Actor Network Theory and its attention to 'assemblage' (Latour, 2006; Jacobs, 2011). Nevertheless, her theoretical construction still lacks a more systematic approach to the various *modes of ordering* the city, in the sense of Descola's 'modes of identification' or Boltanski and Thévenot's 'repertoires of evaluation' (2006) (i.e. the identification of a limited number of historically-constituted, normative ways of producing urban order present and competing within any single city). Without such a broad conceptualization, the risk is to simply observe the multiplication of 'assemblage' without the possibility to truly compare different ways of being an 'ordinary' city and, more importantly, to link those assemblages to political questions.

In order to regain a sense of verticality and power, it is important to take more seriously such legitimate principles and their important impact on the way objects and people are configured (Thévenot, 2011). As Roy suggests (2011), we need to consider the role of state power in defining the boundaries of legitimate urban order.

The quest for a relational approach to modes of urbanization

In her article 'Slumdog Cities', Roy (2011) advocates the symmetrization of different modes of urbanization in order to rethink the field of 'subaltern urban development'. In particular, she argues that what is often labeled as 'informality' and, generally speaking, is overlooked or disregarded, is a mode of urbanization that simply lacks political recognition. Furthermore, informal urbanization should not be considered a feature exclusively inherent to poor neighborhoods, but rather one that is used by rich actors and the state itself to produce the city. The only difference is its recognition by state authorities (legitimizing the informal urbanization of the rich and destroying that of the poor).

For Roy, one motive for rethinking subaltern urbanism is that she finds it too 'ontological and typological'. In other words, in its attempt to recognize the value and qualities of subaltern places such as slums – describing them, for example, as places of vibrant life and entrepreneurialism (as in Srivastava and Echanove's article) – subaltern urbanism, owing to a Bourdieusian perspective, remains bound 'to spaces of poverty, of essential forms of popular agency, of the habitus of the dispossessed, of the entrepreneurialism of self-organizing economies' (Roy, 2011:231).

It lacks a fundamental frame of analysis to understand this 'subaltern' dimension as a mode of urbanization which cannot be reduced or intrinsically attributed to specific peoples and places. Subaltern is neither 'habitus nor territory, neither politically subversive nor culturally pragmatic'. To develop a more relational approach, one must understand subaltern urbanism as pointing to the limits of 'archival and ethnographic recognition', or as an attempt to grasp the 'conditions for knowledge' on which slums are described and understood (Roy, 2011:231). Roy goes one step further in that she develops several major concepts, including urban informality, allowing for a more relational, dynamic conceptualization of subaltern urbanism.

The question raised by this perspective is that of the legitimizing power of the state. Indeed, there is a valorization of elite informalities (i.e. the legitimizing of illegal constructions) and, by contrast, a criminalization of the subaltern informalities that 'produce an uneven urban geography of spatial values' (Roy, 2011:233). Urban informality must therefore be understood in a relational way at the crossroads of 'legal and illegal, the legitimate and illegitimate, the authorized and unauthorized' (Roy, 2011: 233).

This detachment of the characteristics of the subaltern from an onto-logical perspective on people and places is close to the fundamental attempt of French pragmatic sociology to account for differences in people's behav-ior and modes of ordering not linked to the classic loci of sociology. Indeed, Laurent Thévenot and Luc Boltanski analyzed the different historical legitimi-zation principles of 'good' organization (efficiency, equality, tradition, and so on), which can be found in the traditional social entities distinguished by soci-ology, such as the family, school, the company and the state (Boltanski and Thévenot, 2006). Thus, the various 'orders of worth' they distinguish allow us to go beyond the inherited divisions of the world, as they are no longer seen as essential characteristics of a localized culture (Lamont and Thévenot, 2000).

Such frames of analysis are essential when accounting for the hetero-geneity of our contemporary world without losing sight of the limits of this heterogeneity; otherwise, it would not be possible to build a common world. Heterogeneity – i.e. differences between convictions, capacities or rythms – is always challenged and limited by the making of a common world. The issue then becomes to what extent a given political or spatial order is able to cope with difference. As we suggested earlier, hybridity and promiscuity are the intolerable *differences* of the modernist urban order. In other words, identifying and qualifying differences is always based on a specific conceptual and spatial manifestation of a normative definition of 'good' urban order (and therefore of 'good' citizens, practices, spatial settings, etc.).

Developing a broader research strategy, however, implies analyzing how formal configurations relate to the ordering of everyday urban experi-ence *and* to the normative concept of urban order. Linking these two analytical levels is the cornerstone of what could be called a *pragmatic* approach to urban order – that is, analyzing how urban order is developed based on a combination of heterogeneous entities framed by a political and moral model of the 'good' city (Pattaroni, 2007, 2015). We believe that this *pragmatic of urban order* is an heuristic way to generalize Srivastava's and Echanove's attempt to promote an alternative model of urban development, thus ena-bling greater diversity (of ways of life and spatial forms) in the city. We will now present some principles of such an approach by going back to a recent study in Geneva that echoes some of the major questions at the heart of our discussion.

3. The place of difference in the city: elements for a pragmatic of urban order

Our interest in the question of subaltern urbanism is rooted in our own experience and study of urban development in Switzerland, especially in the cities of Geneva and Zurich. Indeed, for the past 40 years, civil society militants and urban development actors alike have strongly critiqued the principles of modern rationalist and functionalist urban planning, be it for their role in capitalist development, the disjunctive dimensions of zoning policies or the standardization of the built environment (Cogato Lanza *et al.*, 2013; Pattaroni, 2011).

A history of urban difference in Geneva

As has been well documented by urban sociology (Castells, 1983), critical urban movements appeared all over Europe at the beginning of the 1970s, in direct response to the counter-culture of the 1960s. In a recent book, we investigated the birth and transformation of those urban struggles in a small neighborhood in Geneva called Les Grottes (located behind the central train station) over a 40-year period (Cogato Lanza *et al.*, 2013, Pattaroni, 2015).

As a typical setting of the European struggles of the 1970s, this popular 19th century neighborhood – partly neglected for decades – was slated to be destroyed to make room for a *modern* urban project. The public presentation of the project in 1975 provoked strong counter-mobilization, not only from neighborhood residents, but also from many militants of the rising new left, who came in solidarity from all over the city, in order to occupy empty buildings, among other actions.

This research allowed us to fully appreciate the profoundly democratic nature of the urban struggles of the 1970s or, in the words of Jacques Rancière, this 'democratic moment', wherein an unheard voice rises to question the established order, in both its symbolic and material forms (Rancière, 2004). This voice spoke for the people, their ways of life, the organizational forms that were excluded, ignored or abolished by the institutionalized 'distribution of the sensible'[6] of the modernist urban order. In the public arena,

---

[6]   See note 5 and also Mustafa Dikeç (2012).

the neighborhood became the symbol of a two-tiered, intense contestation of the established order, both in terms of *political representation* – with the birth of the new left (feminist and ecological movements, residents' associations, more revolutionnary groups like Maoists and artistic ones like the Situationists) – and *urban representation* – with the Lefebvrian critique of the modernist urban planning regime as a tool for capitalist development of the city, which impoverished the quality of everyday life of inhabitants (Lefebvre, 2009 [1968]).

What occurred during those years of struggle in the neighborhood was the invention of an alternative ideal of urban development, a counter-representation of the dominant model of urbanization. However, it was more than a mere counter-representation (a concept that tends to reduce criticism solely to its discursive dimension); it was an enacted and embedded critique of the dominant model through the modification of the built environment and establishment of an alternative social system. It is through the actual occupation of the empty buildings, the creation of collective rooms, the appropriation and setting of public space through direct action that activists were able to forge and defend a new 'grammar of the common' based on such guiding principles as conviviality, creativity, hospitality, collectivism, participation and individual autonomy (Pattaroni, 2007; Breviglieri, 2009.)

We believe these struggles have much in common with those in Mumbai, in particular as regards recognition and acknowledgement of slums as a potential alternative path to urbanization. Both are indeed struggles for the recognition of an urban difference. They fight against every normative layer of the established urban order that is at the same time its epistemological foundations, its material and institutional forms[7].

Ultimately, the struggle was successful in Les Grottes, as in many other cities in Europe. The neighborhood was renovated rather than destroyed, thus preserving the old urban fabric. We believe that it is this alternative conception of urbanization and urban ordering in general, based on the ideals of preserving what already exists, civic participation, collectivization of certain spaces and conviviality that is at the heart of the current concept of sustainable urban development (Pattaroni, 2011). Indeed, what has happened in Europe during the past 30 years is the slow institutionalization of those urban

---

[7]   Thévenot developed the concept of 'investment in forms' to account for the cognitive and material resources needed to extend the validity and formal impact of conventional categories (Thévenot, 1984).

struggles. The integration of the critiques and the struggles waged have contributed to profound changes in modes of production and government (Boltanski and Chiapello, 2005 [1999]).

Nevertheless, the acceptance of these critiques also diminished their subversive power. Our argument in *De la différence urbaine* is that strong differences tend to be eliminated in order to guarantee a liberal composition of well-controlled 'diversity'. In other words, as Marc Breviglieri analyzes it, the epistemological foundations of the modern, liberal urban order tend to be reaffirmed, most notably: 1) the protection of private property and strict division of functions, and 2) the weakening of strong convictions and attachments into opinions and flexible identities (Breviglieri, 2013).

It is here that the dialogue with India finds its full meaning. Indeed, Srivastava's and Echanove's attempt to reverse the perspective on urban planning by starting with the intricate reality of slums has much in common with the critiques of the 1970s; there was something profoundly akin to the subaltern urbanism of Roy in those struggles for a new urban order. The development of an alternative conception of a 'good' city – both as a mode of urbanization and a 'grammar of the common' – is in all likelihood a major concern in both Northern and Southern cities. However, today, this struggle plays out in very different political and economic settings, requiring careful attention and description. Therefore we need to identify and analyze the major alternative ways of conceiving and producing the urban order of contemporary ordinary cities, at play in the major territorial conflicts over the right to the city throughout the world.

Fundamental modes of ordering the city: a dialogue between ordinary cities

In the perspective of a systematic comparison of the fundamental concepts of urban order that both frame and nurture political struggles in ordinaries cities, we must consider both the similarities and the differences in the struggle for a new kind of urbanization as evoked above in Dharavi and Les Grottes. Do they bear only a vague resemblance in their critique of modern urban planning, or are they similar in their legitimization principles and anthropological fundaments? What legitimation principles (i.e. 'repertoire of evaluation' from Lamont and Thévenot, 2000) frame and guide the incremental development of

Dharavi? How do they allow the expression and composition of intimate and public relations? How do public problems arise and how are they handled? What is the relationship to difference? The answers to such questions should enable us to slowly systematize a few major 'modes of (urban) ordering' or 'regimes of urban order'.

Indeed, it is not enough to say that slums are partly – or mostly – the product of state legitimization strategies, as do Roy or Srivastava and Echanove. We need a more systematic analysis of how slums become a public problem and how exactly they are (dis)qualified. That is, how do the critiques of slums vary in relation with the normative idea of the 'good' urban order?

For example, the extension of what is considered a slum in Mumbai is linked not only to the speculative neo-liberal interests and general idea of the city that underlies its development but also to a change in its definition. The definition of 'slums' is no longer based on the issue of legality, but rather on that of 'risk'; parts of the city considered to be a physical threat to inhabitants. The analytical exercise here is not to assess whether or not this is true, but to understand the political, social and planning impact of this framing of the problems. There is wealth of literature on the development of public issues – and their relation to situated experience – that is hardly used in those debates[8]. Paying systematic attention to those questions should provide a sharper edge to the comparison between ordinary cities or else the establishment of an 'urban geography of spatial value' (Roy, 2011:233). In other words, the criminalization of poor, informal developments is not only a matter of the 'qualification power' of the state (Roy, 2011), but also has to do with the specificities of urban forms and the normative conceptions of the common good underlying them.

Therefore, the comparison should not stay at a discursive or epistemological level, but should consider the urban fabric. How it is produced? Which principles nurture it? What aesthetic does it boast? How does it relate to the social and political organization of everyday life? As Srivastava and Echanove have already demonstrated, the narrow streets of Dharavi are, formally speaking, very similar to those of cities in southern Italy. But does that mean that the everyday reality or the way of relating to other is the same? In Geneva, the areas most similar to what we saw in Dharavi are probably the 'porous spaces' of Les Grottes, where the distinction between private and public is blurred (due to the vegetation, the closed but still open courtyards and

---

[8] See all the tradition inspired by the seminal work of John Dewey (1927). For an overview, see Cefaï & Terzi (2012).

the presence of domestic objects in the public spaces). This porous dimension of public spaces must be considered as a critique of the modern urban model and its clear-cut division between private and public. It would be extremely interesting to compare how such spaces are perceived in India and Europe relative to differences in personal boundaries and the engagement expectations resulting from contrasted norms of behavior in public space. It is in such examples that the links between situated experience and the political conception of the common could be investigated.

These questions bring us back to the study of the practical and normative constitution of urban order and its relationship to difference. As we suggested, the *pragmatic of urban order* means fully understanding the ordering dynamics of people and things, which play out in what can be considered as a double pluralism[9] of the legitimization principle and of the ways of engaging in the world. As we already suggested, pragmatic sociology produced a few analytical tools to study 'repertoires of evaluation' and their impact on the world (Boltanski and Thévenot, 2006 [1991]; Lamont and Thévenot, 2000), as well as the 'versatility' of human agency (Thévenot, 2006). Regarding the question of urban planning, we also need analytical tools that place our description and reflection at a more fundamental level than the inherited concept of 'planning' in order to symmetrize the various modes of urbanization. Recent applications of the methodological principles of ANT to architecture (Latour and Yaneva, 2008) help us defend the concept of urban planning as a mobilization process producing collective forms.

Nevertheless, as Jane M. Jacobs (2011) suggests, a strictly Latourian interpretation of the city risks overlooking the political dimension of technological assemblages. This critique converges with the one we made earlier regarding the danger of simply describing networks and assemblages without assessing their political implications. On the contrary, a *pragmatic of urban order* invites us to consider the links between situated experience, built forms and powers at play in this encounter. In other words, it implies a study of the normative principles that orient each type of 'assemblage' along the material and conventional investment translating them into a specific regime of urban order, revealing both its emancipatory but also oppressing dimension.

To summarize, we would like to go one step further in the political and economic analysis of the dominant contemporary urban order we believe is at work in Mumbai as well as in Geneva. In particular, it seems essential to

---

[9]   On the question of double pluralism, see Breviglieri & Stavo-Debauge (2000); Pattaroni (2007).

better grasp the complex relationship it entails between the perpetuation of a modernist, liberal urban order and the major changes in the economic and political tools of urban development.

The disjunctive urban order of the 'warranted city'

As we saw in our discussion of Srivastava's and Echanove's article, the political issue behind subaltern urbanism lies in the fact, that its intricate forms not only oppose the dominant urban order symbolically, but they actually challenge its reproduction and, therefore, the benefits enjoyed by the elites who produce and govern it. Indeed, the strict delimitation and 'linearization' (Raffestin, 1986) of boundaries at the heart of the rationalization of the modern production of space is precisely what allowed for the development of property rights, thus giving land an exchange value[10]. Hence, the enforcement of a strict division of public and private spaces – and, on a larger scale, zoning regulations – helped to lay the foundations for the specific political and territorial order required by the expansion of capitalism (Harvey, 2001).

Nowadays, while 'post-industrial' or 'cognitive' capitalism has a rather different relationship to territory (Brenner, 2013; DuPasquier and Marco, 2009), we can nonetheless argue that it still requires a discretization of spatial entities, conferring them with a market value (as well as clear ownerships rights). This is particularly obvious in the way spatial 'diversity' is produced in what, in French, has been coined as the *macrolot*. The *macrolot* is a large urban project wherein each plot is designed by a different architect with a different program (Lucan, 2012). The aim here is to develop a well-balanced, diverse neighborhood. But this kind of diversity is not the same as in the complex habitats of Dharavi or Les Grottes in Geneva. The promoters of the *macrolot* can think of diversity as only consisting of 'objectified' (rational functioning) sub-parts, and spatially arrange them next to or, at best, on top of each other, reinforcing a strict delimiting of private property (Breviglieri, 2013). There is little or no spatial overlapping or temporal multi-use of space. In fact, the *macrolot* still complies with zoning and its demand for the spatial segregation of functions, though in a more concentrated way. More broadly,

---

[10] This has been well analyzed wtih regard to the development of 'enclosures' in England (Neeson, 1993).

Aihwa Ong suggests that neo-liberal policies are reinforcing zoning practices, as illustrated by China, 'where liberalization coincided with 'zoning fever', as expressed by the multiplication of 'zones of exception' (Roy, 2011:234).

On a more fundamental level, we can argue that this evolution is not 'simply' due to the implementation of abstract neo-liberal principles, but also to major changes in the government of urban order. Indeed as Marc Breviglieri (2013) suggests, contemporary cities throughout the world are increasingly ordered by a 'government through objectives' (Thévenot, 2014). A government that functions based on precise, measurable objectives – as well as the various indicators allowing for their evaluation – that appears unquestionable due to their 'realism' (Breviglieri, 2013). Enforcing this 'government through objectives', we find a plethora of certification agencies, experts, labels and strictly-controlled participatory procedures working to 'guarantee' the quality of urban development. It is the production of this 'guaranteed city', as Beviglieri calls it, which contributes to the negation or transformation of intricate, and somehow shallow, forms that lack the clarity required by the qualification process. This guaranteed city can therefore be interpreted as a reaffirmation of the liberal order underlying the modern city (Breviglieri, 2013) – a liberal order based on mobile and weakly tied autonomous individuals who are fit to enjoy the guaranteed qualities of high-rises and their carefully formatted urban diversity.

Thus, Srivastava's and Echanove's article demonstrates the entangled nature of the speculative interests of contemporary capitalism and the art of separation at the core of modern urban planning. Rehabilitation projects are not only a means of increasing the value of land, but of actually participating in reinforcing the fundamentally liberal urban order of the guaranteed city and its disjunctive production and use of space.

Throughout the world attempts are made to go against this dominant normative and economic framework and to conceptualize and actualize alternative regimes of urbanization of the (ordinary) city. Hence, we need comparative tools to symmetrically and systematically describe the various modes of ordering that compete in contemporary cities, both in their ideological forms (legitimization principles) and their spatial expressions (architectural and urban projects, everyday experiences). This theoretical and empirical challenge is essential, as the distinction between the 'good' and 'bad' urban order is not only an abstract question but, as Srivastava and Echanove reminds us, a story of losses and gains, destruction and eviction, a story in which the building of the city shapes the pluralism of our common future.

References

Adjusting with the Adaptable Cat (2013) *Afternoon Despatch and Courier*. http://afternoondc.in/special-report/adjusting-with-the-adaptable-cat/article_86171

Bapat, J. (2005) *Development Projects and a Critical Theory of Environment*. Sage, New Delhi.

Berque, P. (1997) *Le Sauvage et l'artifice, les Japonais devant la nature*. Gallimard, Paris.

Boltanski, L. (2011) *On Critique: A Sociology of Emancipation*. Polity Press, Oxford.

Boltanski, L. and Chiapello, E. (2005) [1999] *The New Spirit of Capitalism*. Verso, London.

Boltanski, L. and Thévenot, L. (2006) [1991] *On Justification: Economies of Worth*. Princeton University Press, Princeton.

Breman, J. (2006) Slumlands. *New Left Review* 40. http://newleftreview.org/II/40/jan-breman-slumlands, (consulted April 2014).

Brenner, N. (2013) *Implosions/Explosions. Towards a Study of Planetary Urbanization*. Jovis Verlag, Berlin.

Breviglieri, M. (2009) in Pattaroni, L., Rabinovich, A. and Kaufmann, V. (dir.) Les habitations d'un genre nouveau. Le squat urbain et la possibilité du 'conflit négocié' sur la qualité de vie. *Habitat en devenir*. Presses polytechniques et universitaires romandes, Lausanne.

Breviglieri, M. (2013) in Cogato Lanza, E., Pattaroni, L., Piraud, M. and Tirone, B. Une brèche critique dans la ville garantie? Espaces intercalaires et architectures d'usage. *De la différence urbain. Le quartier des Grottes/Genève*. Metispresse, Genève, 213–236.

Breviglieri, M. and Stavo-Debauge, J. (2000) Le geste pragmatique de la sociologie française: autour des travaux de Luc Boltanski et Laurent Thévenot. *Anthropologica* 7, 7–22.

Callon, M. in Law, J. (1986) Some elements of a sociology of translation: domestication of the scallops and the fishermen of St Brieuc Bay. *Power, Action, and Belief: A New Sociology of Knowledge?* Routledge, London, 196–233.

Castells, M. (1983) *The City and the Grassroots: A Cross-Cultural Theory of Urban Social Movements*. University of California Press, Berkeley.

Céfaï, D. and Terzi, C. (ed.) (2012) *L'expérience des problèmes publics*. Editions de l'EHESS (Raisons pratiques 22), Paris.

Census (2001) *Census of India 2001, Series I H-1*. Government of India, New Delhi.

Chandavarkar, R. (1994) *The Origins of Industrial Capitalism: Business Strategies and the Working Classes in Bombay, 1900–1940*. Cambridge University Press, Cambridge.

Choay, F. (2006) *Pour une Anthropologie de l'Espace*. Editions du Seuil, Paris.

Clarke, L. (1992) *Building Capitalism: Historical Change and the Labour Process in the Production of the Built Environment.* Routledge.

Cogato Lanza, E., Pattaroni, L., Piraud, M. and Tirone, B. (2013) *De la différence urbain. Le quartier des Grottes/Genève.* Metispresse, Genève.

Correa, C. (2010) *The New Landscape.* Penguin.

Darshini, M., Zhiyan, L., Xiuming, Y. (2010) *Housing Options and Mobility of Urban Migrants in India and China.* Centre for Urban Equity, Ministry of Housing and Urban Poverty Alleviation, Government of India. http://www.spcept.ac.in/download/cuewp/cue-wp-005.pdf, (consulted April 2014).

Davis, M. (2006) *Planet of Slums.* Verso, London.

Debord, G. (1996) *La société du spectacle.* Gallimard, Paris.

Descola, P. (2005) *Par delà nature et culture.* Gallimard, Paris.

Dewey, J. (1927) *The Public and Its Problems.* Holt, New York.

Dikeç, M. (2012) Immigrants, Banlieues, and Dangerous Things: Ideology As an Aesthetic Affair. *Antipode* 45.1, 23–42.

DuPasquier, J.-N. and Marco, D. (2009) *Le rapport territorial: essai de définition.* 3e forum de la régulation, Paris.

Echanove, M. and Srivastava, R. (2013) Circulatory Urbanism: The Konkan Railway in Mumbai's Urban System. *Forum for Mobile Lives.* SNCF, Paris.

Echanove, M. and Srivastava, R. (2008) The Tool-House. *Mumbai Reader.* Urban Design Research Institute Publications, Mumbai.

Echanove, M. and Srivastava, R. (2008) *The S Word.* http://www.airoots.org/2008/10/the-s-word/, (consulted April 2014).

Foucault, M. (2002) [1969] *The Archaeology of Knowledge.* Routledge, London and New York.

Gupta, D. (2011) *Beyond the Metropolis.* Seminar Vol. 629, http://www.india-seminar.com/2012/629/629_dipankar_gupta.htm, (consulted April 2014).

Harvey, D. (2012) The Urban Roots of the Financial Crisis. *Socialist Register.* The Crisis of the Left, <http://socialistregister.com/index.php/srv/issue/view/1223#.UzELQl5hNz8>, (consulted March 2014).

Harvey, D. (2001) *Spaces of Capital: Towards a Critical Geography.* Routledge, New York.

Jacobs, J. M. (2011) Urban geographies I: Still thinking cities relationally. *Progress in Human Geography* 36, 412–422.

Lamont, M. and Thévenot, L. (eds.) (2000) *Rethinking Comparative Cultural Sociology: Repertoires of Evaluation in France and the United States.* Cambridge University Press, Cambridge.

Latour, B. (1987) *Science in Action: How to Follow Scientists and Engineers Through Society*. Harvard University Press, Cambridge.

Latour, B. (2005) *Reassembling the Social: An Introduction to Actor–Network Theory*. Oxford University Press, Oxford, New York.

Latour, B. and Yaneva, A. in Geiser, R. (ed.) (2008) Give me a Gun and I Will Make All Buildings Move: An ANT's View of Architecture. *Explorations in Architecture: Teaching, Design, Research*. Birkhäuser, Basel and Boston, 80–89.

Leeds, A. (1994) *Cities Classes and the Social Order*. Cornell University Press, Ithaca.

Lefebvre, H. (2009) [1968]. *Le droit à la Ville,* 3 éd. Economica-Anthropos, Paris.

Lewis, C. (2008) Now Buffaloes need to get a Mumbai tag. *The Times of India*. http://articles.timesofindia.indiatimes.com/2008-11-06/mumbai/27897039_1_buffaloes-cattle-mumbai-tag, (consulted April 2014).

Lucan, J. (2012) Où va la ville aujourd'hui: Formes urbaines et mixités. Études & perspectives de l'École d'architecture de la ville & des territoires à Marne-la-Vallée. Éditions de la Villette, Paris.

Neeson, J. M. (1993) *Commoners: Common Right, Enclosure and Social Change in England, 1700–1820*. Cambridge University Press, Cambridge.

Nijman, J. (2009) *A Study of Space in Mumbai's Slums*. Royal Dutch Geographical Society, KNAG.

Padmanabhan, V. (2011) *A Study of the Urban Poor in Navapada, Sanjay Gandhi National Park*. Centre for Development Studies, Tata Institute of Social Sciences, Mumbai.

Patel, S., Arputham, J., Burra, S. and Savchuk, K. (2009) Getting the information base for Dharavi's redevelopment. *Mumbai Environment and Urbanization* 21.1.

Pattaroni, L. (2007) in Bassand, M., Kaufmann, V. and Joye, D. (eds.) La ville plurielle: quand les squatters ébranlent l'ordre urbain. *Enjeux de la sociologie urbaine*, 2ᵉ édition. Presses polytechniques et universitaires romandes, Lausanne.

Pattaroni, L. (2011) Le nouvel esprit de la ville. Les luttes urbaines sont-elles recyclables dans le développement urbain durable? *Mouvements* 65, 43–56.

Pattaroni, L. (2014) in Cattaneo, C., Martinez, M., Squatting Europe Kollective (ed.) The fallow lands of the possible an inquiry into the enacted critic of capitalism in Geneva' squats. *The Squatters' Movement in Europe: Everyday Commons and Autonomy as Alternatives to Capitalism*. Pluto Press, London, 60–80.

Pattaroni L. (forthcoming 2015), "Difference and the Common of the City : The Metamorphosis of the 'Political' from the Urban Struggles of the 1970's to the Contemporary Urban Order" in Alexandre Martin and José Resende (ed.),*The making of the common in social relations*, Cambridge Scholars Publishing.

Raffestin, C. (1986) Eléments pour une théorie de la frontière. *Diogène* 34.134, 3–21.

Ramanujan, A.K. (1990) in Marriot, McKim (ed.) Is There an Indian Way of Thinking? *India Through Hindu Categories*. Sage Publications, New Delhi.

Rancière, J. (2004) *The Politics of Aesthetics: The Distribution of the Sensible*. Trans: Rockhill, G. Continuum, London and New York.

Robinson, J. (2006) *Ordinary Cities: Between Modernity and Development*, Questioning Cities Series. Routledge, London and New York.

Roy, A. (2011) Slumdog Cities: Rethinking Subaltern Urbanism. *International Journal of Urban and Regional Research* 35, 223–238.

Sharma, K. (2000) *Rediscovering Dharavi*. Penguin.

Sharma, S. (1994) *Tribal Identity and the Modern World*. Sage Publications, New Delhi.

Thévenot, L. (1984) Rules and Implements: Investment in Forms. *Social Science Information* 23.1, 1–45.

Thévenot, L. (2006) *L'action au pluriel. Sociologie des régimes d'engagement*. Textes à l'appui, série Politique et sociétés. Éditions La Découverte, Paris.

Thévenot, L. (2011) Powers and oppressions viewed from the sociology of engagements: in comparison with Bourdieu's and Dewey's critical approaches of practical activities. *Irish Journal of Sociology* 19.1, 35–67.

Thévenot, L. (2014) Voicing concern and differences from public spaces to commonplaces. *European Journal of Cultural and Political Sociology* 1.1, 7–34.

Photomontage: J.-A. Boudreau

Part 4

Cultures

The dialogue (albeit long-distance) between the authors of the two texts that comprise this fourth chapter addresses the notion of urbanity and its various uses, first on either side of the Atlantic, and then on its uses around the world.

For Boudreau, urbanity is conceived and used here as a double extension of the historical concept of the Anglo-Saxon (or more precisely Chicagoan) notion of planning – in other words, not planning in the French sense, but urbanity as the life and condition of urban dwellers. It is expressed socially, culturally and spatially, sometimes to the point of transforming the urban space through cultural and social practices diverging from the norm. The term also defines the inherently 'risky' nature of existence. Hence, the figures of urbanity that interest Boudreau are more or less marginal actors (creative workers, biker gangs, etc.) whose logics of action, which are often at odds with the political logics of planning, according to Boudreau, bring them closer.

Carmo *et al.* look at these concepts with regard to their European terrains. In so doing they reveal the social and spatial tactics of 'creativists', engaged, counter-creative artists, travelers and DIYers, and thus their urbanity. The authors propose calling the historic urban spaces they help to shape *punkspace*, a direct reference to Rem Koolhaas' *junkspace* – a space of postmodern logics of actions learned in Las Vegas, providing a jumping-off point for a discussion of the various forms of heroism and post-heroism of different punkspace inhabitants.

Urbanity as a Way of Life: Risky Behaviour, Creativity, and Post-heroism in Canada and Mexico[1]

Julie-Anne Boudreau

Urbanization, Culture and Society Research Center,

INRS, Montreal, Canada

'*Calling for all risk-takers and change makers [...] It's time for the risk revolution*', *the slogan stands out on a flashy brochure from a non-profit, arts-based real estate development organization in Toronto (Artscape 2005). Similar messages are posted on the website corridosalterados.com, featuring downloadable songs and movies glorifying narcotraffickers in Mexico. This artistic genre consists of using traditional songs from the Mexican northern border and changing their lyrics and images in order to feature the exciting life, risks, and pleasures of drug dealing: 'I have money and women/ and friends*

---

[1] This paper was first presented at the workshop *Wassup, Cities: An Interdisciplinary Approach to Contemporary Urbanization*, held in Leysin (Switzerland), November 22–25, 2011, organised by the Laboratoire de sociologie urbaine (LaSUR) of the École polytechnique fédérale de Lausanne. It draws on modified versions of three papers: Boudreau, J.A. (accepted). 'Jeunes et gangs de rue: l'informel comme lieu et forme d'action politique à Montréal' publié en 2013. in *ACME: Revue électronique internationale de géographie critique*. www.acme-journal.org; Boudreau, J.A. and F. de Alba. (2011). 'The figure of the hero in cinematographic and urban spaces: Fear and politics in Ciudad Juarez' in *Emotion, Space and Society* 4.2:75–85; and Grundy, J. and J.A. Boudreau (2008). '"Living with Culture": Creative Citizenship Practices in Toronto' in *Citizenship Studies* 12.4:347–363. I wish to thank Felipe de Alba and John Grundy for their research collaboration respectively in Mexico City and Toronto.

everywhere/ I love day and night/ because there is nothing else/ I laugh about life/ I will be happy when I die'.

The 'creative worker' exhorted by Artscape (following Florida, 2002) as the leading class of the new urbanity is perhaps not so different from the gang member or 'at-risk' youth targeted by prevention programs, or from the corridosalterados blogger. In many ways, they constitute paradigmatic figures of urbanity (see Pedrazzini and Sanchez's work on the figure of the *malandro* in Venezuela for a similar argument, 1998). The city is not only their scene; it is their logic of action, their way of life, to paraphrase Wirth (1938). They act in ways that are difficult to understand from the rational-consequentialist logic of action guiding the modern project of ordering that has (unevenly) dominated state activities for over one hundred and fifty years. In Montreal, for instance, the Youth Secretary of the Ministry of the Executive Council of Quebec is investing $23,025,000 to 'prevent and act on risk behaviour' by promoting healthy and responsible sexuality, countering the neglect of children, supporting young people in distress or with mental health problems, fighting drug abuse, and countering street gangs (www.jeunes.gouv.qc.ca/strategie/defis/sante/prevenir-agir-comportements-a-risque.html). The logic underpinning such programs is one of risk-management more than risk-taking.

This paper is an attempt to better understand these logics of action and their difficult reconciliation, as noted by Artscape:

> On the one hand, leading thinkers everywhere are heralding the arrival of the creative age [...] On the other hand, the ability to make change has never been more challenging, whether in government, business, or non-profit sectors. As if fear of failure was not a strong enough impediment to growth and change, we've created elaborate systems to manage risk or avoid responsibility, and almost any new initiative that hints of boldness is susceptible to being shredded as scandalous waste or a boondoggle. (Jones, 2005:1)

Risk-taking and risk-managing are both appreciated and depreciated forms of behaviour, depending on who is acting, where, and for what purposes. Based on empirical work in Toronto, Montreal, and Mexico City, this paper explores different forms of agency, the constitution of different types of actors, and the resulting forms of social ordering that emanate from the contemporary urban condition. The aim is not to propose a comparison of three cities, but rather to look at three seemingly different groups of actors (creative workers, gang members/at-risk youth, policy-makers) in order to produce a typology of competing but interrelated – and sometimes overlapping – logics of action at play in the contemporary historical period marked by intense and globalized urbanization.

The paper starts with a brief overview of this common urban histori-cal context, before turning to an analysis of three logics of action in light of the empirical material collected. Firstly, the paper interrogates the contractual logic of action guiding the production of safety through new public manage-ment systems as much as through social codes of civility. Secondly, we will discuss the actuarial logic of action guiding risk-management and prevention programs concerning arts as much as youth gangs. Thirdly, the paper turns to a discussion of the urban logic of action exhorted by creative workers and gang members alike.

Living in an urban world

Processes of urbanisation bring new sets of economic, social, political and cultural conditions that affect how people act and interact (Boudreau, 2010). Urban sociology, from Wirth (1938) to Sennett (1970) has sought to qualify the urban way of life and its consequences on individual practices and identi-ties. Others, such as Rémy (1990) or Bourdieu (1979), have insisted on codes that structure relationships in the context of interactional density in cities, with these codes being more accessible to certain privileged groups than to others (*urbanity* defined as *civility*)[2]. Proposed here is a threefold definition: Urbanity is a historically situated and unevenly distributed condition which influences lifestyles, modes of interaction, and collective and individual log-ics of action, no matter where one lives. In other words, urbanity[3] is under-stood here as a common historical condition equally affecting people living in urban, suburban or rural settings.

---

[2] This is at the core of debates on youth violence in France, focused on the notion of incivility.
[3] The word *urbanity* sounds a little clumsy in English, but it has to be understood here as a concept similar to that of *modernity*, the suffix *–ity* designates a historical condition.

The contemporary urban world signifies more needs for mobility, changing the area-based logic of action prevailing in the modern state system. It requires being able to act rapidly and swiftly as urban rhythms accelerate. It creates complex situations entangled with one another. This makes evaluating future consequences of an act more difficult. The complexity, fluidity and rapidity of urban life pose challenges to how people plan and strategize. As more and more people live in urban settings, these characteristics of social, economic, and cultural life come to define the contemporary period (Lefebvre, 1970; Magnusson, 2011).

Urbanity is a paradoxical condition. On the one hand, it is often seen as supporting modern rationality and 'civilization'. This is very present in discourses on urbanization in the Global South: Urbanizing as a strategy for 'developing' and 'catching up' with the Global North. In this case, formal processes of urbanization are emphasized, particularly through urban planning and state entrepreneurialism in constructing flagship projects and infrastructure. On the other hand, urbanization, particularly in the Global South, is also closely associated with 'messy' and 'uncontrollable' slums, 'underground' economies, and illegal power networks (slum lords, drug lords, mafias, corrupt politicians, etc.). In other words, urbanization is closely associated to processes of informalization. As Roy and Ong (2011) suggest, urban informality 'is a heuristic device that uncovers the ever-shifting urban relationship between the legal and illegal, legitimate and illegitimate, authorized and unauthorized. This relationship is both arbitrary and fickle and yet is the site of considerable state power and violence' (Roy and Ong, 2011: 233).

Bauman (2005) argues that this urban fluidity and complexity (which is not exclusive to the Global South) is a source of anxiety because it contrasts with modern rationality. Modern rational action is thought to result from calculating the costs and benefits of anticipated consequences (Darwall, 2002). Anticipating consequences presupposes control of the unknown, of the uncertain. Such rationality, as we will see below, underlies prevention programs and risk-management techniques characteristic of the actuarial logic of action. Similarly, civility and social behaviour is assumed to rest on people's self-control and ability to integrate social norms, that is, to minimize uncertainties and act with strategic precaution (Goffman, 1959). This type of cautious and socially strategic behaviour characteristic of the contractual logic of action is not most prominent in the urban logic of action observed in creative workers and narcotraffickers.

Urbanity is an unevenly distributed condition, meaning that it does not erase modern logics of action such as actuarial and contractual logics. In fact, one individual can mobilize more than one logic of action depending on the situation (Dubet, 1995). Importantly, however, urbanity creates the need to interrogate emerging logics of action that are more attuned to this historical condition. This requires a very different epistemology, being open to realities that are difficult to categorize, map, grasp or explain with linear causalities and temporalities. It requires a completely different conceptual toolbox, displacing central concepts in social sciences such as society, nation-state, or wage labor, while breaking down modernist dichotomies between formal and informal, rural and urban, dominant and dominated, Global North and Global South, good and bad. We will come back to this in the conclusion.

The contractual logic of action

From Rousseau to Locke and into the present day, the idea of a social contract has been guiding democratic states. The idea of popular sovereignty is based on shared decision-making power between governors and the governed whose sovereignty is partly and willingly ceded to the state. This political philosophy is based on the fear that other individuals' liberties will impede on one's well-being, thus legitimizing the need for the social ordering and civilizing techniques of the state. Such contractual logic of action further penetrates the other two spheres of the modern state-society-market triad. In the social sphere, the history of the modern liberal democratic project is testimony to the belief that individual lower passions constitute a threat to social order (Valverde, 1996). De Courville Nicol (2002, 2011) argues that this fear has meant a conceptual shift in the location of 'bad' forces from the environment outside the individual body to an interior psychological space. In order to self-manage risks, the democratic citizen needs to interiorize that which needs to be controlled. S/he needs to constitute him/herself as a sovereign and autonomous actor by managing anxieties, controlling frustrated desires, taming passions and fending off irrational tendencies. In psychoanalytic theory, locating irrationalities and desires within the individual – in a sphere distinct from reason – is a means to facilitate self-control while placing the burden of social order on the individual. The liberal democratic state is thus based on a contract between a sovereign state and sovereign individuals.

These techniques of self-governance coexist with another tradition in modern liberal thought which builds on intuition and experiential knowledge, and which is more visible in the market sphere but is also embedded in modern contract law. Modern contract law (as it developed in the tradition of common law) sees risk-management and risk-taking behaviour as forms of pragmatic and situated calculation based on 'reasonable expectations' and 'everyday prudence [...] with respect to potential harm' (O'Malley, 2000:461). Risk-taking is encouraged insofar as situated knowledge provides enough information for prudent, yet innovative, action. The belief here is that market profit is generated by the creativity of entrepreneurs who follow their intuition and experience to make decisions in an uncertain environment where it is impossible to control all variables. In this modern liberal context, a primary duty of the state is to facilitate the delicate balance between the suppression of interior 'irrationalities' and their utilization for generating profit and wealth.

But beyond the state and the market, people's ability to minimize uncertainty and act with strategic precaution is a defining feature of the social concept of civility. Goffman (1959) ably describes how individuals self-manage to save face in situations of social interaction. They will comply to rules of politeness and civility in order to keep up with the socially-expected behaviour in a given situation. In other words, they will act prudently in order not to experience negative emotions such as regret, shame or guilt, which come when the tacit contract maintaining civil order is broken. Indeed, this risk-management behaviour is premised on the mutual recognition of a social situation by the actors involved. They tacitly recognize a specific situation and the behaviour expected because they understand the codes of the social contract.

This modern contractual logic of action remains operative in the contemporary state-society-market spheres; some of its aspects have been exacerbated with the rise of neoliberalism, while other aspects have less relevance as societies are profoundly transformed by globalization and urbanization processes. As developed in section 4 on the urban logic of action, the state's loss of control over its borders, its declining capacity to monopolize the use of legitimate violence, the rising significance of cities, the declining legitimacy of the nation as urban dwellers' primary allegiance, the multiplication of entangled, interdependent and indefinable situations have shattered the monopoly of the modern contractual logic of action. This is particularly clear in the case of Mexico, where such formal and modern contractual logic of action was never fully and uniformly implemented. After more than half a decade of authoritarian one-party rule by the *Partido Revolucionario Institucional* (PRI), a (neo)liberal democratic state began to emerge in 1989 when the PRI lost power in a northern state. This gave rise to a (neo)liberal social contract between the state and its citizens, but also between the state and the market. Between the 1930s and 1980s, the PRI had governed with a tight fist through a populist, clientelistic, and corporatist regime. The system collapsed in the 1980s when the state abandoned the import substitution model, privatized numerous enterprises, opened its market to external trade and abandoned agricultural subsidies. The authoritarian state gave rise to the neoliberal state, characterized by a contractual logic of action but without eliminating older corruption and clientelistic practices (De Alba, 2009).

If the contractual logic of action largely penetrated (albeit unevenly and more recently) the state and market spheres, it has had more difficulties in the social sphere. The idea of a social contract between the sovereignty of the state and the sovereignty of individuals has been less relevant in Mexico given the strong communal ideas inherited from the Mexican revolution and the dominance of the Catholic Church. The regulation of 'irrationalities' or the 'taming of passions' were less individually-managed than communally or religiously-controlled. But such forms of social management have been crumbling since the 1990s. One-fourth of Mexico's population lives in the United States, legally or otherwise. Through their back-and-forth movements, these citizens transport new values and a more individualistic ethos. At the same time, international NGOs are more and more active in Mexico, carrying a discourse of individual human rights which defies the state's idea of a national and patriotic identity. Mexicans 'are experiencing a passage from identities inscribed in prescribed roles (as men, women, farmers or indigenous individuals who submit to local traditional authorities and are inscribed in a forced political dependence on the PRI) to collectively contested and negotiated identities' (Boudreau and De Alba, 2011:81). A multiplicity of actors is filling the state-market-society formal spaces, competing for legitimacy and power: drug traffickers, new social movements, new religious figures such as the *Santa Muerte*. There is no longer a clear center of power in the capital. Instead, Mexico is governed by mobile and fluid 'capitals': Tijuana, Ciudad Juarez, Monterrey, Mexico City. This is a fertile ground for the emergence of an urban logic of action, as we will see below.

On the other hand, faced with such challenges, the modern state in Mexico, as in Canada, does not abdicate and has responded with an exacerbation of the modern contractual logic of action. It has developed three types of responses: 1) shifting from a protective to a therapeutic role, 2) reinforcing individual responsibilities towards the community, and 3) intensifying risk-management measures through auditing mechanisms.

Firstly, as individuals are faced with an increasingly complex urban and global environment, the state has gradually abandoned its role of protector, dominant during the welfare state period (Castel, 2003), to replace it with what Isin (2004) calls a therapeutic role of appeasing and tranquilizing citizen anxieties. Let us take the example of cultural planning practices devised for marginalized and socially-excluded groups such as 'at-risk' youth. Art-based community development projects are set up as a way to provide them with self-confidence and the power to participate in the social contract. They are conceived as vectors of personal development and autonomy, inculcating in youth self-management. In Montreal, for instance, the Vice-Chair of the Canada Council of the Arts writes that:

> Regular and constant contact with the arts and culture contributes to cultivating the components of creativity, which are a critical sense, the ability to stimulate the imagination, transcending rigid thinking, the ability to dream, emotive distancing, the capacity for transposition, and being able to move away from convention, predictable intellectual and physical behaviours [...] It will be our duty to reinvent, expand, open up, reposition and refinance the cultural systems, programs and tools we possess in order to meet the challenges of today and to stimulate the enormous human development potential that our fellow citizens rightly aspire to. (Brault, 2005:59–60, cited in Grundy and Boudreau, 2008)

Secondly, in addition to fostering individual capacities for self-management in an increasingly complex and risky world characterized by the retreat of state protection, the contractual logic of action requires the reinforcement of individual responsibility towards the community. Individuals are asked to calibrate their behaviour in light of civic virtues such as participation, social capital and social cohesion. As Walters states, 'with ethopolitics, it is a host of previously less tangible things – the civility, the level of trust in society, the intensity of

community feeling, the extent of voluntary endeavor – that become important' (Walters, 2002:390, cited in Grundy and Boudreau, 2008). European
debates on youth incivilities are testimony to this reinforcement of a specific
social contract based on civility and cohesion. The creative and expressive
attributes of youths are bound to a wide variety of governmental objectives
such as 'social cohesion', community renewal and global competitiveness.
In this context, the figure of the creative worker becomes central to manage-
rial and motivational philosophies as much as economic development proposals. The creative worker becomes the 'risk revolutionary' who is not afraid
to take risks in order to produce collective creativity. S/he is celebrated as
courageously tearing down the Weberian 'iron cage' of professional bureaucracy.

Yet – and this is the third type of state response exacerbating the contractual logic of action – these innovative and risk-taking attributes are cir-
cumscribed by what Michael Power (1994, 2004) calls the 'Audit Explosion'
and the 'Risk Management of Everything'. Public administration is now
characterized by multiple performance assessment mechanisms. Cultural
policy is caught up in this spiral. While important resources are attributed to
such programs, they are simultaneously subjected to audit practices through
which they need to specify in quantitative terms their value and outcomes.
In Toronto, for instance, the Culture Division is required to use performance
indicators as a 'benchmark of the health of the Creative City' (City of Toronto,
2003). This entrenches a contractual logic of action between the artist and the
state. As a staff member of the Toronto Arts Council explains the attempt to
assess artistic production through performance measurement:

> You aren't supposed to have deficits, and everyone is supposed to have
> organizational health. In the sixties, if you were just creating, that was
> sufficient. Now you have to have a really well run organization, with
> donations, and government funding, following policies. (Interview, 31
> October, 2005, cited in Grundy and Boudreau 2008)

A growing field of expertise in the area of 'arts stabilization' now assists artists
in negotiating the simultaneous demands for creativity and risk-management.
For instance, in 2003, the program Creative Trust was set up as an example
of 'how to give arts organizations a hand up, rather than a handout' (Creative
Trust 2003, cited in Grundy and Boudreau 2008)

The actuarial logic of action

These examples of how neoliberalism has exacerbated the contractual logic of action are closely related to another emerging logic of action, the actuarial logic based on probabilistic calculative tools used for assisting decision-making. Such logic of action took hold in the 1990s, in the wake of Blair's Third Way ideas. With the elimination of many of the welfare state's regulating tools (monetary policies, protection through social redistribution, etc.) and the state's increasingly visible incapacity to protect citizens from crime, terrorism, natural catastrophes or health hazards, the neoliberal state had to find new ways to legitimate its presence. Its authoritative functions (penal functions) remain fairly intact, or were strengthened through a series of measures criminalizing poverty, for instance. But its social functions evolved from an emphasis on social redistribution to that of individualized responsibilization (workfare, insistence on individual performance, etc.). The neoliberal state no longer promises happiness for all, but rather an efficient management of risks. In this system, the 'good citizen' is required to work on himself, to become useful. Obesity becomes an individual responsibility and being healthy is a duty to society; school dropouts are not victims of poverty but responsible for their lack of motivation, etc.

In this context, social workers and artists are asked to work on developing 'useful' individuals. They are asked to tailor their practice on evidence-based research. The work of R. E. Tremblay (2008), for instance, is influential in Canada. He argues that the development of aggressive behaviour originates in the first five years of life. It would thus be crucial to intervene in 'at-risk' groups very early to prevent and redress aggressive attitudes, in order to avoid an increase in seriousness and the stabilization of such behaviour. In this framework, social work would consist of teaching children emotional regulation and the management of impulsivity, while training parents to impose discipline and control peer influence.

The actuarial logic of action, in brief, consists of identifying 'at-risk' groups in which to socially intervene to prevent future problematic behaviour. It mobilizes actuarial techniques of probabilistic calculations in order to detect risks and act preventively. It is based on the premise that risk is an objective, and thus calculable, element of social life (Borraz, 2008). In the field of police action, this has come to be known as the 'new penology' (Feely and Simon, 1992). It refers to an understanding of the criminal as a bundle of risk factors.

The criminal is not conceived as immoral or deviant, but is rather seen as part of an at-risk group to be managed. The criminal act is no longer seen as an act of transgression, but rather as a statistical probability for a vulnerable group. It is thus a normal aspect of the social system that cannot be eradicated, but that we ought to *manage* through prevention. The goal of the penal system is thus to neutralize danger and not to punish or rehabilitate the criminal. In order to do so, various techniques have been implemented: crime prevention through urban design; social and spatial interventions in at-risk territories; community policing; using at-risk individuals to control others (youth patrols, urban stewards); racial profiling; and zero tolerance zones (regulating delinquency in a space, not regulating the delinquent).

One of the most important consequences of seeing the individual as tributary of a social group (which is classified according to risk levels) is that it strips him/her of all modern liberal and autonomous agency. The individual is seen as a passive victim of his/her social group or living milieu, who ought to work very hard to become a better person (individualized responsibility) because probabilities are that s/he will turn out 'bad'. To prevent the worst from happening, an army of social workers will help those who do not have self-motivation. Youth are particularly targeted by such measures. As Ungar writes,

> Youth thus become objects of collective fear, seen not as individuals but for the anxieties they cause and the jarring cultural changes they are seen to embrace. The particular impulsiveness of youths, wrapped up in their hostility to tradition and authority, only serves to aggravate these tensions. (Ungar, 2009:208)

Since the end of the 1990s, when important police actions were taken against organized crime in Canada (particularly the Hells Angels and criminalized bikers), the media began to shift focus to street gangs (Sheptycki, 2003). What is most striking in this media coverage is the constant comparison between the mafia (organized crime) and gangs, the latter being considered more difficult to infiltrate given that '[t]heir members are young and often drawn from newly arrived ethnic communities', according to a police officer quoted in a January 26, 2008, article in the *Globe and Mail*. The displacement of organized crime from the traditional mafia of adults to the 'uncontrollable' gangs of youths generates much anxiety for police officers, but mostly for the general public.

The threat expressed by the media as much as in government documents can be synthesized as a fear of violence caused by rivalries to control drug markets, but also the use of violence by gang members (often in public spaces) to solve other types of misunderstandings related or not to criminal activities (responding to a provocation, protecting a territory, preventing or punishing denunciation, eliminating competition or strengthening authority) and the visibility of rowdy youths expressing their gang identity through demonstrations of strength (Government of Quebec, 2007).

It is the unpredictability of at-risk youth that worries people, something that has been recurrent in Western society for a very long time. But as Furedi (2001) argues, '[i]nstead of a specific concern, parents [now] seem to be suffering a more general loss of confidence' (Furedi, 2001, excerpts from guardian.ca.uk, 25 April, 2001). In other words, if we apply this analysis to worries concerning street gangs, parents feel more and more anxious that their children will not learn how to become autonomous individuals in full control of themselves. Indeed, a quick look at the information given to youth on Canadian governmental websites dedicated to gang prevention, one can clearly see how gangs are portrayed as a spiral of loss of self-control, either through drug consumption or escalating violence. In both cases, a small initial gesture is portrayed as irreversible in a linear descent to hell.

Yet, as evident in the narco aesthetic conveyed on websites such as corridosalterados.com, acting fearlessly is a way to challenge power relations. As a police officer told us of youths in a barrio of Iztapalapa in Mexico City:

> I feel that if they give importance [to their neighbourhoods] it's because they feel they have power, the power that their family gives them, and the power that the place [delegación] or the situation gives them. They feel incredible, 'cause nothing can be done against them. (interview, March 2011, cited in Boudreau *et al.*, 2012)

Here, a police officer worries about the vulnerability of youth in the barrio, as they are 'victims' of intergenerational criminal influence. It seems impossible to the police officer that youth can escape such influence, especially when they do drugs. As a response to this 'predictable' risk-factor analysis, the police officer explains how youth react by creating for themselves a space of action where they feel empowered and act fearlessly: the neighbourhood.

The urban logic of action

In his fascinating book, Katz (1988) seeks to understand what he calls the 'aesthetic finesse' of the criminal who is able to recognize and elaborate on the sensual potentialities of a situation. He looks at concrete situations experienced by criminals in order to explore what incites someone to commit a crime. Even when youth exhibit (self-)destructive behaviour, they do not necessarily cut off relations with society. Destruction is part of a 'series of tactics for struggling with what the adolescent experiences as a spatially framed dilemma – a challenge to relate the 'here' of his personal world to the phenomenal worlds of others who he experiences as existing at a distance, somewhere over 'there'' (Katz, 1988:112).

But in order to understand such seemingly 'irrational' or 'immoral' logic of action, it is necessary to locate the analysis in the context of the profound transformations we are experiencing as we construct the contemporary urban world. In other words, what new logics of action are emerging in this historical urban context? Perhaps provocatively, this paper argues that criminalized or at-risk youth, like creative workers, are sometimes acting in ways that are difficult to understand from the point of view of the contractual and the actuarial logics of action. After all, as Katz puts it: 'As unattractive morally as crime may be, we must appreciate that there is *genuine experiential creativity* in it as well' (Katz, 1988:8, emphasis from original). What is so creative about the urban logic of action?

In a nutshell, the urban logic of action is characterized by the following: acting swiftly and rapidly (in a reaction more than prevention mode), seizing opportunities emerging from unpredictable situations (rather than trying to predict them), seeking stimulation and loss of self-control (rather than controlling emotional intensity in order to prevent aggressiveness), building on identity differences to construct oneself as an actor (rather than profiling differences for preventive action) (Boudreau, 2010). In contrast to the contractual and actuarial logics of action, the urban logic unfolds in a tactical, more than strategic, mode. That is, it is more reactive, immediate, unpredictable. It does not unfold in a linear temporality (as in: if I do this, the consequence will be that), but on a more experiential register in a specific moment (trial and error, intuitive). Consider two examples, the first concerning youth in Montreal and the second concerning creative work in Toronto. In the first excerpt, a police officer from Montreal describes how a specific gang acts:

Sometimes it is *improvised*. I am thinking of a specific gang that comes
to mind. For them, it is iPods, but we can't even follow them. We can't
in a day detect/ they may do nothing. It is not structured; it is really
improvised. It's like a delinquent gang that do bad things. And hop!
We are going to name ourselves and oh! We are giving ourselves signs.
From there, they can act more. But at the beginning, it is disorganized.
(Interview, June 2011, cited in Boudreau *et al.*, 2012)

In this example, youths act in reaction to specific opportunities that may
come up. They perceive a propitious situation and begin moving in order to
steal the iPod. This is what Katz (1988) calls 'aesthetic finesse'. By aesthetic
he means mutual tuning, the ability to sense a situation and individuals in
co-presence. The youth described by this police officer do not anticipate the
reactions of others; they feel it. They do not rationalize their act; they act
intuitively. Such tactical form of action stands in contrast with the strategy
developed by a journalist who came to that same Montreal school once to talk
about youth in the neighbourhood. She was writing a series of three pieces,
but after the first one, she lost the confidence of the youth because she published a very negative picture of the neighbourhood and their school. They
reacted promptly, writing letters to her. While narrating this anecdote to us, a
police officer concluded:

You know, it is a journalist that I respect very much. She had a strategy.
I knew her conclusion and she chose her way to denounce a situation:
there is a need for more resources in those milieus. This was her conclusion: 'Stop thinking that everything is so easy'. But the way she chose
did more harm [to her relationship with youths]. But at the same time,
I was surprised by youths' reactions. (Interview, June 2011, cited in
Boudreau *et al.*, 2012)

This anecdote illustrates well the clash of two modalities of action: strategic on the one side (the journalist portrays the neighbourhood with pity in
order to politically ask for more resources) and tactical (youth feel betrayed
by the trust they gave her, insulted at the negative stereotype she conveyed
about the neighbourhood). The police officer positioned himself between
these two modes in this specific anecdote: he understood what the youth didn't
appreciate (the journalist's judgment), and he empathized with their feeling of
betrayal, but was surprised by the force of their reaction.

Indeed, in the following second example, what is emphasized is the way the urban logic of action gathers momentum. It is a mode of action energized more by a force of impulse than by antagonism. Nicolas-Le Strat (2008) suggests that the intensification of encounters characteristic of city life can produce radical forms of subversion not through opposition to an 'enemy' external to everyday life (the state, the police, capitalism, etc.), but rather through creation and experimentation. In creative city policies such as the *Live With Culture* campaign of the City of Toronto, this is partly what was intended:

> Envision thousands of canvasses and easels dotting Nathan Phillips Square as Torontonians *congregate* en masse to paint or sketch. One day to come together and celebrate the creativity we all possess and contribute. Now imagine a whole summer of Everyone Create! events. These single day splash events will encourage active artistic participation. Various venues across the city will host these *outbursts of creativity* whether people are painting, dancing, singing or reading. (City of Toronto, 2005, cited in Grundy and Boudreau 2008, emphasis is mine)

These two examples illustrate that an important aspect of urbanity is the *juxtaposition of various rationalities: calculative, affective, intuitive, experiential, experimental*. In a study of how households develop livelihood strategies in Jakarta, Simone and Rao (2012:5) were '*struck by the diverse ways in which households and groups calculated the use of limited resources*'. They suggest focusing on 'everyday practices whereby individuals attempt to find ways of flexibly moving through various scenarios and spaces, rather than consolidating specific zones of affiliation, work and responsibility'. Such flexibility and the juxtaposition of various rationalities are visible in the behaviour of 'at-risk' youth but also of creative workers who walk the thin line between art and performance indicators. The growing popularity of the cult of the *Santa Muerte* in Mexico is another example of this juxtaposition of various rationalities. The *Santa Muerte* is known as the patron saint of narcos. Nearly clandestine in the 1990s as it was rejected by the Catholic Church and the State, the cult became very public around the turn of the century. It is a dispersed and leaderless cult as any devotee can add prayers or initiate ceremonies. Prayers strategically call to the *Santa Muerte* for protection against the police, while carrying a strong affective tone. Ceremonies are intense experiences of subversion, creating affiliation and reciprocity without submission to a formal hierarchy such as the Catholic Church.

The urban logic of action relies on *webs of relations and interdependent situations*. Acting in such context relies on the constant nurturing of multiple relations between people, sites, stories, trajectories. People ensure their sense of security 'by making the practices and actors involved relevant to others' (Simone and Rao, 2012:14). The city is too unpredictable (physically, culturally, economically) to fully grasp. We often explain cities by their center. What happens downtown is set up as the general dynamic of the whole urban and periurban area. This shortcut is to be displaced as it prevents us from seeing the urban logic of action at play outside the center, in liminal spaces, in margins, beyond the neat formerly planned city. When we begin scrutinizing those physical and metaphorical spaces, it becomes clear that they are beyond rational grasp. '[R]esidents imagine security and stability as located beyond what they can see and figure out – in dense entanglements of implication, witnessing and constant acknowledgements of other residents, whether physically present or not', write Simone and Rao (2012:17).

This requires being mobile. Cities are characterized by *multiple movements at various scales*. Bourdin (2005, translation is mine) defines mobility as 'the fact of changing position in a real or virtual space that can be social, axiological, cultural, affective, cognitive'. In other words, urbanity is about moving around, from daily commutes to migration, but it is also about upward or downward movements on the socioeconomic ladder (social), moving value systems (axiological) through changing party affiliation or religion, for instance. Urbanity is also about moving across cultural habits (attending an ethnic festival, for instance), moving affective relationships (family recomposition for instance), or again cognitive movements (changing fields of work or study). The combined effects of these multiple movements concentrated in cities is a profound challenge to modern bounded and immobile definitions of societies, nations and communities.

In the case of Montreal, the importance of such multiple movements is exemplified by the need expressed by police officers to go beyond their institutional framework in order to develop personalized relationships with youth. The trust relationship they built with 'at-risk' youth was made possible by the elaboration of a flexible, unbound common space of action. The physical limits of this space were constantly moving depending on the situation to be resolved. It was a conception of space based on common attachment rather than physical boundaries. Such attachment became visible to both youth and police when they went out of this common space of action (in other neighbourhoods, in other local police stations). As opposed to the immobile framework of formal territorialized institutions, mobility was very much part of what happened in that neighbourhood.

Multiple mobilities is also at the core of the narcotrafficker life and the artistic production that follows this lifestyle. Pop songs about drug dealers depict them as 'border-crossing social bandits, tragic heroes, and daring rags-to-riches entrepreneurs' (Campbell, 2005:327, cited in Boudreau and De Alba, 2011). The narcos draw their power from the border, but also from machismo and *caudillismo* (the idea of individual-centred agency, which confronts directly the more communitarian and collective ideals promoted by the Catholic Church). Stories about drug dealing are ubiquitous in many Mexican towns, particularly border towns. Everyone has a story to tell about a brother, cousin, friend. Just as the narco is a very mobile figure continuously crossing the border, the stories about them circulate extensively in daily settings. They imprint the material space of the city as bars, restaurants, used car lots, junkyard 'become important landmarks used by people to orient themselves or give directions, as in "I'll meet you next to restaurant X, you know, the place where so-and-so was shot"' (Campbell, 2005:328, cited in Boudreau and De Alba, 2011). They also imprint the virtual space of digital artwork, music, homemade videos circulating on the internet. These websites are interactive sites where people can post comments, download films and songs, post personal ads, pictures, drawings, etc. They create a common space of action.

Conclusion

This paper began by briefly describing the contemporary condition of urbanity in order to ask: How does this historical condition influence the way we act politically and socially? Are there emerging logics of action that coexist with modern logics of action? Revisiting empirical work conducted in Montreal, Toronto, and Mexico City, the paper proposed a typology of three overlapping and sometimes conflicting logics of action: the contractual, actuarial, and urban logics (see Table 1 for a brief overview). In order to illustrate the workings of each of these modes of agency, various examples were mobilized, looking specifically at three types of actors: the creative worker, the 'at-risk' youth (and/or the drug dealer) and the policy-maker. The objective was not to present a systematic analysis of this empirical material, but rather to reflect theoretically about the way different social groups in different

Table 1   An overview of three logics of action.

Contractual	*Individualism*: Political philosophy of (neo)liberalism based on a contract between a sovereign state and sovereign individuals + self-governance and the integration of social norms = heroic conception of the actor as a willing and coherent self. *Individual responsibility:* Under neoliberalism, individuals are increasingly required to self-carry the burden of responsibility in the face of risks, as an ethical requirement for the community (more than the state). Increasing audit mechanisms and performance indicators. *Strategic precaution:* Acting with prudence, anticipating the consequences of an act in order to avoid a rupture of the contract, which would constitute a political act of transgression. *Linear temporality*: Centrality of the idea of progress and a causal rationality. *Area-based, territorialized space of action*: The contract takes place in a bounded space: the country, the society. *Politics*: Political action is considered to take place between competing interests under the rules of the contract (constitution).
Actuarial	*'At-risk' groups:* The use of actuarial calculations to determine 'at-risk' groups or spaces. Such vulnerable individuals lose their liberal sovereignty and are conceived as statistical bundles of risk factors. *Systemic responsibility*: Abnormalities are part of the social system; they are not considered acts of transgression but predictable occurrences that the state needs to manage. *Strategic and preventive action*: Based on probabilities of future abnormalities, preventive interventions are designed to 'redress' vulnerable individuals before they become adult. *Linear temporality*: A combination of risk factors is considered to lead to predictable consequences. *Area-based, territorialized space of action*: Some forms of intervention are geared towards 'at-risk' spaces and not only 'at-risk' individuals. *Politics*: There is no room for political acts; this is a technical logic of action where actuarial evidence leaves no room for contestation.
Urban	*Post-heroic actors*: Actors are diffuse and leaderless, embedded in a web of relationships, ambiguously good and bad. The focus is displaced on situations of action more than actors per se. *Risk-taking more than risk-management:* More than a simple focus on responsibilities; stimulation and loss of control are valorised for their creative potential and juxtaposed with various other rationalities, depending on the situation. *Tactical action*: Action is intuitive, reactive, unpredictable, and sensible. *Multiple temporalities and rhythms*: The immediate present dominates as it determines situations of action that are entangled with other situations at various scales and rhythms. *Unbound and mobile space of action*: Multiple movements fostering a fluid, but common, space of action. *Politics*: Political action is decentred from individual or collective actors. It appears by a force of impulsion more than antagonism, through the multiplication of encounters and experimentations.

cities act in a common urban world. Although not explicitly comparative, the paper is nevertheless a gesture towards what Tilly (1984) called 'encompassing comparison', that is, looking for each group's relation to a common globalizing system. As MacFarlane recently wrote, the paper asks *what might be the implications for urban theory when we take comparison not just as a method, but as a mode of thoughts that informs how urban theory is constituted?* '(MacFarlane, 2010:726).

In order to 'see' the urban logic of action, the researcher needs to operate two kinds of displacements from the prevalent social scientific gaze. Firstly, it requires adopting a situational approach whereby the analytical lens is directed towards the process of acting per se, not the actors themselves. A situation is a moment defined by the actors who give a shared meaning to what is happening. 'Each person enters a situation and leaves it not so much according to the places and institutional setting where it occurs', writes Agier (2009:55, translation is mine), 'but according to the fact that he or she shares the meaning that is at stake in the situation and understands it enough to be able to get involved in one way or another in the interactions that are present'. These interactions pertain to those with other individuals just as much as to the material space of the city[4]. Some situations are commonplace, those that go unnoticed in daily urban relations. However, there are also situations that assume a special meaning for the people who experience them.

A situation is either 'dynamic' (strategic plotting) or 'aesthetic' (tactically adjusting). For de Fornel and Quéré, 'a dynamic situation emerges when a plot takes shape thanks to an event, an initiative, or a combination of circumstances, and it is resolved when an outcome is produced (de Fornel and Quéré, 1999:21, translation is mine). While this strategic logic is definitely central to the contractual logic of action, the urban logic of action unfolds more visibly in aesthetic situations mobilizing tactical action, that is, the ability to move and react to these unpredictable and vague situations characteristic of city life, to know how to take advantage of these commonplace situations that are 'entangled' in each other and create new, unexpected situations (Lefebvre, 1970 [2003]:39).

---

[4]   Goffman defines a situation in a similar way: 'I would define a social situation as an environment made of mutual possibilities of control, within which an individual finds himself completely accessible to the direct perceptions of all those who are "present" and who are similarly accessible to him' (Goffman, 1988, quoted in de Fornel and Quéré, 1999:9, translation is mine).

Secondly and relatedly, 'noticing' the urban logic of action requires abandoning the heroic conception of the individual actor and adopting what Innerarity (2008) calls a 'post-heroic' approach. A situational approach means observing how action unfolds more than focusing on actors per se. It is a processual approach based on a displacement of what we called elsewhere the 'heroic conception of the actor'. Heroes are generally understood as 'self-confident subjects, imbued with hope and believing in their own ability to act on a situation' (Boudreau and De Alba, 2011:78). They generally act with the aim of bringing justice, based on the idea of progress. Heroism is thus a form of action based on a project, that is, action is projected in an imagined future, and the actor moves with the aim and will to affect such future. Such modern actors evolve on linear temporalities and move with a coherent conception of the self and a stable morality. In this modern vision, politics exists only in dissent and rupture from the 'bad' or the 'enemy', in the heroic act of claiming equality. Consider this example:

> What is central to Balibar's and Rancière's vision is that neither freedom nor equality are offered, granted or distributed, they can only be *conquered*. The political, therefore, is not about expressing demands to the elites to rectify injustices, inequalities or unfreedoms, but about the enunciation of the right to égaliberté [...] Put simply, politics (or a political sequence) arises when, in the name of equality, those who are not equally included in the existing socio-political order, demand their 'right to equality', a demand that both calls the political into being, renders visible and exposes the 'wrongs' of the police order (Swyngedouw, 2009:606, cited in Boudreau and De Alba 2011, emphasis is mine, except for the word égaliberté)

In this excerpt, Swyngedouw's conceptualisation of political action is 'heroic': the political sequence emerges when the conquering hero appears and by his/her presence exposes 'wrongs'. With the example of the global consensus on the need to fight climate change, Swyngedouw demonstrates that we have entered a 'postpolitical' period dominated by consensus and management. He speaks of postpolitical times to lament the delegitimization of oppositional claim-making practices to the benefit of systemic risk-management and consensus-building.

If we adopt a post-heroic approach to political action, however, we might not necessarily qualify the contemporary period as postpolitical. Indeed, in the post-heroic context, 'the state is no longer a hero that can make sovereign decisions. It depends too much on shared knowledge, on shared decision-making capacity and on shared financial means' (Innerarity, 2008:131, cited in Boudreau and De Alba 2011, translation is mine).

> In a post-heroic period, political action remains, but it is decentred from individual or collective subjects (which constitute the focus of heroism). Action takes place through an unfolding situation produced by actors and objects in relation to one another. (Boudreau and De Alba 2011:79)

The urban logic of action proceeds through unpredictability, multiple choices, shared knowledge. We saw how such logic governs narcotraffickers, their cultural followers, and their religious beliefs in the *Santa Muerte*. Narcos, just like the *Santa Muerte*, are ubiquitous post-heroes, ambiguously good and bad, diffuse and difficult to identify in recognizable individuals. This is why such logic of action is most detectable when we focus on situations of action, rather than actors per se.

If there is a specifically urban way of acting in this urban world, it is perhaps time that we enact a specifically urban way of doing research.

[Heroic] Figures of Urbanity, 'Creativists' and Travellers: New (Post)Heroes in Town

Leticia Carmo, Yves Pedrazzini, Maude Reitz

Laboratory of Urban Sociology,
Ecole Polytechnique Federale de Lausanne, Switzerland

Introduction: punk situations in creative cities

Based on the assumptions of Montreal geographer Julie-Anne Boudreau described above, we have chosen to respond to the issues and proposals most likely to trigger innovative thinking about 'the city', its 'inhabitants' and those who shape it today – a process that involves relative violence that, nonetheless, is fundamental to the creation of spaces with the specific qualities (Pedrazzini, 2005, 2007). Hence, our discussion with J.-A. Boudreau focused primarily on what she calls 'post-heroism', 'urban action' along with figures of contemporary urbanity (of which we have chosen the most 'outsider', whom we will refer to as 'punks'). As we begin our thinking about urbanity and its oxymoronic 'heroic' figures, we will liberate the 'punk' from his coffin – caricaturistic Mohawk, studded-belt and all – and use the term to describe a rebellious, unruly, messy and raw space. This space is characterized by its irremediable incompatibility with the capitalist, democratic urban order of the early 21st century – in short, an urbanity that is irreconcilable with artistic productivity and contemporary creative wage systems, which we will refer to as *punkspace*.

For her part, Julie-Anne Boudreau (2010) calls urbanity the result of confrontations, arguments and agreements between the different logics of action of urban dwellers. After a period of urban modernity, in which these logics at times violently opposed one another, becoming a permanent part of the spaces they often radically transformed, we finally come to the era that Boudreau calls 'post-heroic'. This urbanity − 're-negotiated' and seeking to protect itself against the risks, that seems to threaten its moral, political and formal foundations on all sides − is the subject of her analysis. As a result, using Boudreau's theory of urbanity in risk society, we would like to illustrate how the torch of social and urban 'heroism' − virtually extinct today − is carried on by the outsiders of our urban worlds. Boudreau analyzes this contemporary abandonment of political heroism and the fluid or liquid slide towards what David Innerarity (2012) describes as post-heroic society through figures of 'maximum urbanity', meaning not only drug traffickers and gangs along the Mexican border but also creative workers of Toronto and policy makers of Montreal.

For our part, we decided to use other figures of the new deconstructed urbanity to show that not all heroic forms of urbanity (as a way of life) have disappeared from the faces of cities, but rather have been reincarnated in certain outsiders groups and their punk (i.e. 'risky', by Boudreau's definition) practices. We chose two groups in this category: the first are 'artivists', or 'creativists', referring to artists or creative people who, faced with a complex, chaotic, potentially at-risk world, become activists in their way of inhabiting and transforming the city and its interstices, and of dealing with the market system, corruption and social injustice; the second are 'travellers' and other neo-nomads who, against a backdrop of market and housing crises, creatively self-design and self-build mobile homes, combining technical, social and spatial knowledge, skills and experiences gleaned during the course of their travels. Because of their ability to react via confrontation (and not the bargaining so characteristic of our postmodern, post-democratic societies), we consider these two urban figures as heroic and have united them under the banner of 'punk', a term that emerged in the 1970s but that is used here to describe a common culture of urban figures that inhabit parts of cities that are still insubordinate to order.

More than 'historical' quality or other attributes, it is punk's philosophy − a direct, raw relationship to creation (artistic, political and social), spatialized implementation of a 'non-future' leading to real-time DiY (do-it-yourself), DIN (do-it-now), and more or less spontaneous, primal action within the social and spatial environment, like a post-industrial 'container' of action – that interests us here. This container is the residue of the 20th century, of modernity and political heroism supported by a raw energy. It is also, as Greil Marcus theorized (1990), the random fusion of situationist, DADA and Dostoevskian anarchism[5]. And we add to this the 'world' of the punk, the wasteland in which his rock culture vernacular is rooted, which perhaps is what Marcus means when he refers to 'the art of the collapse' of punk. The capacity – heroic to say the least – to destroy cultivated cities like Berlin, Paris, London and Zurich (between 1910 and 1980), and to appropriate ruins they have not themselves helped to create, but which were given to them by industrial society. This is a commando operation, urban guerrilla warfare against postmodernism which later, in the 2000s, we realize was only a red herring, meant to distract public attention from the phasing out of popular proletarian culture.

Here is the punkspace: resistance to the transformation of the uncertain space into junkspace (Koolhaas, 2000), resistance to the transition toward post-heroism, to what we call punk and to the orthodoxy of creativity for all (disguised in the form of bohemian bourgeois, hipsters or contemporary artists working in pubs) – in other words, the haphazard, determined players that are different kinds of punks (underground, radical and anti-aesthetic, deconstruction workers, etc.). More than the actors in this resistance movement, it is the punkspace itself that best resists.

After reading Boudreau's text and its approach to the concept of urbanity, we also observed that the relationship of 'urban' figures to the materiality (objects and urban forms) of the environments in which their own was relatively 'peripheral', if not marginal. Considering urbanity within the scope of materiality naturally leads us to question the uses of material culture in a transdisciplinary way, focusing on the sensitive logics and practices that connect people and things. Thus, we felt that in order to understand urbanity in all its dimensions, it was necessary to focus on the acquisition and transmission of specific and unique skills, techniques, daily practices and knowledge, whose 'destructive' capacities should also be interpreted from this technical standpoint.

---

5   Already in 1980, sociologist René Loureau associated somewhat similar ideas in his book *Auto-dissolution des avant-gardes*, in which DADA, Surrealists, punks, Leninists and Trotskyists are mingled.

Creativists and interstices

Are we all post-heroes?

Taking the Zapatista slogan, 'We are all Marcos'[6], for specific examples of urban actions performed by post-heroic actors in the urban space, our analysis will focus on the concept of urbanity and the post-heroic figure. To begin, we identified three types of post-heroic actors in two European cities (Lisbon and Ljubljana[7]), to explore the matter of urban action in spatial terms: the common man, the committed artist and the creative person. More specifically, we will examine the ordinary man confronted with sudden and drastic changes in his living conditions (i.e., modern economic crisis), the committed artist faced with the incompetence and corruption of politicians (and consumption in general), and the creative person faced with uncertainty. While, as 'collective' actors, each has distinctive characteristics, they need to confront – and solve – the problems that arise by challenging the risks that unite them (Boudreau *et al.*, 2012).

Without necessarily having a leader or political party to channel their participation in events, these figures can be considered post-heroes. In Lisbon, for example, the current economic crisis has affected the entire population, making it take to the streets regardless of political beliefs, as if they were screaming, *We're all in crisis!*, united by a common cause, however vague. Their aim is not to start a revolution, perhaps, but at least to protest government policies. Yet, the response logic and strategy of the ordinary man – which is unclear, dispersed and often impulsive – is also intense, since it is based on a reaction to the immediate present. We find these characteristics (fluidity, dispersion and impulsivity) in one of Boudreau's logics of urban action. Thus, using flash mobs as an example of contemporary urban action to which a political dimension has been added, we will focus on an event that took place in downtown Lisbon in 2012: during the 'in situ' presentation, by a group of seemingly harmless housekeepers, a policeman stopped them on the grounds that such actions were not allowed, and then summoned them to the Court. Two days later, a flash-mob was convened in solidarity via a blog to 'fight

---

[6] In Mexico, while the Zapatista guerrillas in Chiapas spread to cities across the country during the 1990s, protesters shouted in the streets: 'We are all Marcos', creating a new collective myth at the global scale (Autonomous afrika-gruppe *et al.*, 2011:41).

[7] This is Leticia Carmo's architecture thesis project, entitled 'Alternative Cultural Spaces: A study of the contemporary dynamics in the cities of Lisbon, Berlin & Ljubljana'.

censorship and reaffirm the right to freedom of expression'. This action was a form of impulsive action-reaction that, though organized virtually, reacted spatially and symbolically – a reactive response to actions seen as authoritarian, a subversive artistic act based on the principles of guerrilla-communication, wherein ordinary post-heroes shouted, *We are all housekeepers!*

A second paradigmatic work of creative contemporary urbanity is the 'artistic happening'. We refer here to a recent performance (2007) by three artists from Ljubljana, all of whom legally changed their names to Janez Janša, the name of the highly contested Conservative Slovenian Prime Minister. In this case, *We are all...* no longer reflects an act of solidarity with a national hero or victims of the system but rather, ironically, is a critique of political power and consumer society in general. In Slovenia, it is both common and easy to change one's name, as if names were disposable. Hence, this name – well known by Slovenians – becomes a 'ready-made' in Marcel Duchamp's sense (ready to be used by anyone and everyone), a common name. This action proved to be a work of art, diffused as a concept in the form of an exhibition at the Kunsthaus Graz in 2008, under the name 'NAME ready-made'[8]. This logic of urban action reflects both modern-day recycling (of objects, spaces, names, etc.) and the history of art (Duchamp), and is used by this other post-heroic actor (the committed artist), who dabbles in punk (Dada, DiY, etc.) without actually adopting it. The committed artist is first and foremost an artist who believes in art in spite of it all, just as the creative person – our most recent post-heroic actor – believes in creativity (and marketing).

In the two cities mentioned, creative people (or the 'creative class', as dubbed by Richard Florida, 2002) act as post-heroic urban actors at two levels: 1) in a perspective close to that of Boudreau, they are informed by the prevailing system (universities, colleges) to cope with everyday challenges (risk management), using their creative abilities (Keil and Boudreau, 2010). Affected by the contemporary economic crisis (as reactive victims), creative people take to the streets in protest mode, alongside the ordinary man (or ordinary post-hero). At both levels, the spaces of action coincide with the spaces of production, which usually develop in the interstices of the city, either in public spaces or in former factories that have been occupied and transformed (industrial wastelands), like LxFactory and Fábrica do Braço de Prata in Lisbon or Rog and Metelkova in Ljubljana.

---

[8]   http://www.aksioma.org/name/

Metelkova Mesto, Ljubljana 2012 (Picture by L. Carmo, 2012).

For Richard Florida, the creative person is the 'scientist or engineer, and architect and designer, a writer, artist or musician', but also those who work in 'business, education, health care, law or some other profession' (Florida, 2002:9). Hence, we might conclude that 'we are all creative people' (or almost), given that broad range of professions included in Florida's proposal. Since the early 2000s, everyone wants to be or become a 'creative person', and almost has a duty to be so, if they want to keep up with the formidable competition of the job market.

Thus, in the words of Charles Landry[9], 'ordinary people can be creative', not so much for the love of art or artistic criticism, but because an economic crisis like the one in Portugal can prove vital to the process of creative stimulation. The idea here is that creative people are used to dealing with unstable[10], precarious situations in innovative ways, but also have the ability to envision a brighter future (however difficult, in the moment).

---

[9]   During his statement/presentation at/in the 'Creative Cities' conferences, Leipzig, November 29, 2012.

[10] This idea started, nevertheless, to be used almost as a slogan by the dominant political speech somehow in a distorted way: as if the economic crisis had a positive impact in people's life after all, since the lack of funding drives people to find solutions, other than the ones they are used to deal with, which will force them to use their creativity; this way, polititians use this speech as an excuse for applying their austerity measures and financial cuts in cultural affairs.

The deterioration of the worker's condition to one of precariousness is the driving force behind the creative class' transformation into the proletariat, also causing it take to the streets alongside ordinary people who, in times of economic stability, would have nothing in common with this rather privileged creative class. Everything is reversed, everything converges. The three actors (ordinary people, committed artists and creative people) become activists or creative people and, 'while not artists from the beginning, may soon become so' (Petrescu *et al.*, 2007).

The spatialization of urban actions

We have just considered the evolution, spread and globalization of the political expression *We are all...*, which was and could (still) be (re)adapted, (re)appropriated and (re)transformed in diverse situations, by an infinite number of social actors. We also looked at different logics of urban action in conjunction with specific urban spaces:

-   the city center, during flash mob events (mentioned above) and anti-crisis protests/demonstrations; the city center as a 'space representing social order through its buildings, political authority and official culture' (Autonome a.f.r.i.k.a.-gruppe *et al.*, 2011:33–36);
-   the interstices of the city and urban fringes, often transformed into 'creative industries', in the form of abandoned factories, where certain creative people settle but which have also become the headquarters for protest actions carried out in the city center.
-   the global space of communication networks as physical space (@-spatial), which are nevertheless urban, as these networks are the result of our urban condition. The work of artists in Ljubljana mentioned earlier is largely developed and exhibited via Internet and the cinema, though they also use more conventional modes like museums. @-space is crucial because of its power of immediacy, for the calling to and carrying out of protest acts at the global scale, such as those led by movements like global springtime, Indignados and Occupy Wall Street[11].

---

[11] '...mass protests in Cairo, in Madison, Wisconsin...Madrid...Barcelona...Athens...Oaxaca... Cochabamba...El Alto...Buenos Aires...Santiago (Chile)...; Rome...London...Berlin... New York and Melbourne ... 2000 cities in Asia...Africa...world-wide demonstration against the threat of war in Iraq.... Youth-led movements throughout the world... followed by an "Occupy Wall Street" movement that began in New York City before spreading to innumerable cities in the US and now around the world' (Harvey, 2012:116).

Thus, we can see that, similar to certain expressions or concepts, various spaces are appropriated, transformed and used for characteristic forms of urban action.

DiY and scenic sensibilities

Focusing now on the interstitial spaces of the city center and the spatial re-creation these areas undergo, one might wonder if this is not part of a DiY process of recycling destroyed, abandoned, neglected urban spaces by non-professionals (ordinary people). The occupying of these spaces (sometimes improvised and/or illegal) and subsequent spatial transformation are, in fact, informal architectural projects grounded in an often obscure, chaotic, melancholy underground world that is also poetic and beautiful (what we call *the city*). We can also find all kinds of aesthetic issues associated with these places, which are updated via visual and spatial patterns – the physical evidence of a critical, subversive yet convivial ideology for a better, more harmonious, undoubtedly nostalgic world dedicated to the memory of the city and respectful of its various historical strata. In addition to derelict factories, there are also more discrete forms of occupation directly in the city center and its interstices (basements, garages, balconies, roofs, decadent palaces or abandoned buildings). These places are often not visible to the eye but rather are located in dark hidden streets and can almost be likened to a theatrical performance, resulting in the kind of marginal ambiance associated with mystery and the city's underground (further reinforced by the almost exclusively nocturnal use of these spaces).

In this context, we believe that some of the ideas developed by the situationists in the 1960s find their actualization in the use of this type of space, if we accept that, with them, the city became the place of the 'revolutionary transformation of existence through the participation of citizens and the reintegration of the poetic in the ordinary' (Simay, 2008). If this is the case, a question then arises: is urban action necessarily spatialized? If we consider urban action in spatial terms, we could say that it is generally comprised of three phases: occupation, appropriation and transformation (of space). Following Boudreau's thinking, one could then speculate that this course of action occurs via *post-heroic actors* but is nonetheless *situated*.

Travellers and their trucks:
Do It Yourself as a logic of action[12]

The road as an alternative

Using as the basis for our observations an Internet discussion forum for owners of outfitted Mercedes trucks (*mercotribe.net*), we will look at some of
the principles characteristic of the creative and constructive art of turning
commercial vehicles into living spaces – a practice that lies at the heart of
the neo-nomadic lives of 'travellers'. We will then evaluate their punk (and
perhaps heroic) potential. Practically speaking, we put the notions of creativity, urbanity and logic of (urban) action developed by Julie-Anne Boudreau
into perspective by placing them against the larger backdrop of the principles
of the DiY ethic, reflecting on the question of the acquisition and transmission of knowledge and skills as regards housing and mobility. The *mercotribe.
net* forum is an initiative of MERCOTRIBE, a French association (Law of
1901) created in 2005 to encourage discussion among owners of converted
Mercedes vans and trucks. The forum has thematic sections, combining user
posts ranging in subject matter from the specs of different models of trucks
to accounts of life on the road (with helpful hints for outfitting thrown in),
uniting sedentary people with a bit of *wanderlust* who are fixing up a truck to
use to travel in their free time, and 'fanatic nomads' who live in their trucks
year-round. Also called 'travellers' (in reference to the British New Travellers movement[13]), they are part of a wider movement for a voluntary return
to more nomadic forms of habitat (i.e. yurts, cabins and caravans/trailers) at
a Europe-wide scale (Jeanjean and Sénépart, 2011). Having made the choice

---

12   This chapter reports on the first phase of an ethnological study being done in France on values
and practices surrounding contemporary mobile habitats. Following in particular seasonal and
'intermittent' nomads living in trucks, this study aims to shed light on knowledge and know-how
relative to habitat and mobility in this emerging lifestyle.

13   This phenomenon began in Britain in the wake of protests by the rock counter-culture of the
1960s, and then punks in the late 1970s. Many young people, following the ideals of living
preached by the protest culture (hence, critical of the values of the capitalist system) chose to
adopt a lifestyle on the margin, opting for new values and practices including a mobile habitat,
traveling in converted trucks, vans, caravans and buses. In the late 1980s this movement
intersected with the nascent rave movement, thus incorporating the production of electronic
sounds and the organization of clandestine parties in their lifestyle. Following the adoption of
the Criminal Justice and Public Order Act by the Thatcher government, which drove them out
of the United Kingdom, the phenomenon gradually spread throughout Europe and France, in
particular, through the organizing of techno music festivals (Frediani, 2009).

to leave downtown areas and invest in less fixed living spaces, many people (mostly young) have taken to the road and adopted 'alternative lifestyles' between ephemeral living places and the edges of woodlands.

DiY ethic: sharing and action as principles

DiY is a term generally used to describe the construction, modification and repair of various artifacts, without the help of experts or professionals. In common use since the 1950s (in reference to home improvement projects), the term took on a much broader meaning to include (in the context of critical movements of the 1960s) a set of skills allowing one to provide for one's own basic needs, thereby bypassing relationships of production and exchange based on profit. Largely rooted in a desire for independence, autonomy and self-management, the DiY ethos involves creative practices that likewise take a 'reactionary' and critical stance as regards the professionalization and institutionalization of production practices and the consumer system[14]. While these practices were highly valued and popularized by the punk movement in the domain of music, this form of action invented *in situ* to respond to the demands of everyday life and individual/collective aspirations that have been part of the human experience since the dawn of time. In the first chapter of *The Savage Mind*, Levi-Strauss uses the idea of *bricolage* to describe how primitive societies have developed in practical terms, what he calls a 'science of the concrete' (Levi-Strauss, 1962:30–49) – namely a system of classification for interpreting the world, the beings of nature and everyday objects of the environment (natural and social). This 'DiY thinking' functions around a practical logic linking beings and things. It is an 'instrument that also contains bits and pieces through which structural arrangements are created (Lévi-Strauss, 1962:51). These arrangements of fragments 'refresh the possibilities' and project models of intelligibility. Bringing them back to a more specifically urban context, Michel de Certeau (1980) characterizes these DiY activities using play areas, creative cunning and tactics of resistance. In short,

---

[14] In this context, people inspired by anarchism and the punk movement chose to self-produce and self-distribute their musical creations. Extended to all aspects of life, the DiY ethos then became a tactic and objective of individuals and communities wishing to organize and provide for themselves, without relying on the market or the state. This approach is reflected today in many creative practices, including music, painting, filmmaking and software, to name only a few (Hein, 2012).

the idea of *bricolage* expresses the condition of ordinary people who, in their lives, must constantly build and rebuild, using any means available; in other words, a form of practical intelligence whose implementation takes place without the consent of any authority (Marsault, 2010).

Turning a vehicle into a home requires, among other things, architectural, mechanical, design and artistic skills. On the *mercotribe.net* website, diverse profiles of the community members cover a wide range of experiences in the art of converting trucks ranging from 'inspirational' experiences to tips for buying your first truck, to 'veteran' who have already converted several models. Many of the posts are thus aimed at sharing knowledge and experience gained 'in the field'. The creative practice discussed on the website also emphasizes the importance of human contact based on the principles of networking and open access to knowledge, skills, tools and techniques through the sharing of individual experiences[15]. The *mercotribe.net* forum is also an invitation for us all to take action. Through the various tales, the art of converting trucks is presented by the members as an experience accessible to anyone and everyone. From the project on paper to its practical realization, all of the steps are done by ordinary users – sometimes with the help of more experienced users – debunking the idea that the construction of a home (a very small one) is reserved for experts.

Converting a truck: a scalable, flexible art

Perusing the forum, one can access a description of the entire process from A to Z (i.e. from idea to realization), albeit in piecemeal fashion. The topics and content are grouped by topic. While there are 'fun' items (such as photos of members and their trucks, travel diaries and ads for festivals and gatherings), most items concern technical and practical issues (mechanics, bodywork, electricity, etc.) linked to the different models of Mercedes trucks and their conversions. When one chooses to live in a truck, the first step (meaning the choice of truck and the purchase) is crucial, since one subsequently takes

---

[15] This way to exchange can be compared to hacking phenomena and 'participative' media, which use different methods of production and editing based on self-production and self-regulation of content. Free, open source software and various forms of open publications (blogs, social networks, forums, wikis, etc.) now allow anyone to create information, share knowledge and update so-called free press publication (i.e. fanzines), so popular in libertarian counter-culture circles of the 1970's.

ownership of this space and configures it to meet one's needs. Of course, the choice of model depends on the initial budget, but above all it depends on the buyer's ability to assess his or her needs, determine the resources available on the market (used vehicles, spare parts) and seize opportunities. Constitutive of travellers' experiences, learning through practice, exploration and investigation for many begin upon the purchase of their first vehicle. The conversion stage is a time of freedom that embodies the physical possibility of living differently, outside the lifestyles and rhythms imposed by society. Along with the 'mechanics' section, the 'conversion' section has the most posts. Elevated to virtues and transformed into principles, DiY and recycling are at the heart of the travellers' daily lives. Doing it yourself from A to Z means engaging directly and physically with the material, getting hurt, getting dirty, sweating, making mistakes and starting again. While the members do proudly display their finished vehicles, the conversion process itself is no less important, and even contributes to the experience and to the traveller's ethos: 'over time, it changes because you change, so you adapt'. (*mercotribe.net*).

Thus, this form of mobile housing reflects in its very principle the transformation of both the everyday world and the movement and evolution of the individual and family over the course of travels and based on new finds. It is a scalable architectural work, combining improvisation, imagination, exploration and constant adaptation. Adapted to change, such habitats are intrinsically part and parcel of movement – veritable works in progress – because of their improvised and scalable qualities. Hence, movement should not only be considered in terms of the mobile dimension of the habitat but also in the habitat's capacity to evolve over time. Both new and old material can be found (one finds a number of ads on the *mercotribe.net* website), but more often than not, materials are acquired through salvage (chance discoveries and meetings, used objects with chips from dumps and scrap yards, etc.). Just as practices are gleaned, assorted routines and techniques gradually become skills for recycling the world's treasures and refuse. A solar panel is built out of an old refrigerator. An oil drum is converted into a wood-burning stove. Cooking oil becomes fuel. By combining resourcefulness and the ability to make something new out of something old, contingency becomes a driving force for creation, and improvisation becomes a tool.

The principles surrounding the skills and art required to convert trucks can be likened to what Boudreau describes as an urban logic of action. Nevertheless, it seems important to stress the coexistence of rationalities that the urban logic of action characterizes. Effectively, in reference to the extremely

Renault G230, Hautes Alpes, France, 2013. (Picture by M. Reitz, 2013)

binary contrast that Levi-Strauss made between the ideal figures of the engineer and the *bricoleur*, we prefer to place the creative arts of travellers within the framework of an ambivalent rationality that is *calculated* (relative to calculating the project's costs, risks and opportunities), *experiential, experimental* and *intuitive* (improvised). In other words, the traveller-*bricoleur* works on a specific project (an extra 'room' for the birth of a first child, for example), designs (3-D drawings on *SketchUp*), innovates, organizes, sees projects through to completion, evaluates and corrects mistakes and examines *what is* in order to imagine what *can be*, all the while fumbling, seizing and creating (in this case, often at the limit of legality) the opportunities afforded by random finds. Thus, they explore the multiplication and extension of uses of the objects they collect and, if hard economic times call for resourcefulness, this resourcefulness can also reveal a certain form of autonomy. *Becoming* and *being* autonomous is therefore a question of necessity, though the experience may also be rewarding or may be used to apply certain values. In short, the constructive, creative practices of travellers allow for rich comparisons in terms of research issues, between 'technicality and cunning, organization and vagueness, project and contingency, the determined and the negotiated, the sensitive and the intelligible' (Odin and Thuderoz, 2010:7). In this, the nomadic traveller is not only ingenious when it comes to transforming objects (trucks and everyday objects) and acquiring knowledge and skills, but also has the potential to resist social and urban order – a potential for 'resistance to the resistance of reality' through the social practices that contextualize them (Dupont-Beurier, 2006:139).

Creating, occupying and transforming as a mode of critical action

Truck conversion is the product of small, daily acts, everyday practices, tactics, uses and performances. Both a 'furnished backdrop and a theater of operations' (Serfaty-Garzon, 2003), the truck-home is a witness to everyday life and constructive practices – an object at the junction of the technical, the aesthetic and the affective, which can potentially serve as a platform for a range of social and technical practices and experimentation of technical forms, associations and configurations related to habitat and mobility. An intimate and transformative experience, the building of these moveable homes – like the mobility in which they are actualized – is often part of an existential journey;

both a spatial and an ideological statement, they tell stories and convey values through which travellers invent a culture and an identity. These practices and experiences, which extend from desires, moreover underscore the fact that the critique of daily life does not always take the form of a conscious, organized, straightforward battle against dominant structures. These micro-initiatives aim for and result in conquests and infiltrations of spaces at *their own* level, however small. Often invisible in the urban environment, these refurbished mobile habitats (disguised as converted refrigeration and moving trucks) perfectly blend into the environment, like any other commercial vehicle, without calling attention to themselves, especially when parked in the city. When conditions are favorable, these habitats are deployed, thereby extending and expanding the vehicle's space beyond its four original walls and roof to create new spaces. From this inside-out movement emerge living spaces: fragile micro-territories that, with rare exception, are transitory and unstable. These urban forms in the making and the emergence of these contingent, unstable 'cities' have a critical, committed, creative dimension in that they embody the potential for each of us to follow our own path, find our own space, choose where we live, and thus to leave our own mark.

Conclusion: punkspace, the final critique of urbanism

Despite obvious differences between creativists and travellers, each offers a critique of modern urban development. The punkspace is both the place of criticism *and* the embodiment of the critical space. Hence, it is not only a type of autonomous zone – a land of informality that somehow escaped laws and norms before being overtaken by the forces of urban order – but is also a heterotopia made by its own users.

    According to Boudreau, urbanization (and thus urbanity) are closely linked to informal processes. In terms of a logics of action, it is questionable whether this term still has any epistemological relevance, or if its continuance (most notably in the urban sciences) is solely due to the leftover ideological shreds of urban planning. *Urban* refers to a specific space or a territory (the city, neighborhood, road, etc.) whose character no longer encloses it within the confines of urbanization, or even of *cities*, for that matter. Thus, what we have precisely attempted to analyze and think about throughout this chapter are spatialized acts and actions whose spatialization is a radical critique (the most radical possible today) of the ways of inhabiting our urbanized world and (re)producing it, spatially and politically.

This brings us back to punkspace, that is to say the ability to define the spatial qualities where the punk logic of action can find its place and, at the same time, criticize it using DiY techniques. A punkspace theory, so far as it postulates the existence of a specific spatialization of the punk as a heroic comeback actor, helps us understand (in contemporary ways) areas in transition (from industry to ruin, and inversely from ruin to industry) today as they almost inevitably pass into the hands of 'culture' to survive as culture and as ruin. It also helps us understand how DiY recycling (and resistance to it) succeeds in actualizing itself in a certain spatial container whose primary trait is that it is an historical part of a process of destruction and of the gradual (sometimes programmed) transformation of the built environment into a destroyed environment: modern urbanity that is neither postmodernity nor post-heroism. The era of urbanity destroys itself in order to reinvent itself for the benefit of the 'other' inhabitants of these cities who are the punks, the dismantlers of the sterile urbanity of planning and modern urban order (*destructive* workers, after all). However, mere destruction does not please outsiders.

If one believes in the possible survival of heroic urbanity, we must build on at least two aspects of the theory. The first (which is sociological) deals with the concept of punk post-heroes (an actor theory). Throughout this text, we observed variations in the definition of 'post-hero', from Julie-Anne Boudreau's definition to ours in which the urban post-hero and ordinary post-hero are becoming extraordinary (creative post-hero, creative ordinary post-hero, etc.). Might this not be further proof of this contemporary instability – instability that produces plural personalities, the result of a world where trends coexist and choices are combinable, stackable options? The question is the following: can a postmodern hero still fight the system? To tell the truth, we have no idea. What we do know (because it is what the modern city has experienced over the past fifty years) is that true heroes should be resistant to the social and physical normalization of modernity. Moreover, as guarantors of urban uncertainty, they are a necessity. This resistance is, above all, a way of challenging spatial order and contesting order spatially through pirated use of ready-made spaces (the objects of a process of occupation, appropriation and transformation) through a collective dynamic of actors who defend recycling and DiY approaches. Herein lies the paradoxical seductiveness of the punkspace. According to Petrescu *et al.*, interstices are one of the morphological figures of urban action that prove that desires, other than those of speculation, do exist. However, these practices (initially of resistance or from marginal actors) are then often reclaimed by the dominant ideology and as a common form of individual action (Petrescu *et al.*, 2007:14–15), to which we can attest through the 'creative class' propensity to settle in such spaces.

The second aspect (spatial this time, and which, it would seem, is not a fundamental dimension of urbanity) can be developed around the concept of punkspace, and leads to another theory of urban action: the concept of 'interstice' could very well represent the notion of punkspace. As a self-taught situationist, the punk critiques rational urban planning by appropriating its remnants. What they do with it is what we call the punkspace, which ultimately is more of a radical criticism of contemporary urbanism than a response to Koolhaas' theory of junkspace or a critique of other architects' contributions to the creation of this junkspace over the past fifteen years, or even since the 1970s.

It is this terrifying, extreme side of punks – from Iggy Pop to the present day, in fact – that gives them eternal legitimacy as deconstructionists and sets them apart (*real* punks, that is, not *a la* Billy Idol punks) from fashion and fads[16]. The punk is, by definition, the contrary of the alienation of popular classes due to his (voluntary) lack of access to consumption; the punkspace provides nothing and is in no way a shopping center, unlike the creative spaces of today which are summoned to contribute to the creative city. The punk is still capable of subversive practices, only when they are spatial practices. Relative to the 'crisis of modern life' (unemployment, depression, austerity, complexity, postmodernity, etc.), punkspace offers a rather meaningful synopsis of the city to come. At the same time, its critique of space is a form of resistance to consumer society, business, neo-liberalism, the real estate market and the extinction of diversity[17]. Moreover, even if the biker gangs studied by Boudreau were theoretically, as 'sons of anarchy', closer to the punk spirit, they would nevertheless remain good little soldiers of savage capitalism, violently defending free enterprise without the irony that makes punk an eternal deadbeat of *Das Kapital*.

Punkspace, because it raises questions of architecture, urban planning and real estate, is political, anti-aesthetic and should be irreconcilable with

---

[16]   The punk (un)fashion, a 'Style in Revolt' (Hebdige, 1979).

[17]   '...challenge the hegemony of the "dominant culture". Punk's hegemonic challenge involves a defiant attitude, real and assumed moral transgression and the anarchic refusal of dominant values' (Moore and Roberts, 2009:273).

Western art, culture and civilization. As a result, considering the contemporary city requires us to constantly reposition ourselves, to re-contextualize our
social and cultural prejudices, and to understand that subversion is not always
part and parcel of invention and novelty and that the negative reinvention of
urban forms and the practices of inhabitants themselves (recycling, pre-fabs,
manufactured objects, DiY) is perhaps far more subversive, given the strategies of cognitive capitalism. Faced with capitalism, the last poetics possible
in the city are punk poetics: the abandoned city, the stranger, the unaware/the
ruins[18]. All that obviously attracts the eye but remains resistant to salvaging
by the market pressure – the poetry of catastrophe, of abandonment, of the
forgotten. This poetry that the biennials will never manage to retrieve completely, because the imaginary scenery (even for Georges Bataille) is never
able to survive the sincere, truly negative rejection of the artistic posture. And
in making it so, urbanity nonetheless follows its path toward the destruction
of the conventions of urban planning and the city as it is so violently produced
in our world.

---

[18]   'Coming of age in the heyday of punk, it was clear we were living at the end of something – of
        modernism, of the American dream, of the industrial economy, of a certain kind of urbanism. The
        evidence was all around us in the ruins of the cities. Vacant lots like missing teeth gave a rough
        grin to the streets we haunted. Ruin was everywhere, for cities had been abandoned by the rich,
        by the politics, by a vision of the future. Urban ruins were the emblematic places for this era, the
        places that gave punk a part of its aesthetic' (Solnit, 2005).

References

Agier, M. (2009) *Esquisses d'une anthropologie de la ville: Lieux, situations, mouvements*. Academia Bruylant, Louvain-la-neuve.

Artscape (2005) Creative Places + Spaces 2, risk revolution Artscape. www.torontoartscape.on.ca/mydocs/media/pdf/riskrevolutionconferencebrochure060805_120545.pdf?myrand¼673, (consulted February 2006).

Autonome a.f.r.i.k.a.-gruppe, Blissett, L. and Brünzels, S. (2011). *Manuel de communication-guérilla*. La Découverte, Paris.

Bauman, Z. (2005) *Liquid life*. Polity, Cambridge.

Borraz, O. (2008) *Les politiques du risque*. Presses de Sciences Po, Paris.

Boudreau, J.A. Jeunes et gangs de rue: l'informel comme lieu et forme d'action politique à Montréal. *ACME: Revue électronique internationale de géographie critique*. www.acme-journal.org, (consulted April 2014).

Boudreau, J.-A. (2010) in Davies, J. S. and Imbroscio, D. L. (eds.) Reflections on Urbanity as an Object of Study and a Critical Epistemology. *Critical Urban Studies: New Directions*. SUNY Press, New York.

Boudreau, J.A. and de Alba, F. (2011) The Figure of the Hero in Cinematographic and Urban Spaces: Fear and Politics in Ciudad Juarez. *Emotion, Space and Society* 4.2, 75–85.

Boudreau, J.-A., Davis, D. E., Boucher, N. and al. (2012) *Constructing youth citizenship in Montreal and Mexico*. UCS/INRS, Montréal.

Boudreau, J.-A., Diane, E., Boucher, N., Chatel, O., Clémence, É., Janni, L., Philoctète, A. and Salazar Salame, H. (2012) *Constructing youth citizenship in Montreal and Mexico City: The examples of youth-police relations in Saint-Michel and Iztapalapa*. Institut national de la recherche scientifique. <www.ucs.inrs.ca/sites/default/files/centre_ucs/pdf/MontrealMexicoCityreport.pdf >, (consulted April 2014).

Bourdieu, P. (1979) *La distinction. Critique sociale du jugement*. Éditions de Minuit, Paris.

Bourdin, A. (2005) *La métropole des individus*. Editions de l'Aube, Paris.

Brault, S. (2005) The arts and culture as new engines of economic and social development. *Policy Options* March–April, 56–60.

Campbell, H. (2005) Drug trafficking stories: Everyday forms of Narco-folklore on the U.S.-Mexico Border. *International Journal of Drug Policy* 16, 326–333.

Castel, R. (2003) *L'Insécurité sociale: qu'est-ce qu'être protégé?* Seuil, Paris.

Certeau, M. (1980) *L'Invention du quotidien, 1. Arts de faire et 2. Habiter, cuisiner*. Gallimard, Paris.

City of Toronto, (2005) Live with culture signature events City of Toronto. www.livewith-culture.ca/content/view/full/4822#Create_anchor, (consulted July 2007).

City of Toronto. (2003) Culture plan for the creative city. City of Toronto, Toronto.

Proven Success, Creative Trust. http://www.creativetrust.ca/files/proven.htm, (consulted July 2007).

Darwall, S. L. (ed.) (2002) *Consequentialism.* Blackwell, Oxford.

De Alba, F. (2009) ¿Que lugar para los nuevos liderazgos? El político 'moderno' del espacio metropolitano. *Desafíos* 19. Universidad del Rosario, Colombie, 105–134.

De Courville, N. V. (2002) La production de l'homme moderne: ou le passage de la peur à l'intérieur. *Sociologie et sociétés* 34.1, 175–197.

De Courville, N. V. (2011) *Social Economies of Fear and Desire: Emotional Regulation, Emotion Management, and Embodied Autonomy.* Palgrave Macmillan, New York.

De Fornel, M. and Quéré, L. (eds.) (1999) *La logique des situations: Nouveaux regards sur l'écologie des activités sociales.* Éditions de l'EHESS, Paris.

Dubet, F. (1995) *Sociologie de l'expérience.* Seuil, Paris.

Dupont-Beurier, P.-F. (2006) *Petite philosophie du bricoleur.* Editions Milan, Toulouse.

Feely, M. M., and J. Simon. (1992) The New Penology: Notes on the Emerging Strategy of Corrections and Its Implications. *Criminology* 30.4, 449–474.

Florida, R. (2002) *The Rise of the Creative Class: And How It's Transforming Work, Leisure, Community, and Everyday Life.* Basic Books, New York.

Frediani, M. (2009) *Sur les routes. Le phénomène des new travellers.* Imago, Paris.

Furedi, F. (2001) Making sense of parental paranoia. An extract from Paranoid Parenting. *The Guardian*, 25 April, 2001.

Goffman, E. (1959) *Presentation of Self in Everyday Life.* Doubleday Anchor Books, Carden City.

Goffmann, E. (1988) *Les moments et leurs homes.* Seuil, Paris.

Gouvernement du Québec (2007) Plan d'intervention québécois sur les gangs de rue, 2007–2010. <www.msp.gouv.qc.ca>, (consulted April 2014).

Grundy, J. and Boudreau, J.A. (2008). 'Living with culture': creative citizenship practices in Toronto. *Citizenship Studies* 12.4, 347–363.

Harvey, D. (2012) *Rebel Cities, from The Right to the City to the Urban Revolution,* Verso, London.

Hebdige, D. (1979) *Subculture: the Meaning of Style.* Routledge, London.

Hein, F. (2012) *Do it Yourself! Autodétermination et culture punk.* Le passager Clandestin, Paris.

Innerarity, D. (2008) *Le futur et ses ennemis, de la confiscation de l'avenir à l'espérance politique*. Climats, Paris.

Innerarity, D. (2012) *The Future and Its Enemies*. Stanford University Press, Standford.

Isin, E. (2004) The Neurotic Citizen. *Citizenship Studies* 8.3, 217–235.

Jeanjean, A. and Sénépart, I. (2011) Habiter le temporaire: habitations de fortune, mobiles, éphémères. *Techniques & Culture* 56.1. Maison des sciences de l'homme, Paris.

Jones, T. (2005) Calling all risk-takers & change-makers… it's time for the risk revolution. *Creative places + spaces news journal* 1, 1–2.

Katz, J. (1988) *Seductions of Crime: Moral and Sensual Attractions in Doing Evil*. Basic Books, New York.

Keil, R. and Boudreau, J.-A. (2010) Le concept de la ville créative: la création réelle ou imaginaire d'une forme d'action politique dominante. *Pôle Sud* 32.1, 165–178.

Koolhaas, R. in Koolhaas, R. *et al.* (2000) Junkspace. *Mutations*. Actar & Arc en Rêve, Centre d'Architecture, Barcelona.

Landry, C. (2012) Open Innovation in Creative Industries. *Creative Cities Conferences*. Leipzig.

Lefebvre, H. (1970) *La révolution urbaine*. Gallimard, Paris.

Levi Strauss, C. (1985) [1962], *La pensée sauvage*. Plon, Paris.

Loureau, R. (1980) *Auto-dissolution des avant-gardes*. Galilée, Paris.

Macfarlane, C. (2010) The Comparative City: Knowledge, Learning, Urbanism. *International Journal of Urban and Regional Research* 34.4, 725–42.

Magnusson, W. (2011) *Politics of Urbanism: Seeing Like a City*. Routledge, Oxford.

Marcus, G. (1990) *Lipstick Traces: A Secret History of the Twentieth Century*. Harvard University Press, Cambridge.

Marsault, R. (2010) *Résistance à l'effacement – Nature de l'espace et temporalité de la présence sur les Wagenburgs de Berlin entre 1990 et 1996*. Presses du Réel, Dijon.

Moore, R. and Roberts, M. (2009) Do-It-Yourself Mobilization: Punk and Social Movements. *Mobilization* 14.3, 273–91.

Nicolas-Le Strat, P. (2008) Multiplicité interstitielle. *Multitudes* 31, 115–121.

O'Malley, P. (2000) Uncertain Subjects: Risks, Liberalism and Contract. *Economy and society* 29.4, 460–484.

Odin, F. and Thuderoz, C. (2010) Des mondes bricolés? Arts et sciences à l'épreuve de la notion de bricolage. Presses Polytechnique Romandes, Lausanne, Lyon.

Pedrazzini, Y. (2005) *La violence des villes*. Collection Le Livre Equitable, Editions de l'Atelier, Paris.

Pedrazzini, Y. (2007) in Mohammed, M. and Mucchielli, L. (eds.) Fonctions du gang: pauvreté et violence dans les métropoles d'Amérique Latine. *Les bandes de jeunes, des «blousons noirs» à nos jours*. Collection Recherches, La Découverte, Paris, 287–308.

Pedrazzini, Y. and Sanchez, M. R. (1998) *Malandros: Bandes, gangs et enfants de la rue – la culture d'urgence dans la métropole latino-américaine*. Éditions Charles Léopold Mayer/Desclé de Brouwer, Paris.

Petrescu, D., Querrien, A. and Petcou, C. (2007) Agir urbain. *Multitudes* 31.4, 11–15.

Power, M. (1994) *The Audit Explosion*. Demos, London.

Power, M. (2004) *The Risk Management of Everything: Rethinking the Politics of Uncertainty*. Demos, London.

Rémy, J. (1990) in Bastenier, A. and Dassetto, F. (eds.) La ville cosmopolite et la coexistence inter-ethnique. *Immigration et nouveaux pluralismes. Une confrontation de sociétés*. Éditions universitaires De Boeck, Bruxelles, 85–105.

Roy, A. and Aihwa, O. (eds.) (2011) *Worlding Cities: Asian Experiments and the Art of Being Global*. Wiley-Blackwell, Oxford.

Sennett, R. (1970) *The Uses of Disorder: Personal Identity and City Life*. W.W. Norton, New York.

Serfaty-Garzon, P. (2003) *Chez soi, Les territoires de l'intimité*. Collections Sociétales. Editions Armand Colin, Paris.

Sheptycki, J. (2003) The Governance of Organised Crime in Canada. *The Canadian Journal of Sociology / Cahiers canadiens de sociologie* 28.4, 489–516.

Simay, P. (2008) Une autre ville pour une autre vie. Henri Lefebvre et les situationnistes. *Métropoles*, revue électronique.

Simone, A. and Rao, V. (2012) Securing the Majority: Living through Uncertainty in Jakarta. *International Journal of Urban and Regional Research* 36.2, 315–35.

Solnit, R. (2005) *A field guide to guetting lost*, New York: Viking.

Solnit, R. (2002) *L'art de marcher*. Actes Sud, Paris.

Swyngedouw, E. (2009) The Antinomies of the Postpolitical City: In Search of a Democratic Politics of Environmental Production. *International Journal of Urban and Regional Research* 33.3, 601–620.

Tilly, C. (1984) *Big Structures, Large Processes, Huge Comparisons*. Russell Sage Foundation, New York.

Tremblay, R.E. (2008) *Prévenir la violence dès la petite enfance*. Odile Jacob, Paris.

Ungar, M. (2009) in Jones, G.A. and Rodgers, D. (eds.) Policing Youth in Latin America. *Youth Violence in Latin America: Gangs and Juvenile Justice in Perspective*. Palgrave Mcmillan, New York, 203–224.

Valverde, M. (1996) 'Despotism' and Ethical Liberal Governance. *Economy and society* 25.3, 357–372.

Walters, W. (2002) Social Capital and Political Sociology: Re-Imagining Politics? *Sociology* 36.2, 377–397.

Wirth, L. (1938) Urbanism as a Way of Life. *American Journal of Sociology* 44.1, 1–24. Reproduced in P. Kasinitz, P. (1995) *Metropolis: Center and Symbol of our Times*. The New York University Press, New York, 58–82.

Dubaï. Source: Hor Al Anz Street Project.

Part 5

Image

The reflection on post-heroes – yesterday, marginal urban groups; today, central to contemporary urbanity – calls us to look beyond dominant cultures and thus to question what global cities show us, often in too obvious a manner. This is what the fifth and final chapter proposes: to go against the obvious in order to provide a more comprehensive, varied and more genuine view of urban reality.

In this sense, the empirical example of Dubai supports a methodological and theoretical analysis that highlights 'little' spaces and everyday places of the 'little' people, rather than 'urban spectacle', for which this global metropolis is famed. This proposed shift in perspective – a kind of plea for inclusion of the urban ordinary – is supported by the use of visual techniques (notably photography and film), methods which are no mirror of reality observed but rather, like text, reflect the subjectivity of the researcher and the intentions of the theoretical demonstration.

This last chapter thus questions not only the manner in which the urban researcher addresses urban reality, but also how this specific method influences description and interpretation. The authors of both pieces in this chapter then go on to reiterate the fundamental epistemological question of this book: does what we call *city* depend on the academic discipline and tools used to consider it, and if so, to what extent?

Informal Urbanism & Limited Mobility: Lessons from Dubai

Yasser Elsheshtawy

Faculty of Engineering
UAE University, Dubaï, United Arab Emirates

In this paper I am examining the impact of migration on Gulf development from an urban planning perspective, looking at the extent to which the presence of migrants within Gulf cities have shaped their built environments and the degree to which migrants adapt spaces in their daily interactions. My focus is on the city of Dubai, which, more than any other urban center in the Gulf, is known for its multicultural and cosmopolitan character.

The literature on Dubai emphasizes the city's excessive developments and megaprojects. A passing visit would seemingly confirm that Dubai is not a city in the conventional sense. It is more of a set of cities connected by a network of highways, where there is hardly any pedestrian circulation and everything is geared towards consumption. This is, of course, the planners' view – a view from above, where successful cities are conceived as nodes on a network, command points in a global economy. Then there are those who try to follow or emulate them. Here, there are no real people – merely passive consumers, following the dictates of global capitalism.

This view from above will show that Dubai is primarily a city of migrants. Also, the city has been subjected to severe criticism for the abject conditions under which its low-income workers live, thus situating these practices as another example of capitalist exploitation. However, the city's low-income population is not merely composed of unskilled laborers living in 'Dickensian' labor camps. In the extremes – the super-rich living in exclusive multi-million villas or Asian sub-continent laborers toiling in labor camps – only a partial picture is revealed.

To truly understand the city of Dubai, or any city for that matter, a closer look is required in places where everyday life is taking place. There one will find a series of vibrant spaces which offer a sense of comfort and inclusiveness for the city's migrants, thus creating a 'migrational city' which 'slips into the planned city', according to Michel de Certeau (de Certeau, 1984). The significance of these spaces stems from their being a 'haven' for the city's multiethnic community, a setting where users from lower socio-economic backgrounds can interact without having to enter into the more exclusive zones reserved for higher-income segments of society. They are imbued with meaning by becoming a way to connect to home countries. Territories are marked through traces such as paper lights celebrating the Indian Diwali festival, advertisement geared towards compatriots, the playing of culturally specific sports such as cricket in parking lots and graffiti.

In the following sections I will be summarizing both previous research done on these spaces and an ongoing study, 'The Hor Al Anz Street Project', which represents a systematic attempt at mapping activity patterns within a street in a low-income community. This will be grounded within a theoretical framework that responds to a shift in global city research, emphasizing the everyday, as well as transnational connections in which both the local and the global are closely intertwined. I am arguing that such processes are observable in these 'forgotten' settings, utilized by Dubai's low-income migrant community for the exchange of information and as a major gathering point. This analysis of users, their activities as well as the morphology of these spaces situates them within the overall development of Dubai.

Theorizing the everyday: little space vs. big space

Cities are becoming highly complex with an increasingly diverse range of inhabitants. As a result there has been a fragmentation of space, a prevalence of ethnic enclaves and a segregation of uses (Graham and Marvin, 2001; Marcuse and van Kempen, 2000). Mono-functional buildings dominate cityscapes and result in an impoverished public realm, particularly in rapidly urbanizing centers. Urbanists, alarmed by such developments, began focusing their attention on the degree to which inhabitants make sense of these spaces and reclaim the city – hence the renewed focus on everyday urbanism (Stevens, 2007; Hou, 2007).

Historically, everyday urbanism, i.e. finding poetry and significance in the quotidian and the mundane daily activities, has been propagated as a counterpoint to the modernist city with its attempts at imposing strict order, separation of uses and fragmentation of urban space. The French movement Situationist International (SI), in particular, was concerned with the deadening quality of contemporary urban life. They advocated the act of drifting (or *dérive*) – a form of aimless wandering that seeks to discover a city's hidden spaces that may not have any strictly functional value. This would include bypassed spaces where unexpected events or encounters may happen (Sadler, 1999).

The SI were trying to undermine planning practices which, according to Quentin Stevens, '… generally tend to organize and circumscribe human action in space, to limit the risk of incursions upon intended, conventional urban behaviors by making alternative acts more difficult' (Stevens, 2007:207). Situationism shared a determination to penetrate the outward, spectacular, commercialized signs of mass culture and explore its interior. There, one examined the everyday patterns of life such as people's use of buildings and urban space (Sadler, 1999). Ultimately the SI remained an elitist movement with little or no practical use for their critique of the modern city, yet they did highlight some of its main shortcomings. The theoretical underpinnings for these efforts were provided by a series of French intellectuals such as Henry Lefebvre, Guy Debord, and Michel de Certeau who, according to Crawford, identified the everyday as an important arena of modern culture and society. Motivated by what they saw as the oppression of daily life, they discovered '… its potential as a site of creative resistance and liberatory power' (Crawford, 1999:9).

Such focus on the daily practices of city residents resonated with the writings of influential urbanists such as Jane Jacobs, who extolled the virtues of daily living in Greenwich Village, Manhattan, and Richard Sennett, who also discussed these spaces. They constitute an idealization of traditional neighborhood life – and may find little relevance outside their North American context (Jacobs, 1961; Sennett, 1977; Sorkin, 2009; Zukin, 2009). Some have thus expanded the definition of *public*. Of particular note is the work of Margaret Crawford who writes about the spatial expressions of informal economies, as in street vending and garage sales in U.S. cities, seeing such manifestations of a spatiality of occupation as offering a counter-argument to the dominant spaces of malls. She explores the survival of spaces of public association and exchange despite the encroachment of privatised spaces on a more conventionally defined public realm. She writes that 'Woven into the patterns of everyday life, it is difficult to even discern these places as public space'; however, located behind the private, commercial and domestic realms they '… contain multiple, and constantly shifting meaning rather than clarity of function' (Crawford, 2005:28).

Crawford argues that in contrast to clearly defined arenas of space with coherent formal characteristics, everyday space is a '… diffuse landscape. It is banal, it's repetitive, it's everywhere and nowhere, it's a place that has few characteristics that people pay attention to… it [is] a zone of possibility and potential transformation' (Crawford, 2005:19). The everyday is 'ambiguous like all in-between spaces' and it 'represents a zone of social transition and possibility with the potential for new social arrangements and forms of imagination' (Crawford, 1999:9).

These theoretical frameworks and depictions of daily life were written primarily by those working in the social sciences – geographers, sociologists, anthropologists and so on. But they were also echoed in the work of city planners and architects such as Kevin Lynch, William Whyte as well as Jan Gehl, among many others. More recently, Quentin Stevens introduced the idea of the Ludic City, exploring the ludic – i.e. play – potential of city spaces. He notes that the idea of 'play' within urban settings poses a threat since it is '… evidence of a non-instrumental, non-commodifiable basis for urban social relations'. Echoing Lefebvre, he argues that play transforms everyday experience and that 'people appropriate space as they see fit, and uses overlap' (Stevens, 2007:12).

His focus is on leftover spaces which are 'underdesigned, difficult and abandoned spaces such as alleyways, floodways, tunnels, the underside of bridges, the backs of billboards, the edges of footpaths, kerbs, excessive plazas, locked doorways, staircases, blank wall surfaces, buildings' loading docks and undercrofts'. These spaces provide, as Stevens puts it, 'the best opportunities for play precisely because they often do not have a function and their affordances are unknown … they are outside the functional, managed environment; serious uses and meaning are absent' (*ibid.*:199).

In my interrogation of Dubai I will be relying on these conceptual frameworks as well as adopting some of their methodological approaches.

Similar to what Crawford forcefully advocated, I will focus on 'the possibility of reclaiming elements of the quotidian that have been hidden in the nooks and cranies of the urban environment', looking at overlooked 'marginal places, from streets and sidewalks to vacant lots and parks'. This is prompted by the belief that 'lived experience should be more important than physical form in defining the city' (Crawford, 1999:10). To locate these differences in everyday lives, it is crucial to map the 'social geography of the city'. Thus, by identifying sites of multiple social and economic interactions where multiple experiences accumulate, we highlight 'the most potent sites for everyday urbanism' (Crawford, 1999:11). As urban sociologist Abdoumaliq Simone keenly observes, in our effort to make cities more livable for all, we should not just focus on the 'misery' of its inhabitants, which inevitably makes their conditions worse. Instead we need to uncover the world that these residents inhabit 'however insalubrious, violent, and banal they might often be' (Simone, 2010:199).

Contextualizing Dubai

1) The physical city

Looking at Dubai's urban growth is revealing. Its first phase of urban development extended from 1900 to 1955. The city's urban growth in this period reflected a pattern of slow and limited physical expansion due to constrained economic activities and marginal growth in population. The entire population of the city was confined to three small enclaves located at the mouth of the creek. The second phase of Dubai's urban development can be characterized as compact growth, extending from 1955 to 1970. Developments were extended to the outskirts of towns, aided by the use of the automobile. A 1959 British prepared master plan (by architect John Harris) called for an increased development of the central business district and limiting outer development to industrial use. Dubai then underwent what some have called 'planned suburban growth', a period of rapid expansion, which began in 1970 (AlShafieei, 1997). The current phase of its development has extended the city further towards the Jebel Ali port (its border with Abu Dhabi). This phase is characterized by both the emergence of vertical towers as well as horizontal gated communities. The juxtaposition of these different phases and the pace in which they emerged contributed to an urban form that has been characterized as fragmented and splintered (Graham and Marvin, 2001). Moreover, the city has been criticized as catering primarily to upper income segments of society while neglecting or marginalizing the poor. Many of these opinions and viewpoints rely on anecdotal evidence, based on short stays or a cursory reading of media reports.

One of the first impressions of the city is its fragmentary nature and its reliance on cars as the primary means of circulation. The city is composed of multiple, disconnected centers that are separated by multi-lane highways. This precludes any meaningful pedestrian circulation or, for that matter, a conventional urban fabric which can only be found in the 'traditional' areas of Bur Dubai/Shindagha and Deira. Given these developments it is compared to Los Angeles and other U.S. cities; furthermore, it is cited as a prime example of what is termed 'splintering urbanism' by Stephen Graham and Simon Marvin – thus placing it squarely within worldwide urban trends. Yet there are certain aspects to its growth that are unique. They pertain to the city's rapid urban development and its land use and distribution policy.

This *tabula rasa* type development has resulted in large gaps or patches between developments: vast expanses of sand that need to be filled. The general feeling of the city at its present state is that of a construction site – work is still in progress. Furthermore, lacking the high population density that would sustain such momentous growth, many areas appear empty, without a sign of life. Its neighborhoods lack a sense of community; they have a transitory feeling. This is further compounded by the 2008 financial crisis that has led to a decline in population and has halted about 50% of construction projects.

Further compounding the problem of unchecked growth is the absence of a master plan. Instead, Dubai Municipality is employing a 'Structural Plan', identifying areas of growth, land-use, etc., with the possibility of change based on potential future needs. The existence of multiple agents and real estate agencies – all owned to varying degrees by the Dubai government – such as Nakheel, Emaar, Dubai Properties, as well as private enterprises such as Futaim, is another factor causing this uneven, and sometimes conflicting, development. While Dubai Municipality is nominally in charge of coordination, developments are often given the go-ahead, and approval obtained after-the-fact and then incorporated into the structural plan.

2) The social city: migrant living conditions

Dubai's unique population structure is skewed if one considers the ratio of males to females. Out of Dubai's total population of 1.422 million, around 1.07 million are males while just 349,000 are females. Furthermore, it is estimated that around 500,000 people in Dubai live as 'bachelors'. According to Dubai Municipality, all single men and women are categorized as 'bachelors'. However, many so-called bachelors are married, but cannot afford – or are not allowed – to bring their families. They usually rent rooms in villas located in a variety of neighbourhoods in the city. Given the hazardous conditions under which people live in these settings, a policy of 'one family-one villa' is being implemented.

Similar situations can be observed all over the Gulf. Yet in Dubai it has acquired much more acute and intense dimensions. Indeed the problem came to the fore in 2006 when a fire broke out in an old house in Naif, a neighbourhood in Deira, resulting in the death of eleven people and the injury of dozens of others. The house was a two-storey villa complex in which as many as 400 labourers may have been living illegally. An *Associated Press* report observed that the house had been partitioned into at least thirty rooms, with as many as twenty workers living in some of them. Also, the second storey was a modification to accommodate the extra workers. The report notes that 'Foreign workers are officially supposed to live in labor camps or industrial zones that have been specifically designated for them'. Most of the people living in the house were unskilled labourers who earned up to 800 dirhams (U.S. $218) per month working as janitors or garbage collectors.

The living conditions of these people are characterized by poverty and overcrowding; this is as close as one gets to a slum in Dubai. The fire took place in an area known locally as Satellite Street for its sale of television satellite equipment and other electronic products. The villa was an old 'Arab-style' traditional home with two floors (one floor was added to the original to accommodate more people). Each room had just enough room for bunk beds, three or four beds high, and a radio or television set. Surviving workers told reporters that they took turns to sleep on the beds while the others slept on the floor. Even within such misery there was a sense of community and attachment, what Suleiman Khalaf and Saad Alkobaisi, in their examination of the lives of migrants in the UAE, have referred to as 'reinforcing a sense of identity' by being close together in such a crowded environment. Thus, there was a small kitchen area on all the floors, which the workers used to make their meals. A palm tree growing in the middle of the villa provided workers with a sense of comfort. The neighbourhood around the villa is a busy area populated largely by workers, but tucked behind the busy main road are several old villas that are home to some of the poorest residents of the city (Khalaf and Alkobaisi, 1999).

Within these spaces are smaller lanes and alleyways, and it is here that the overall morphology becomes irregular, following the historical street layout, as it existed prior to the city's modernization. Walking through these alleyways opens up different vistas and surprise encounters: pedestrian alleys containing outdoor seating for a coffee shop; an outdoor display area for a textile shop surrounded by mannequins; a street corner filled with laborers from South Asia; a gathering of people around a restaurant showing a live cricket match from India; a man selling bootlegged Bollywood movies on a blanket in a side alley. Restaurants serving South Asian cuisine are spread throughout and cater to both low and middle income users, in addition to supermarkets and grocery stores stocking items from India and Pakistan. Places opposite these food retailers become gathering points that attract visitors and residents.

These scenes evoke a very different city. Walking through these spaces, a sense of the city's true nature becomes apparent as a merging of the formal and informal: flyers indicating a search for a room; graffiti on the walls of its darker alleys; or paper lights hanging from balconies to celebrate the Diwali festival. What makes all of this even more remarkable is the understated architecture in which these activities unfold, thus allowing for a certain amount of personalization.

Mapping the city: transitory settings

Seeking to go beyond the city as spectacle, the aim of this ongoing study is to document and map the city's informal spaces. In surveying these spaces, my main criteria for identification was that they should be central gathering points for the city's migrants, easily accessible, and contain a variety of activities as well as users. The proposed methodology, in addition to answering the research questions, aims to capture the flavor and dynamics of the city of Dubai. To that effect various innovative techniques involving photography (still and time-lapse), ethnographic mapping, and video have been used. The overall outcome will be an urban portrait of Dubai, which navigates between the macro and the micro level. Moreover, an attempt will be made to move from a strictly documentary perspective to one that involves and captures the subjective perceptions of city dwellers as they move through the urban environment. Various modes for a graphic representation of space will be used for this purpose. The following represents a summary of my initial attempts at documenting these spaces, which I will then follow with a detailed description and preliminary reporting of an ongoing study in the Hor Al-Anz area of Dubai.

In the initial survey I employed a methodology of participant observation, which entailed observation of activities, taking field notes, interviews with selected informants and photography. In addition, archival information was used to contextualize these settings; governmental reports, maps and aerial photographs were used to conduct a social and morphological analysis of these spaces. A brief ethnographic description of these spaces follows (Elsheshtawy, 2011a, 2011b, 2010, 2008).

Baniyas Square

Baniyas square is surrounded by well-off and middle-income zones in addition to being in close proximity to the poor district of Naif. It is located in a section of the city called Deira. One informant told me that the square was known for the presence of a cinema, as well as shops offering luxurious fashion items. However, as locals have moved out from the city center and into suburbs, it has become a setting mostly associated with expatriates.

The square and its surroundings – particularly the space surrounding the Sabkha bus stop – is a setting for the exchange of messages and receipt of news from home. This has become prevalent as surrounding areas are divided by nationality and ethnic backgrounds. Each member of a group would therefore know where to find compatriots (Kutty, 2002:7). The space is relatively empty during the day; however, in the evening it is crowded with people. This reaches a climax on Friday. Particularly attractive are the green lawns in the middle of the space, which are a place for people to sleep, eat or simply chat with others. Also, street corners are gathering nodes for people, who simply stand there and talk while observing passersby.

The square was closed off for two years due to the construction of Dubai Metro. In 2011 it re-opened to pedestrians, and has over the years become a major gathering area again.

Ghubeiba and Satwa

These two spaces are closely associated with low-income users, primarily from the Indian sub-continent. Ghubeiba is located in Bur Dubai, near the historic Shindagha district. Satwa, on the other hand, is further away, bordered by the two wealthy areas of Sheikh Zayed Road and Jumeirah/Um Suqeim, both of which contain high-end residential villas and ultra-luxurious towers. These two settings have major bus stops, which draw people from all over the city and contribute to the crowded feeling, particularly on weekends. These bus stops are surrounded by commercial establishments that cater to the con-stantly moving, transient users. They include eateries, cafes and newspaper stands which display mostly Hindi magazines and newspapers. There are also seating areas. The food and drinks served in these places are a reminder for these workers of home. In some instances they become sites for illegal con-sumption of alcohol (Menon, 2006).

In close proximity to these bus stops are zones which act as a major hangout for passersby. They include hundreds of people simply standing, talk-ing to each other or watching others. Interviews revealed that people come to these settings on a regular basis to interact with others, meet friends and receive news from back home, thus serving an important communication function (Kutty, 2002). In addition to these informal modes of communica-tion, more advanced means exist as well. For example, I observed a heavy use of mobile phones, which many of these workers have; there are also a number of Internet cafes close by that are heavily used. Thus, ties to home countries are retained, and these spaces become settings where such transnational con-nections are nurtured. Highlighting this transnational connection is the ubiq-uitous presence of money exchange operators[1]. There is also a large presence of ethnic restaurants; however, aware of the multi-cultural nature of potential clientele, advertisements entice users by noting that the menu contains Indian, Chinese and Philippine specialties. Other restaurants are restricted to a certain

---

[1]   For an excellent analysis on the role of remittances see S. Raymer, "Dubai's Kerala connection," *YaleGlobal Online*, July 12, 2005

ethnic group (e.g. a Karachi restaurant) and make this clear through decorative elements and other signs. Furthermore, spaces are imbued with meaning by becoming a way to connect to home countries.

Given its centrality Satwa is a particularly interesting area. Delving into its back alleys, one encounters a different world. Migrants congregate in small houses and gather in small alleys. Signs of an active street life are present throughout – for instance couches are placed in front of houses, forming an outdoor living area. Yet one of the most memorable sights for me in Satwa was during Ramadan in 2007. It is quite common to set up in various parts of the city what are known as *Iftar tents*, which is the designation of an area for the city's low-income Moslem population who would otherwise not be able to afford breaking their fast; it also serves as a communal gathering space where they can reinforce their sense of religious identity and belonging. While these are usually indoors, a large parking space adjacent to the Satwa bus stop was used for this purpose. The ground was covered with large pieces of cloth, and volunteers were dispensing food to hundreds of people. In the background to this rather remarkable scene was the Sheikh Zayed Road skyline – representing a stark contrast to the more down-to-earth activity occurring in front of me. Also, on my way to the Iftar area, I passed various street vendors selling traditional food typical of India or Pakistan. Here it seems were scenes that represented a counterpoint to the flashy image of Dubai. Poor and not-so-poor immigrants gathered together to celebrate a religious event, which, in some way, subverted the surrounding spectacle.

Rashid Colony

Rashid Colony in Al Ghusais, a neighbourhood near Dubai International Airport, was built in the 1960s. It comprises a series of repetitive 4-storey residential blocks. In 2006, eviction notices were issued to residents, comprising a mix of low-income expatriate families. My visit to the area in Spring 2008 showed a vibrant community alive with residents from many nationalities. Yet, moving closer to the buildings, another picture emerged. Signs of deterioration and foreboding notices of eviction were plastered throughout the complex. There was also an eerie silence as I moved to the inner parts of the colony, as if the place had been abandoned by its occupants. More telling were graffiti signs – always a sure sign of resistance – with one explicitly stating (in English): 'We won't leave'. The passageways within the buildings were dark and narrow, but there were smells of food, sounds of people, footsteps. Emerging from these passageways, residents moved from one block to another, seemingly oblivious to my presence. They were wearing 'house clothes' as if the spaces inside the colony constituted a semi-private area allowing them to wear less 'formal' clothing, with the building blocks somehow protecting them from preying eyes. Around noon, schoolchildren accompanied by their mothers arrived; they engaged in various play activities at the colony's outer edges. Moving further inside the colony, elderly women wearing elaborate saris accompanied by their husbands – perhaps parents visiting their children – were taking a walk across the rather inhospitable streets. Clearly, Rashid Colony served an important function in providing affordable accommodation, but the complex did stand in stark contrast to its luxurious surroundings – multi-million dirham villas and apartment blocks.

The area also has restaurants catering for the South Asian community, and associated with similar settings back home, including places known throughout their respective communities, such as Karachi Darbar or Bombay Fast Food Restaurant. The presence of these two eateries, in addition to several others, enhances the ethnic character of the district to the extent that a place such as Bombay Fast Food becomes a destination visited by people from different parts of the city – and even from different Emirates. This latter establishment has been in operation for more than 30 years, thus creating a sense of identity for the city's migrants. Due to the familiarity of the food and its low cost, some, such as Karachi Darbar, become a hangout or a place for a break for the city's low-income population. For example, they are frequented by a large number of taxi drivers.

Al-Quoz District: labor camps

The issue of labor camps continues to dominate the discourse on Dubai. Indeed the city has three large camps: Sonapur, Jebel Ali and Al Quoz. Policies are currently being implemented to construct labor cities that would follow international standards with respect to proper accommodation for office workers.

While Sonapur and Jebel Ali are located at the city's outskirts, Al Quoz is in western Dubai, bordered to the north by Al Wasl and to the west by Umm Al Sheif, Al Manara and Al Safa (all upscale residential neighbourhoods), and thus occupies a central position within 'Greater Dubai'. The area comprises four sub-communities that make up the Al Quoz Industrial District. These industrial areas, occupying much of the southwestern city limits, service development projects such as Dubai Marina and Emirates Hills as well as the free zone in Jebel Ali. Al Quoz is being developed by Dubai Municipality as an exclusive industrial area and thus contains labour accommodation units as well as factories and storage facilities. Some of the accommodation units – or camps – accommodate close to 2,000 labourers.

Al Quoz is not immediately accessible but must be reached from more well-known areas of the city. One means of access is from behind the Mall of the Emirates (with its Ski Dubai). The area is characterized by a rigid street system that discourages any kind of pedestrian movement. Most activities observed were around these labour camps and around the newly constructed Grand City Mall. The mall itself is located at a traffic intersection and is not surrounded by any buildings. Close by are a variety of housing structures and labour camps, but its location at the edge of the industrial area, rather than in the centre, makes it somewhat difficult to access. Despite its relative remoteness, I observed a sizeable number of users. In fact, the area around the entrance, wider than a typical sidewalk, was used by many people who stood around talking, and so on. Also, a large South Asian restaurant, 'Pataan', faced directly onto the open space in front of the mall. Various notices and flyers were mounted on the centre's wall, put there, for instance, by people seeking accommodation, as can be found in many other places in the city, which cater to low-income users. Inside, the mall is clean and well organized. A security guard stands at the entrance. Users are mostly male, although I did see a few female customers. Overall, by adopting the strategies of larger malls, the center attracted users not just for shopping, but also as a gathering place, a setting for reinforcing one's sense of identity (for example, in an ethnic restaurant) – even in an area as desolate and grim as Al Quoz.

The camps are relatively well maintained, although they have an almost 'military' character in the sense that they are surrounded by fences and walls, clothes are left out to dry in outdoor corridors, and many of these residences are marked by large numbers and letters. Beyond toilets and showers, there are no facilities in the camp. Workers must find and pay for their own food. In one camp Chinese paper lanterns hung on a rope strung along the interior courtyard, indicating the ethnicity of labourers, which confirmed an official policy of segregation 'according to nationality to avoid disputes and fights breaking out'.

There were some lively scenes around the entrances to the residences. In one instance I saw a labourer having a haircut; he was hidden from the main street behind a tree; other labourers were standing and sitting nearby. There were other areas, which were gathering points such as a mosque, grocery and health clinic complex – outside the actual camps. Overall, the entire district appeared lifeless, yet hidden behind these foreboding walls are stories of real people with aspirations and dreams.

The Hor Al Anz Street Project

Hor Al Anz is a district located in Deira. Originally planned as a neighbourhood in the 1970s for locals who have since moved out, it is now dominated by inhabitants from South Asia. Looking at the city's 1959 masterplan by John Harris, one sees that the area was nothing more than a patch of sand. Following a policy of constructing housing for nationals, the district was designed similar to Satwa, with identical one-storey buildings. Some of those still remain, while others have been torn to make way for multi-storey apartment blocks.

Currently the district is divided into two parts: East and West. The eastern part is considered to be deteriorating, with its inhabitants mostly consisting of low-income workers from Pakistan, Bangladesh and India. Its population is about 60,000 people within a relatively small sized area, making it one of the most densely populated districts in Dubai. Streets are arranged on a grid system and are relatively well maintained, with the exception of back alleys, which have as of yet not been upgraded. Hor Al Anz Street is a major commercial thoroughfare running through the length of the neighbourhood and is considered a main focal point for residents. This street contains various outlets such as restaurants, grocery stores, electrical appliance maintenance, and so on. My study in this area is related to a research fund by UAE University and the National Research Foundation, which is part of a three-year study of such sites in Dubai. The following is a concise summary of the data that has been captured so far along with preliminary interpretation of some of the findings.

The methodology has been designed to capture the dynamics of everyday life in Hor Al Anz Street. To that effect I am adopting tools of environment-behavior research, specifically behavioral mapping in addition to videography. For the actual mapping the research team used a walkthrough method, which entailed walking along the street focusing either on the western or eastern side. Stationary activities (any activity taking more than 1 minute, rather than simply walking) would be recorded on a sheet. To ensure trustworthiness (that what is being recorded on the sheet is actually what is taking place) students were instructed to take photographs using GPS enabled cameras, which would later be placed on the electronic mapping sheet. Once one particular time segment was completed, another would take place, and so on.

While behavioral maps offer a compelling visual image of how activities are distributed over time and space, they do not reveal the inner dynamics and subtleties of everyday interactions. To achieve this a technique of time-lapse video was used. Based on initial site visits, one particular street corner has been identified as offering strong potential for observation. The objective was to capture activities on that corner across a typical day. Accordingly, a locale opposite the corner was marked for placement of the video camera. Recording took place according to specific time-segments, in 2-hour intervals, with the video camera switched on every 15 minutes for 5 minutes. Given the practical difficulty in conducting this in one day, video capture was done over a three-week period. The resultant high numbers of video clips were then combined in a video-editing program. The time-lapse effect – compressing several hours of footage into a 5-minute clip – was done by speeding up the sequence frames. Further analysis was done by stopping the animation at select intervals that captured key events, such as a particular gathering, behaviour or user. Annotations were used to highlight these.

Resultant data can be seen in Figures (…), illustrating a dynamic and vibrant setting. Findings suggest the urban vitality of the street, as it acts as a node for its inhabitants. Surprisingly, it also is a meeting point for elderly locals, who frequent one of its cafes on a regular basis. Some places, such as the Peshawar restaurant, are known throughout the city and, as a result, acquire an iconic status. Located on a corner it acts as a node, drawing residents and outsiders who interact in front of this store. Such sites defy the typical narrative of Dubai as a lifeless city without a soul.

In discussing the meaning of these findings and observations, one of the main issues emerging from this study is that the street has developed beyond its functional aspects to become a social place. Furthermore, such interactions take place at street corners. The sidewalk is the heart of the district. These interactions serve an important purpose, since they sustain cultural patterns and nurture a sense of belonging. Denied the presence of an extended family, migrants rely on each other for support, exchange of news and so on (Khalaf, Gardner). The large number of those migrants within a relatively small space is an important factor since it reinforces their sense of community. The space is filled with cultural indicators: cricket games, smell of food, drinking traditionally prepared tea, signs and advertisements in native languages, a relaxed dress code. Forced to be insulated from the rest of the city, and limited in their movement, the neighborhood becomes a backstage to the city's glitzy and spectacular sites. Inhabitants' sense of separation is strong to the extent that some walk in the traditional undergarment called lunghi, further accentuating the district's enclave-like status.

What is of particular interest is the extent to which the physical environment supports or inhibits the formation of these activities. The literature suggests that such spaces merely offer affordances for events to take place. Additionally, the idea of having what is called in urban theory a 'loose space' or 'liminal space' promotes open-endedness and ambiguity to cater to varying levels of street use, which are present in the street. While the sidewalks are quite narrow, once one reaches the corner, it opens up significantly. Minimal interference in terms of street furniture – and the resultant wide-open space – allows for gatherings to take place. Incidental features such as large trees offer protection and shade. Empty sites provide further opportunities for gathering. Small modifications made to storefronts, such as the addition of stoops and placement of chairs, suggest an informal character typical of such sites. These corners thus seem to embody the very definition of looseness and liminality. They act as a threshold, and their open-endedness removes restrictions placed on behavior.

Conclusion

At the beginning of the 2008 movie 'Slumdog Millionaire', under the pulsating rhythm of composer A. R. Rahman's score, the camera swoops down on Mumbai, taking us through the city's slums, breathlessly following the movie's protagonist as he moves along through the city's teeming alleyways, snaking his way through its hidden spaces. This scene, in all its vitality and dynamism, captures the essence of the modern urban condition – the existence of a teeming 'other' city, what architect Rahul Mehrotra calls a *kinetic city* (Mehrotra, 2008). This is a city of movement, temporality and transience, fully alive – a living, breathing organism. One can easily imagine such scenes elsewhere, in the dense urban canyons of Manhattan as portrayed in

Ramin Bahrani's 2005 film 'Man Push Cart', or Hong Kong's Central area, marvelously captured by filmmaker Wong Kar Wei in his 1994 'Chungking Express'. Such scenes and movies shape our urban imaginary. They suggest a certain urbanity or 'cityness' that seems to be a model for places aspiring to be the new urban centers of the world.

This urban imaginary is unthinkable in the gleaming, immaculate urban centers of the Gulf. The desire for order and control overrides any notions for an informal – yet viable – alternative urban order. Yet, ultimately people are not passive; the built environment does not have a deterministic quality, despite what planners may envision. What I have attempted to show in this paper is that city residents display resilience in the face of an oppressive and restrictive context. Moreover, the sheer fact that locales in the city are almost hidden and known only by word of mouth indicates that they exist outside a specific geography; they are almost virtual. Abdumaliq Simone notes (within the context of African cities) that such sites have 'no specific location, but yet can still be located'. These are ephemeral spaces given significance by inhabitants through sheer proximity and density. The street, as Simone puts is, acts as a 'switch' or a 'conduit for something else' (Simone, 2010:232).

Through this the lives of migrants acquire meaning, and they are able to retain vital binds that enhance their lives. These are not unsightly gatherings that must be relocated to the fringes and the margins. Rather, they are critical to maintaining a livable and healthy city.

Imagining Dubai:
Methodological Explorations of
Everyday Urban Life

Hossam Adly, Stéphanie Vincent Geslin

Laboratory of Urban Sociology,
Ecole Polytechnique Federale de Lausanne, Switzerland

Dubai – city of grandeur, monumental architecture and spectacle – sprang forth from a lifeless desert. Dubai is the result of the work of monarchs and the elite, perfectly embodying the city as planned by policy makers, investors and urban developers. This spectacular, over-the-top urban development has brought Dubai international fame. As if a new 'American dream', the Persian Gulf emirate presents itself as a land of opportunity where anything is possible. Dubai is known and studied for its skyscrapers, artificial islands and malls. This side of Dubai, which often serves to showcase the city, is defined by Yasser Elsheshtawy in this work by the concept of 'big space'. Big space refers to Dubai's position in the world – the spectacle that the city offers to the world and the steel and glass exuberance that makes its existence in the middle of the desert surreal, almost magical.

In his article, however, Elsheshtawy wishes to introduce us to another Dubai, to make us experience the city *as it is lived* – a city of usages, of *arts de faire* (everyday practices) and DIY, in other words, the city on the small scale. This little-known Dubai, which the author defines as informal, lurks on street corners, is hidden at the backs of shops, masked by bus stations, or is hastily stuck on a wall or lamppost.

According to Elsheshtawy, it is this other dimension of the city – of little places, small things and details – that requires special attention. Thus he compares the notion of 'little spaces' with spaces of grandeur, to highlight both the existence of forms of appropriation in this city and the socialization within the urban space that are not the result of top-down planning.

Our reading of Elsheshtawy's text aims to follow its looking-glass way of observing Dubai. The first part of the article is based on the concept of big and little spaces, to discover what city the author's approach reveals. However, we could not help wondering: isn't the sharp contrast between big and little spaces reinforced by the lack of symmetry in the theoretical and methodological treatment of these two types of space?

1. Behind the scenes: the ordinary in an extraordinary city

One urban reality, two levels

The article proposed by Elsheshtawy in this volume is based on a conceptual distinction between big spaces and little spaces, a distinction which he has already treated in other works (Elsheshtawy, 2010). This dichotomy enables him to distinguish between urban space as it is *planned* and urban space as it is *lived*, between the city 'seen from above' and the city 'seen from below'. The Dubai of big spaces, however, is not limited to luxury hotels and highways junctions. By himself assuming a 'view from above', he describes Dubai as a 'migratory city', polarized between rich foreigners living in outrageously expensive homes and workers from the Indian subcontinent living in camps. A fragmented, exuberant city, Dubai elicits as much fascination as it does criticism from the international community. However, for Elsheshtawy, these aspects are only part of the reality.

To 'truly understand the city of Dubai', Elsheshtawy invites us to come closer in order to observe spaces where daily life unfolds. At the local level, the little spaces show the appropriation of different types of urban space by low-income migrant workers, as well as the transnational links with the country of origin for which these spaces become the support. The author places the distinction between big and little spaces in a global movement of specialization and segregation of urban areas, of which Dubai – a city characterized by massive inequalities – is emblematic. According to the author, contemporary planning practices should respond to the loss of social and ethnic diversity in urban centers brought about by global capitalism by acceding to the demands and needs of inhabitants too often ignored by developers.

This defines Elsheshtawy's research project and justifies its dual approach from both architectural and social science perspectives. For the author, it is important to understand customs and daily practices in order to plan a city that is in harmony with its inhabitants. This perspective is in keeping with the tradition of French philosophers and intellectuals such as Michel De Certeau, Henri Lefebvre and Guy Debord. Based on the position taken by these figures, and particularly as it pertains to the Situationist International (SI) movement, Elsheshtawy makes an observation of the daily practices of migrant communities in Dubai and their appropriation of built space as the basis for 'everyday urbanism' (this volume: 191).

Traces of an informal city

Elsheshtawy's article continues with yet another distinction, which echoes that made between big and little spaces: the 'physical city' vs. the 'social city'. The first refers to the urban evolution of Dubai in several stages since the beginning of the 20th century, an evolution that has led to the fragmented situation that characterizes the city today. The planning that has prevailed in the emirate for more than a century focuses on car traffic and neglects pedestrians, according to the author. Thus, to strengthen the comparisons that pepper his text, Elsheshtawy takes us through the maze of the 'social city' by foot (this volume: 195).

What Elsheshtawy calls the little spaces of the social city are the hidden, marginal, under-planned spaces, recalling the Situationist framework he employs for this argument. The descriptions of the spaces the reader is invited to peer into reveal 'a very different city' that, when explored on foot, reveals its 'true nature' (this volume: 196). This mainly consists of spontaneous encounters in public spaces not designed for this purpose, advertising posters and graffiti on walls in areas where migrants live. These 'informal' productions – pasted on walls that were not intended for this use – belong to the ephemeral, the illegitimate, even the illegal, and can therefore be contrasted with the lasting, 'official', 'legitimate' traces resulting from urban planning processes (buildings, advertising spaces, etc.). Nevertheless, for Elsheshtawy, through their superimposition and their resistance to capitalist urban development that reflect a 'desire for order and control' (this volume: 205), it is these traces that reveal the city's 'true nature'.

Elsheshtawy thus compares the distinction between big spaces and little spaces to that of formal versus informal. His use of the term *informal* in this paper is appealing because, unlike many studies equating informal spaces with the presence of slums or shantytowns, the author explores how neighborhoods that have been planned in a top-down manner can also bear the marks of informal appropriation and, hence, how these two dimensions – too often described as opposites – in fact intermingle and are actually interconnected. Nevertheless, in our view, Elsheshtawy's text would benefit from a more precise definition of 'traces of the informal'. While it seems quite clear to us, with regard to the graffiti and ads posted on walls, the appropriation of public spaces by migrants does not necessarily constitute an informal practice. While these acts are not planned or organized, we nonetheless assume that they comply with rules that reflect a social organization in terms of hierarchies, networks and social divisions of space.

Indeed, it seems to us that the formal/informal distinction is significant and indicative of planning policies and thresholds of tolerance for certain forms of habitat. It does not necessarily have to do with a difference in terms of quality or type of building but rather a legal classification of who has the right to occupy which space. In a slightly older article based on the city of Cairo, Mostafa Kharoufi (1992) shows that a significant portion of habitat, like business practices, is often defined as 'informal', even though these forms of urbanity do not, he says, represent an anomaly, and that they are neither marginal nor exceptional (Kharoufi, 1992:83). According to this anthropologist, the term *informal* – a concept that was popularized by the International Labour Office in the 1970s – strongly influenced institutional discourse regarding urban practices and spaces, as well as the discourse in Egyptian social science research.

More recently, authors have tried to capture the confusion, entanglements and interdependencies of the formal vs. informal and legal vs. illegal categories by empirically proving that these dichotomies do not reflect the full complexity of contemporary cities (Azaïs and Steck, 2010). In light of this, to us it seems difficult to consider the polarization between formal and informal as a category of analysis, as the fabric of the contemporary city is based on a dialogue between the margins and the norm, the legitimate and illegitimate (Sierra and Tadié, 2008; Adly, 2014).

Showing that rules (i.e. a modus operandi) do exist in the margins of Dubai is precisely what Elsheshtawy attempts to do by highlighting daily practices in these little spaces. However, the lack of deconstruction of the 'informal' category is not entirely convincing. His use prevents us from questioning the meaning that users of these spaces give them and the manner in which they organize their relationship to the built environment (also see the following section). We believe that this deconstruction is all the more necessary, given that the very role of urban research in social science is to challenge the categories established by institutional actors and city government policies and their normativity. The goal then becomes to understand the complexity of contemporary cities that, beyond categories, reflects an infinite variety of practices and ways of being in the city and to analyze mechanisms that allow for the creation of a common universe beyond national differences.

In the shadow of globalization

The abovementioned contrast between 'big spaces' versus 'little spaces' and 'formal' versus 'informal' spaces harkens back to another conceptual binomial that has sparked important debates in the social sciences: 'local' versus 'global' (Appadurai, 1990; Kearney, 1995; Friedman and Friedman, 2008). We can now sense the conceptual architecture that Elsheshtawy proposes us. The city of Dubai has 'formal' planned spaces, whose meaning and symbolism resonate throughout the world within a network of 'global' cities. The form of these spaces is guided by the exigencies of a capitalist economy with little regard for users and inhabitants.

On the other hand, nestled within the interstices of the global village, in the Deleuzian fold, are invisible yet extremely diverse worlds with strong territorial links. Therefore, if 'big spaces' serve to describe spaces of capitalism, 'little spaces' must then be understood as spaces where oppressed or relegated populations live and evolve.

In Elsheshtawy's text, this contrast is supported and justified by an epistemological stance that is in the tradition of approaches to everyday life. In so doing, he puts himself at odds with the dominant approach to research on Dubai (Davidson, 2009; Sampler and Eigner, 2003). The author indeed refers to the works of Guy Debord and the Situationist critique of The Society of the Spectacle – a critique that can be found in the very title of Elsheshtawy's most recent book, *Dubai: Behind the Urban Spectacle* (2010). According to him, this urban spectacle, celebrated by the expression 'big spaces', defines so-called global cities designed according to the demands of economic capital, and of which Dubai is one of the most striking examples. In this way, the relationship between 'big spaces' and 'little spaces' is not unlike the relationship between 'non-places' and 'anthropological places', as proposed by anthropologist Marc Augé (Augé, 2008). This author, who worked for the development of anthropology 'at home' (or 'of the near'), or of 'contemporaneous worlds' (Augé, 1999), is outraged that the physical and spatial markers of globalization (like airports and shopping malls) cause societies to lose their cultural specificity. According to Augé, these places are thus 'non-places', where the anthropological richness of human societies.

However, unlike Augé, Elsheshtawy's binary argument is less politicized. More than a critique of the Dubai of capitalism, he instead provides us with another scope that helps us to analyze – even perceive – the city another way. Elsheshtawy proposes that we focus on the materiality of the city, on the relationship between urban street furniture and social practices. In the manner of a Roland Barthes, his description of Dubai likewise deciphers the production of representative objects from the society. The appropriation of public space by street vendors, an ad stuck on a lamppost or a tag on the façade of a building all say as much about the customs of migrants in Dubai as the Citroen DS did about the modern lifestyle in France in the 1950s (Barthes, 1957).

Indeed, for Elsheshtawy, the city offers the opportunity to play with mechanisms of control and repression. In this respect, he is like Michel De Certeau, whose strength consists in focusing sociological analysis on the 'practices of everyday life' and the everyday creativity of ordinary citizens (De Certeau, 1990). Thus, the migrants of Dubai develop tactics for 'making do'. A certain malleability in a technocratic and functional framework. Consequently, for Elsheshtawy, the little spaces are the 'real' Dubai – the city of humans of the urban ordinary, the inhabited city, as opposed to the city of big spaces, which is only consumed: 'Here, there are no real people – merely passive consumers, following the dictates of global capitalism' (this volume: 189).

However, can a city without veritable human beings, built only on the dictates of global capitalism, really exist? Might the author's radical critique of this city primarily be the result of the observer effect? What would Elsheshtawy see if he focused (as he did with low-income migrant communities in ethnic enclaves of Dubai) on the daily practices and everyday urban life of white collar citizens living in the city center, that economic elite who gather atop those glass towers, the developers in the government? Wouldn't he meet just as many 'real people'? Aren't big spaces, if looked at up close, in the same manner as little spaces, also inhabited and appropriated by individuals who, above and beyond the transnational ties they may have with the Shanghai stock exchange or heads of American companies, have routines and daily local habits? In other words, don't they also have a local life? Could it be that this distinction Elsheshtawy makes is based primarily on differentiation and methodological bias?

2. From the extraordinary to the ordinary: the city in images

In his works on Dubai, Yasser Elsheshtawy puts visuals, such as maps, photographs (see especially Elsheshtawy, 2010:32–60) and video, at the heart of his analysis. Thus, as he explains in his text, he and his team conducted video observations of certain parts of Dubai, which were then compiled in the form of time-lapse videos[2]. It was this extremely rich visual material that served as a support for his presentation during the workshop, giving it life and grabbing the audience's attention, and literally revealing the reality (or at least *a* reality) of urban spaces in Dubai. Yasser Elsheshtawy gives us not only the typical image of Dubai – that international archetype of grandeur and architectural modernity – but also draws our attention to the small spaces, the very ones that escape the notice of international spectators. Unlike the exuberant image traditionally vehicled by the country, his visual approach focuses on the city's small spaces.

Thus, by using images in his research this way, Elsheshtawy ultimately adopts a method that is relatively common in architecture. He photographs the streets of Satwa as though he were making a sketch of a building, and introduces us to the public spaces of Ghubeiba using time-lapse video in the same way he would show us the plan of a neighborhood or city. This apparent indifference is one of the major qualities of Elsheshtawy's work,

---

[2]   Time lapse videos are compilations of the action that takes place in a fixed frame that are then sped up.

and makes him undoubtedly bolder and more creative in his methodological and analytical approach. He likewise offers us aesthetic and aestheti-
cized data, which greatly contributed to the quality of his presentation. While
the author shows relatively little reflectivity on the visual methodologies
that are the basis of his work (including his book [2010]), he nonetheless
positions himself, in spite of himself, at the heart of the debates that animate
the field of visual methods in social sciences (and visual anthropology in particular) by his very use of such methods. Since the invention of photography and cinema, sociology and anthropology have gradually used these techniques in the production and dissemination of knowledge. However, it was not
until after World War II that 'there was substantial film activity by anthropologists' (Ruby, 1996:1348), while sociology very seldom used video (Harper,
2000:143).

Photos and video: merely illustrative?

Thus, the author uses video as early anthropologists did – for its heuristic
qualities, to literally show cultural events that are difficult to describe in words
without betraying their meaning (Ruby, 1996). Nevertheless, in terms of communication, the inclusion of visual elements has an attractive, captivating quality that moreover greatly contributed to the favorable view of Elsheshtawy's
presentation during the workshop. Images, both still and live, have an illustrative dimension. To begin with, they facilitate the appropriation of research
findings. 'The presentation of images, along with commentaries in a report,
book or article, enhances the restitution of the research results and may clarify
them by incorporating elements from the visible world that help us to better
understand a description' (Conord, 2007:20). Images likewise enable us to
connect with the object of study (Conord, 2002), making the distant appear
close and familiar, and are not necessarily redundant with text because they
directly communicate feelings and emotions. 'Through direct communication,
a feeling of empathy transcends to a certain degree, and not without risks or
pitfalls of otherness' (Colleyn, 1993:21). 'The image illustrates (the text) by
making the strange familiar. By giving body to the respondents, it arouses our
interest' (Pezeril, 2008).
     In this regard, the use of images in Elsheshtawy's work lends itself
to the scientific objectives of his research and serves as an illustration: by
showing the little spaces of Dubai, he makes them close, familiar and alive

for those who are unfamiliar with the context. The images of Dubai describe the city in a way that is directly apprehensible, thus recreating the familiarity and lives of these little spaces. By showing us the 'lived experience' of Dubai, Elsheshtawy is in keeping with the authors to whom he refers in his work (such as the Situationist International movement and Jane Jacobs [1961], best known for her work on little spaces in New York). All highlight the informal spaces and cultural objects of everyday life that give depth and diversity to the urban and make it engaging, areas too often forgotten by those who plan the city. This aim is particularly well served by photography and the use of images in general: time-lapse video 'illustrates a dynamic and vibrant setting... the urban vitality of the street' (this volume:203). Thus, the use of images, which could be seen as redundant with the written description of the streets of Dubai, serves the author's goal of showing another reality of Dubai, 'represent[ing] a counterpoint to [its] flashy image', (this volume:199).

A neutral memory support?

Beyond the illustrative dimension that could potentially be redundant with a written text, Elsheshtawy's work gives images a more important, nobler role. The images here also have a heuristic function, becoming material for analysis in themselves. Videos taken in several parts of the city show that 'the street has gone beyond its functional aspects to become a social place' (this volume:203).

For the author, the systematic recording of street movement serves as a memory support for the researcher, who cannot capture as many details from a scene of observation as photography or video can. This memory function of images has existed since the origins of anthropology as a discipline, because 'In his ethnological lessons (Mauss, 1947), Marcel Mauss introduced the idea that the photographic process allowed one to gather visual data and thus memorize multiple details relating to observed facts – information that the naked eye alone can not retain' (Piette, 1996). With this memory function, images become 'tools of investigation in their own right, rendering visible the insignificant actions and gestures that might otherwise escape the researcher's attention' (Pezeril, 2008). The researcher's gaze, though attentive, remains selective, and does not reflect the wealth of action taking place around him, especially in public spaces. Thus, the desire to record this reality in a compre-hensive manner, through images, allows the anthropologist 'to increase [his] storage capacity' (Conord, 2007:16).

This is indeed the desire apparent in Elsheshtawy's work. The systematic recording of movement in specific urban spaces captures a wider, more comprehensive view of the 'multiple social and economic interactions... multiple experiences' (this volume: 193). Using this method of observation, the author seems to seek comprehensiveness, but also a more objective mode of observation by reducing his interaction with the field and subjects observed. The recorded video data tends to erase the researcher's involvement in his field, as though he were trying his best to expunge his presence and the resulting interactions. This search for objectivity is reminiscent of the positivist utopia that marks the origins of the use of video in anthropology, and which implied that video could provide objective research data (Ruby, 1996). And yet, is this search for objectivity and comprehensiveness not merely wishful thinking?

Indeed, images are not simply a mirror of reality (Conord, 2002), firstly because they are always the result of the technical and esthetic choices of the person photographing or filming (Conord, 2007), and secondly because they always require interpretative work (Piette, 2007). Thus, the images collected are automatically a construction of reality, and while they tell us about the elements being photographed or filmed, they also tell us about the person holding the camera and their relationship with their field (Tornay, 1991). This is also the anthropological critique of positivist theory: 'Films and photographs are always concerned with two things – the culture of those filmed and the culture of those who film' (Ruby, 1996:1345).

The use of continuous video recording in public spaces in Elsheshtawy's work seems to act as a kind of exorcism of the researcher's presence and its impact on observed realities. However, this desire for neutrality in the production of images is utopian, if not impossible; the images produced inevitably reflect research decisions. Thus, the urban planning of spectacle – the big spaces – seems to be observed at a more macroscopic scale, the scale of history and plans. Elsheshtawy describes the rapid growth of the city since the 1970s, but also the spectacular construction of certain buildings, such as the Burj Al Arab and Palm Islands project (Elsheshtawy, 2010:127–128). The big spaces are thus approached based both on plans, which reflect the extremely rapid development of the city and magnitude of urban development projects (i.e. the Palm Islands mega-structure), and images of large projects whose framing lets us see the contrasts and fragmented spaces.

These images, taken from afar or by plane, provide a macro-social view of the city – an aerial view, a 'view from above'. The interstitial spaces in front of malls and major architectural projects hint at a contrasting reality. Like a camera zoom, the author moves in on this contrasting reality to explore the little spaces in greater depth and thus show another urban reality of Dubai. In contrast, the little spaces – the impromptu meeting spaces – are observed from the street, shop windows, bits of sidewalk, or 'one particular street corner in Al Quoz district' (this volume:203). The researcher's gaze is still present in the asymmetrical treatment of these two realities of Dubai that he proposes. This treatment therefore is based on a methodological bias that ultimately proves useful, since it serves the author's theoretical purpose: to show the diversity of life and urban spaces in the city of Dubai.

Nevertheless, one cannot help but ask: is not the sharp contrast between big and little spaces enhanced by the lack of symmetry in the methodological treatment of these two types of space? Were we look more closely at the big spaces in order to observe them more carefully, similar dynamics might very well appear, although originating in quite a different context from those observed in the so-called little spaces. What would we see were we to hide a camera inside a CBD tower in Dubai for 24 hours? Would we not observe processes of appropriation of space, traces of occupation or even uses likely to be defined as informal like those in the public spaces in more relegated neighborhoods?

From image to discourse: towards a subjective view of Dubai?

We should nonetheless emphasize the analytical dimension of collected visual data. In Elsheshtawy's work, it is indeed the image that produces the data and enables the mapping of the activities that take place in public places, and the movement of people in particular. As the very source of the analytical process, the images are used to analyze the appropriation of public space in Dubai by migrants. In a very fine, very relevant way, in an article that combines the perspective of both an architect and an anthropologist, intersecting grandeur and detail, stillness and movement, Elsheshtawy manages to make us part of the dialogues and exchanges that take place every day between migrants in Dubai and the built environment through the original usage of video footage. The recording of repeated gestures and movements, their duration and how space is used allow us to see these *petits riens urbains* that, for Thierry Paquot, comprise the city's richness (2010).

Beyond observation choices that serve the author's theoretical goals, the use of images puts this research at the heart of the debates regarding objectivity and subjectivity that have troubled the anthropological field for many years. The issue of reflectivity on the data and knowledge generated has always been fundamental in anthropology, especially around acceptance of the fact that anthropologists never observe an objective reality, and that the latter is inevitably altered and transformed by the former's presence, gaze and interpretation. The knowledge generated is therefore inevitably subjective as well, as reflectivity can be neither avoided nor eradicated. 'Subjectivity should be engaged with as a central aspect of ethnographic knowledge, interpretation and representation' (Pink, 2007:23).

Therefore, the data thus generated appear to be social constructs in which the observed and the observer are equal actors. In this sense, one way of accepting the subjectivity of the data generated is to fully assume the role of subjects observed in this production. The images collected here, though diverse and rich, remain largely unexposed to the subjects in them. Thus do some social scientists choose to take advantage of the unique interaction that photography and video allows for in the field, and use images as an interview support, or, like counter-gifts, offer their subjects the right to examine, even question the images produced. One example is what some call photo-elicitation (Rose, 2007). Others allow their informants to co-produce their photographic or film works. These are very contrasting methodological biases compared to Elsheshtawy's work, which seeks to give a more or less neutral account of visible movements in certain public spaces in Dubai.

Beyond the utopia that is the production of objective data, one of the major limitations of this method of observation, designed to be neutral, is the absence of verbal input from the subjects observed. Indeed, the images themselves bear no inherent or obvious meaning; their explication can give sense to the images, as well as to the context in which they were taken, 'what is shown' and 'what is outside of the frame' (Conord, 2007:16). Moreover, photo-elicitation provides access to other records of knowledge and information about the elements and people observed by mobilizing memory and emotions, rather than by built, structured, rational discourse (Rose, 2007). Thus, 'the photographic image has many meanings, and the meaning ascribed to it is the result of a construction, a process that is neither natural nor universal' (Conord, 2007:19), hence the need to question social actors about this meaning. Elsheshtawy's research method is largely based on more or less systematic observations in which the researcher has little involvement and, moreover, that leave little room for inhabitants to comment on what is meaningful for them in the practices observed or, more simply, *if* these practices have meaning for them. One wonders, for example, how migrants would describe their urban experience in general and the spaces they frequent every day. In this way, a subjective view of the little spaces of Dubai' is missing and could, methodologically speaking, support the author's theoretical proof.

Conclusion

Elsheshtawy's paper thus leads us to focus on the little spaces of Dubai, offering an unexpected, productive counterpoint to urban planning of spectacle typically conveyed by this megalopolis. In the tradition of Situationist International movement, he takes us with him into the streets of migrant neighborhoods, these areas of everyday life that reveal the richness of the daily urban experience. In so doing, his analysis calls our attention to the small, the close – those spaces he calls *informal* – in which relegated immigrant populations that literally and figuratively build the city of Dubai evolve daily. To do this, he draws on the ethnography of these little spaces, especially through the use of images that make them familiar and alive. The patient observation of how urban space is occupied on a daily basis, by seemingly commonplace gestures and movements, reveals the dynamics at play in a more relevant way, particularly in a megalopolis as diverse as Dubai.

However, he contrasts two very different realities in this movement. On one hand there are the big spaces – a sort of simulacrum of a city driven by global capitalism, inhabited by consumers and planned in such a way as to showcase the tallest, boldest, most modern buildings for the world to see. On the other hand, the little spaces – inhabited by migrants – are the spaces of everyday practices, sociability and the real life of the city. This contrast is overwhelmingly supported by observations made at different scales: a macroscopic, top-down view for big spaces and a microscopic view, attentive to detail and movement, for little ones. This dichotomy is further reinforced by the chosen methodological device: visual observation techniques that are attentive to public spaces and the movement, exchanges and sociability perceptible in little spaces. However, we sense in the author a strong desire for neutrality in the way the images are collected, including the systematic recording of video footage in public spaces. Nevertheless, the tradition of visual anthropology is there to remind us that such an enterprise is, by definition, impossible, and that any image, like any text, is the result of choices made by the person photographing or filming and, hence, the result of the relationship between the researcher and the reality observed. This fact then justifies the need to question the meaning individuals give their practices, to what is shown in images and all they cannot capture.

Thus, the 'little' and 'big' spaces do not distinguish the 'real' city from the 'spectacle', but rather two scales of analysis, two focuses, two different approaches. This, ultimately, is the contribution of Elsheshtawy's paper, which shows us a contrasting picture of Dubai through a theoretical and methodological construction of small-scale observation. The microscopic observation methods used here demonstrate the theoretical questions raised regarding this dual urban reality.

References

Adly, H. (2014) «La vieille ville du Caire à l'épreuve du patrimoine: quelle réception sociale à la "revitalisation" des marges urbaines?», in Nora Semmoud, Bénédicte Florin, Olivier Legros, Florence Troin, *Marges urbaines et néolibéralisme en Méditerranée*, Tours: Presses Universitaires François-Rabelais, 232-257.

AlShafieei, S. (1997) The Spatial Implications of Urban Land Policies in Dubai City. Dubai Municipality (Unpublished report).

Appadurai, A. (1990) Disjuncture and Difference in the Global Cultural Economy. *Theory, Culture and Society* 7.2–3, 295–310.

Augé, M. (1999) *An Anthropology for Contemporaneous Worlds*. Stanford University Press, Stanford.

Augé, M. (2008) *Non-Places: An Introduction to Supermodernity*, trans. John Howe. Verso, London and New York.

Azaïs, C. and Steck, J.-F. (eds.) (2010) Les territoires de l'informel. *Espaces et sociétés* 143.3.

Barthes, R. (1957) *Mythologies*. Le Seuil, Paris.

Colleyn, J.-P. (1993) *Le regard documentaire*. Centre Pompidou, Paris.

Conord, S. (2002) Le choix de l'image en anthropologie: qu'est-ce qu'une 'bonne' photographie? *Ethnographiques.org* (Vol. 2, novembre 2002), *ethnographiques.org*, (consulted August 2012).

Conord, S. (2007) Usages et fonctions de la photographies. *Ethnologie française* 37.1, 11–22.

Crawford, M. (1999) in Chase, J., Kaliski, J. and Crawford, M. (eds.) Introduction. *Everyday Urbanism*. Monacelli. New York, 9, 8–15.

Crawford, M. (2005) in Mehrotra R. (ed.) Everyday Urbanism. *Everyday Urbanism: Margaret Crawford vs. Micheal Speaks, Michigan Debates on Urbanism I*. The University of Michigan, 28.

Davidson, C. M. (2009) *Dubai. The Vulnerability of Success*. Columbia University Press, New York.

de Certeau, M. (1984) *The Practice of Everyday Life*. University of California Press, Berkeley.

de Certeau, M. (1990) *L'invention du quotidien, I: Arts de faire*. Gallimard, Paris.

Elsheshtawy, Y. in Edensor, Tim & Jayne, Mark (eds.) (2011) Urban (Im)mobility: Public Encounters. *Urban Theory beyond the West*. Routledge, London.

Elsheshtawy, Y. (2011) Little Space/Big Space: Everyday Urbanism in Dubai. *Brown Journal of World Affairs*.

Elsheshtawy, Y. (2010) *Dubai: Behind an Urban Spectacle*. Routledge, London.

Elsheshtawy, Y. (2008) Transitory Sites: Mapping Dubai's 'Forgotten' Urban Public Spaces. *The International Journal of Urban & Regional Research*. 32.4, 968–988.

Friedman, K. E. and Friedman, J. (2008) *Modernities, Class, and the Contradictions of Globalization: The Anthropology of Global Systems*. AltaMira Press, Lanham.

Graham, S. and Marvin, S. (2001) *Splintering Urbanism: Networked Infrastructures, Technological Mobilities and the Urban Condition*. Routledge, London.

Harper, D. (2000) The image in sociology: histories and issues. *Journal des anthropologues*. http://jda.revues.org/3182, (consulted May 2013)

Hou J. (ed.) (2007) *Guerilla Urbanism*. Routledge, London.

Jacobs, J. (1961) *The Death and Life of Great American Cities*. Random House, New York.

Kearney, M. (1995) The Local and the Global: The Anthropology of Globalization and Transnationalism. *Annual Review of Anthropology*, 547–565.

Khalaf, S. and Alkobaisi, S. (1999) Migrants' Strategies of Coping and Patterns of Accomodation in the Oil-Rich Gulf Societies: Evidence from the UAE. *British Journal of Middle Eastern Studies* 26.2, 271–298.

Kharoufi, M. (1992) Secteur 'informel' et activités urbaines en Egypte: le point sur quelques travaux. *Egypte-Monde arabe* 9, 83–99.

Kutty, S. (2002) Meeting point, message circle. *Khaleej Times*.

Marcuse, P. and van Kempem R. (eds.) (2000) *Globalizing Cities: A new spatial order?*. Blackwell Publishing, Oxford.

Mauss, M. (1947) *Manuel d'ethnographie*. Payot, Paris.

Mehrotra, R. in Huyssen, A. (ed.) (2008) Negotiating the Static and Kinetic Cities: The Emergent Urbanity of Mumbai. *Cities, Other Worlds: Urban Imaginaries in a Globalizing Age*. Duke University Press, Durham and London, 205–218.

Menon, S. (2006) Move out, board tells Rashid colony tenants. *Gulf News*.

Pezeril, C. (2008) Place et intérêt de la photographie dans une étude anthropologique sur l'islam au Sénégal. *Ethnographiques.org* 16. *ethnographiques.org*, (consulted August 2012)

Piette, A. (1996) *Ethnographie de l'action, L'observation des détails*. Métailié, Paris.

Piette, A. (2007) Fondements épistémologiques de la photographie. *Ethnologie française* 37.1, 23–28.

Pink, S. (2007) *Doing Visual Ethnography*. Sage, London.

Raymer, S. (2005) Dubai's Kerala connection. *YaleGlobal Online*.

Rose, G. (2007) *Visual Methodologies, An Introdution to the Interpretation of Visual Materials*. Sage, London.

Ruby, J. (1996) in Levinson, D. and Ember, M. (eds.) Visual Anthropology. *Encyclopedia of Cultural Anthropology* 4. Henry Holt and Company, 1345–1351.

Sadler, S. (1999) *The Situationist City*. The MIT Press, Cambridge.

Sampler, J. and Eigner, S. (2003) *Sand to Silicon: Achieving Rapid Growth Lessons from Dubai*. Profile Books, Exeter.

Sennett, R. (1977) *The Fall of Public Man*. Knopf, New York.

Sierra, A. and Tadié, J. (eds.) (2008) La ville face à ses marges. *Autrepart* 45.

Simone, A. (2010) *City Life from Jakarta to Dakar: Movements at the Crossroads*. Routledge, London.

Sorkin, M. (2009) *Twenty Minutes in Manhattan*. Reaktion Books, New York.

Stevens, Q. (2007) *The Ludic City: Exploring the Potential of Public Spaces*. Routledge, London.

Tornay, S. (1991) Photographie et traitement d'autrui: réflexions d'un ethnographe. *L'ethnographie* 109, 87.1, 97–104.

Paquot, T. (2010) Petits riens urbains. *Revue Urbanisme* 370.

Zukin, S. (2009) *The Naked City: The Death and Life of Authentic Urban Places*. Oxford University Press, New York.

CITIES IN TRANSLATION, URBAN RESEARCH IN TRANSITION (TOWARDS A CONCLUSION...)

Stéphanie Vincent-Geslin, Yves Pedrazzini, Vincent Kaufmann

Thinking about cities ought to be willing to travel widely, tracking the diverse circulations that shape cities and thinking across both similarities and differences amongst cities, in search of understanding the many ways of urban life. (Robinson, 2006:169)

This quote from Jennifer Robinson's *Ordinary Cities* aptly sums up our goal in this book. While it is true that the tools for describing and understanding the urban phenomenon have multiplied and diversified over time, it is the object itself – the city – that has become infinitely complex. This work, however, attempts to give the city a name – or rather, *names* – and to reformulate the urban question: what is a city? What is an ordinary city, a city 'without qualities' that, nevertheless, is habitable by the fact that it is inhabited? What city cannot be reduced to the order imposed by paranoid authorities, nor abandoned to chaos, to the absurd or to civil war? What is a city in a world plagued by uncertainty, a city where it is a pleasure to stroll aimlessly, to lose oneself (at least a bit) along the way? And, conversely, what is not a city? What *can't* it be, regardless of its geographic location?

In the book you have just read, Dear Reader, researchers of international renown question what we should call this enigmatic character we refer to as the city. Our first goal in this conclusion, therefore, is to use the various articles to shed light on this conundrum, on the basis of three key questions designed to delineate the contemporary urban phenomenon. Then we will attempt to clarify the role of the urban researcher by using the notion of 'translation' before offering some final thoughts for a better understanding of the city of tomorrow.

Where is the city?

In 'Man of the Crowd' (1840), an extraordinary short story by Edgar Allen Poe (translated into French by Charles Baudelaire), the author posits that it is not so much people who make the city, but rather the city that produces people through its urbanity, density and fatal appeal, to the point of making them 'men of the crowd', 'the type and the genius of deep crime. He refuses to be alone. He is a man of the crowd'. Here is a story – a cautionary tale, as filmmaker Eric Rohmer would call it – that we might consider the first hypothesis on the origin of *urbanity*, that morbid attraction for late nights spent in cafés and wandering the crowded boulevards – but not the *city*. Baudelaire unmistakably draws his inspiration for the figure of the *flâneur* in 'The Painter of Modern Life', an article published in 1863 in which the author of 'Les fleurs du mal' at once praises the dandy, the artist and he who 'becomes one with the crowd'. Later, in his famous (French) exposé entitled 'Paris: Capital of the 19th century' (1939), Walter Benjamin uses the figure of the *flâneur* to develop both a theory of aesthetics (similar to that of the Surrealists, with their love of 'arcades') and a critical theory of the capitalist city. Before him, other thinkers of *Mitteleuropa* considered that cities were nothing more than a pile of stone and steel beams, without the crowds that wander within them, giving them life. We are obviously referring to authors such as Georg Simmel and Siegfried Kracauer, who considered the *passant*, the *flâneur* and the *affairé* (busy person) the archetypes of modern man and the main actors on the urban scene, and the 'big city' as the hyper-realistic backdrop for capitalist overproduction.

This beautiful image was obviously undermined by the fall of Berlin in 1945, but nonetheless contributed (in addition to deep melancholy) to the invention of the city and the figure of the urban dweller. We might have stopped there, but a few years later, the *flâneur* became Tarkovski's stalker, followed by the invention – cinematographic (1979) and then real (Tchernobyl 1986) – of a degraded environment as urban landscape. *Flânerie* became suspicious, dangerous, self-serving – a poor survival strategy in a zone where, before long, all that would remain of the city were sections of radioactive walls. Perhaps it is more urban planning itself that is in question here...

However, might this be what makes the city so very European and 20th century? Since the fall of Berlin, one has witnessed the 'officialization' of Paris and the transforming of London, Barcelona and Rome into registered trademarks, nowadays. Are these really the places where we should be looking for the city? One hundred fifty years after the great beginning of the modern European city and those of the veritable plethora of urban sciences that fol- lowed in its wake, should not the question be: *What city is the capital of the 21st century?* Does the *flâneur*, or bohemian artist even more so, have anything to do with the liquid urbanity of large cities? More than we think perhaps, if we recall, for instance, this excerpt from 'The Painter':

> The crowd is his element, as the air is that of birds and water of fishes. His passion and his profession are to become one flesh with the crowd. For the perfect *flâneur*, for the passionate spectator, it is an immense joy to set up house in the heart of the multitude, amid the ebb and flow of movement, in the midst of the fugitive and the infinite. To be away from home and yet to feel oneself everywhere at home; to see the world, to be at the centre of the world, and yet to remain hidden from the world – impartial natures which the tongue can but clumsily define. (Baudelaire, *1863*)

The crowd and the *flâneur*. This is what gives a city its urbanity – the fact of being in the world and not *alone* in the world. In the 19th century, Paris gave up the title to Berlin, Rotterdam, Le Havre and, later, Kabul and Baghdad (barely). Today, in the 21st century, we are forced to look at India, China and Brazil as being on par with Canada, Switzerland or France. Hanoi: capital of the 21st century! Lagos: capital of the 21st century! Manila: capital of the 21st century! Mumbai: capital of the 21st century! Or Mexico City, Sao Paolo, etc. Capital of the informal *Kapital* has taken shape, even where one does not expect it.

How is the city born, and who makes it?

Returning to this question – often hushed and seldom discussed – requires overcoming the two-fold conclusion that the city either results from a top-down process (in other words, domination) or that it is entirely the product of bottom-up processes (in which case we dream of a fairer urban tomorrow). Neither of these visions is better than the other because neither one is real, for at least two reasons. The first is that both are the result (albeit somewhat artificial) of the observer's view of the city, of her perspective and the way she questions it. Secondly, because the city, in all its complex reality, is built through encounters, interactions and the conflict born of these two processes. The authors in this book have not overlooked this fact. Thus, in Chapter 5, Yasser Elsheshtawy shows how Dubai is a multi-faceted city, the product of an urban planning of spectacle, but also a city of immigrants who come from all over Southeast Asia *en masse* to build its skyscrapers, and thereby participate – albeit behind the scenes – in the production of this spectacle, thereby altering the urban reality of Dubai by their very presence and practices.

Planning helps produce the city through the ordering of spaces and inhabitants. Through the chaotic, irregular but novel migratory paths and the practices they bring with them, inhabitants also invent the city, their city, or at least parts of it. Planning attempts to reamalgamate the parts with the whole. Without planning, there would be no transportation infrastructure to break down barriers between spaces and promote urban mobility, which facilitates the social and spatial integration of excluded populations (i.e. the poor) through a more cohesive urban project, as Hanja Maksim, Emmanuel Ravalet, Xavier Oreiller and Yafiza Zorro demonstrate in Chapter 2 through the example of Medellin. The implementation of planning also proves to be a complex process, taking on different, even contradictory meanings depending on the urban policy history and geographical scale. As such, Susan Parnell and Owen Crankshaw consider the segregating effect of urban planning in South Africa as the result of the complexity of the scales of governance and conflicts of territorial policies – and not the failure of planning itself.

Nevertheless, most of the chapters in this book lead us not only to question urban planning but also to rebel against it, theoretically and politically. Marie-Paule Thomas' and Alexandra Thorer's article analyses the traumatic effects of bulldozer-type functionalist urban planning on the city of Addis

Ababa, where little consideration was given to indigenous habits and practices. Both articles in Chapter 1 thus call for general wariness with regard to the imperialism of urban planning, which does not have equal impacts on all cities, depending on their context and history, and regardless of their geographical proximity. This mistrust of turnkey, all-purpose solutions transferred indiscriminately from one context to another (because *our* solutions are not necessarily *their* solutions) immediately raises the issue of translation from one context to another, particularly when it comes to applying Northern, colonial or post-colonial methods to Southern cities.

Aware of the difficulty of translation, many of the authors in this book took seriously Jennifer Robinson's (2006) appeal to focus on the ordinary of the city (and, hence, a bottom-up approach). So we discover the small spaces of Dubai in Chapter 5, Dharavi and its tool-houses in Chapter 3, and creative workers, travellers and gang members in Chapter 4. All call attention to the forgotten, excluded, marginal and illegal residents of the globalized city, giving them the chance to show how they, too, help to create the city according to their own models. This 'good' city includes them and, as articulated by Hossam Adly and Stephanie Vincent-Geslin in Chapter 5, gives them a voice. Methodologically and epistemologically, a 'good city' is not a single, unequivocal reality but rather is the sum of its actors' (subjective) viewpoints and experiences. Thus, a 'good city' is not the same for the urban planner as it is for the Grottes resident. Effectively, Luca Pattaroni's and Tobias Baitsch's article (Chapter 3) shows how people in this neighborhood in transformation developed a new kind of urban project, demanding greater autonomy and freedom in managing their neighborhood and greater acceptance of different urban lifestyles.

A good city is perhaps not the global city of skylines and skyscrapers, economic competition and tourist attractions – in other words, not the city of dominant, neoliberal, functionalist capitalist order. A city does not necessarily win by being overly ordered if this order does not reflect its inhabitants' perceptions and needs. Indeed, the latter is often out of sync with the plans of those who think they know what's best for a neighborhood (though they themselves do not live there), especially with regard to popular neighborhoods. This is above all the case because order stifles creativity, disorder, DIY – all of the little urban nothings that are not merely the beauty and allure of the city, but are its very essence.

What is the city?

The different chapters of this book brought us to Rio, Johannesburg, Montreal, Dubai and Mexico City. After this trip around the urban world, the fundamental question remains: of what is the city the name? From a geographical standpoint, is what we call 'city' the same in the Grottes (in Geneva) as it is in Dharavi (in Mumbai)? Just as Rem Koolhaas (2002) was able to affirm that bigness 'fucks' context, is the city just a city, a generic city, regardless of the context?

In light of the ideas presented in this book's chapters, and in keeping with the analyses of M. Storper on the uniqueness and non-generalizability of context (Storper, 2013:157), we can say that Rem Koolhaas got it wrong and, in fact, quite the opposite is true. *Context fucks bigness!* Or at least context is not so vulnerable to architecture and urbanism, especially when it has already been built, urbanized and planned. Therefore, the city has formal and informal capacities of resistance, as much for building big things as for destroying them, which is obviously an important quality, even in cities 'without qualities' (i.e. ordinary cities).

As such, the analyses presented by South African researchers Susan Parnell and Owen Crankshaw greatly differ from those of their respondents, Marie-Paule Thomas and Alexandra Thorer. Hence, Chapter 1 shows mixed results regarding the impact of planning on 'the city' and its impact on social and spatial segregation phenomena. Such findings highlight the need to translate the concept of urban planning based on the specific historical, political, economic, social, etc., contexts that shape different urban realities, and likewise require the use of different terms. Similarly, in Chapter 5, Yasser Elsheshtawy demonstrates that, beyond its spectacular architectural image which became globalized in the 2000s, Dubai is not just another emerging city, but rather has distinct urban features shaped by its unique position at the crossroads of several continents, cultures and religions, along with its immigrants, who characterize it as much as, if not more than, its skyscrapers.

Thus, an urban reality is produced by the specific, unique relationship to the territory in which it exists, as well as the historic, economic and political dynamics that created it. However strong the desire may be of those who run the city to remove it from the local reality that, historically, governed its creation and development in order to project it in the space-time of globalization, the city somehow continues to grow roots in the most ordinary places, in the daily lives of its most modest, most 'unsophisticated' citizens. What is more, these people and places not only resist eviction from the city and erasure from its collective memory, they are the only recourse against the cultural uprooting of spaces due to urban marketing and the creative planning of global agendas.

This is not the least of the paradoxes in a book aimed at understanding what 'the city' names. Cities are worlds, at once unique and generic. On the one hand, they increasingly conform to the historical development of the capitalist city by liberalizing, deregulating, deformalizing and fragmenting themselves into social sectors and zones with diverging interests and, thus, sometimes violent conflicts. On the other hand, albeit more rarely, they can reinforce their distinctiveness by staging it to attract tourists, showcasing that which belongs to them and them alone, albeit producing negative effects that escape their control. In so doing, they often sacrifice their true idiosyncrasies to the stereotypes and misconceptions that then imprison them, depending on how this distinctiveness is presented by those in charge of their promotion. What follows is every possible misunderstanding about local identity, beauty and the truth of one city versus that of another.

The tension inherent to all cities becomes apparent from the analyses in this book. On the one hand, one witnesses the universal, globalized aspiration of wanting to be a 'great' city (or at least to look like one from an architectural and morphological point of view); on the other hand, a city needs that 'local touch', the specificity of the geographical, political and (dare we say) cultural context. The city is therefore not only a globalized economic center – symbolized by a Centralized Business District and a skyline – but is also, above all, defined by its uniqueness, its 'small spaces' (to use Yasser Elsheshtawy's expression), its 'post-heroes' (to use that of L. Carmo, Y. Pedrazzini and M. Reitz), its disorder and its margins. Many of the authors in this book agree with the idea, clearly stated by J-A. Boudreau in Chapter 4, that those *groups of actors* who sidestep urban order through conflict, marginality or innovation are nonetheless 'paradigmatic figures of urbanity', because 'the city... is their way of life'. Herein lies the specificity of the lifestyles of *homo urbanus* (Lorrain, 2011).

Punkspaces, the Dharavi slum, the favelas of Rio and the *communas* of Medellin. Creative workers, gang members, at-risk youth, travellers, migrants in Dubai and inhabitants of tool-houses are too often seen as marginal – even undesirable – spaces and people, from the point of view of the neo-liberal urban social order that seeks to pacify and secure the city, or at least certain parts of downtown areas, and thereby participate in the homogenization of urban spaces and lifestyles.

These urban spaces and groups are not undesirable components of the contemporary city; they are its essence. The contemporary city is not merely the functional dimension of the 'warranted city' (Breviglieri, 2013), built of certifications, evaluations and standardization. It is also a product of the regenerating otherness of the margins (Cogato Lanza *et al.*, 2013:215). The urbanity of today – and undoubtedly that of tomorrow – does not lie in an ordered, legitimate urban organization that adheres to pre-established rules, but rather in the diversity of disorder, illegality, counter-order, the unexpected and the unplanned. This key idea that runs through our book proposes another kind of universalism with regard to contemporary cities, far from skylines and Centralized Business Districts – that of the urban way of life common to these distinct groups and spaces: the ordinary as a way of life.

The arguments put forth in this book demonstrate with great clarity that the global city of Saskia Sassen, according to Richard Florida, is not a 'good city' from the point of view of inhabitants. In many regards, this formal urban order that is standardized, dominated by money and abundantly described (and in some ways magnified by research), develops to the detriment of its population. Our entire book illustrates this point: urbanity and the city are built of informal practices that elude plans and planning. The creative vitality of cities is stronger than the urban order. The sad lifelessness of downtown areas of major cities that have been normalized, standardized and gentrified – where excess and all traces of life itself have been erased, and all that remains is the built morphology – attest to this. The city has therefore had to rebuild itself elsewhere, in spaces that are more hospitable to the expression and crea-tivity of inhabitants. Thus, the city's essence is not necessarily that first, easy impression it flaunts on the globalized stage, but often what hides where we don't expect it, forcing us urban researchers to look more closely and, often, elsewhere. Perhaps it is precisely in this change of perspective and scale that the city's future resides – or at least that of urban research.

Translating the city

Urban researchers thus call attention to that which is hidden, giving voice to residents and makers of cities, expressing their idea of the 'good city' and the modalities of its implementation. So yes, the urban researcher *is* a trans-lator. It is in this role that the eponymous name of our network takes on its full meaning. Just as it is useful (and necessary) to translate from one language to another, it is likewise crucial to translate empirical phenomena into theory and from one context to another, taking care to safeguard the integrity of the findings and ward off the exoticism and picturesque, on the one hand, and apocalyptic realism and paranoia, on the other. Translation also involves breaking down not only disciplinary boundaries, in order to compile diverse and complementary cognitive resources, but also the barriers between academic and profane knowledge. As such, the empirical knowledge regarding the Dharavi slum provided by Rahul Srivastava and Matias Echanove is no less valuable than that stemming from the Hor Al Anz Street Project in Dubai. For us urban translators, urban knowledge is produced not only in academic circles, but also among activitst networks, provided this knowledge is based on empirical data and the debunking of certitudes and contributes to the development of a critical theory on the urban phenomenon. In other words, there is no hierarchy in the modes of production of urban knowledge because, regardless of whether the knowledge comes from the academic world or elsewhere, the methodology and resulting opinions inherently reflect the intentionality of its creator. Even when the tools used seem only to reflect the reality, they are nonetheless always the product of researchers' choices, with the goal of empirically supporting the objectives of their approaches, as Hossam Adly and Stephanie Vincent-Geslin demonstrate in Chapter 5 (with, for better or worse, the emotional burden of the person analyzing these unique realities).

The texts gathered here also show that it is difficult to go beyond the dominant references in urban studies, regardless of one's standpoint and despite the inherently local nature of the study field and its 'traditions' in interpreting facts. Yet, translating Foucaldian concepts to the favelas of Rio, or those of Debord to Dubai, proves to be an extremely perilous exercise, especially given that Brazilian and Saudi urban realities – even more so than those of old Europe – are in a period of transition. Hence, there is an irremediable need to seriously embrace the urban knowledge produced in the 'labs' that, today, are Rio, Dubai and Mumbai, much like Chicago at the beginning of the last century. Citing Indian authors when analyzing Mumbai, or Latin American authors when discussing Rio or Bogota, would allow us to move away from this kind of scientific imperialism (often tinged with postcolonialism) that pledges allegiance to the founding fathers of urban science, even when the relevance of their concepts is highly questionable due to the geographical and historical specificity of the context. In this work we have only partially succeeded in this exercise of translating local scientific theories, regardless of Rahul Srivastava's and Matias Echanove's frequent references to Indian authors in analyzing Dharavi and Rachel Coutinho's appeal for a local approach to urban science in her methodology.

The strong presence of classic authors of European and North American urban science through its historical origins may also mark the need to return to the basics, to adhere to established and shared knowledge in these times of urban turbulence. In this urbanized world that is gradually becoming the global norm, we sometimes forget that only a few, select parts of Shanghai, Singapore or Los Angeles actually reflect the implacable qualities of contemporary architecture – of that which is best, most innovative and most captivating in what it reveals and suggests about a possible world – and that these areas, in fact, stand alongside vast terrains dotted with container homes, vaguely fenced playgrounds and cardboard shacks erected in an architecture of survival. While this cohabitation of uncertain boundaries is precisely what encompasses the beauty of the whole, it is difficult now to say what the name of the city of tomorrow will be, of which we will immediately be consumers, given the chance (if we can call it that) to be there to see it in 2033 or 2057. Because tensions between supporters of order and marginalized peoples are strong, the latter are demanding a more central and rightful place in this city, along with more flexible structures. Are these signs heralding a new urban era, much as Hanja Maksim, Emmanuel Ravalet, Xavier Oreiller and Yafiza Zorro analyze mobility in this book? Are we transitioning from an era of fixity to one of mobility?

The city tomorrow

So what, then, constitutes the city? Urban research is tentative, even helpless, in addressing this fundamental question. For twenty years, whole fields of urban sociology seem to have lost their purpose – namely the city and urbanity – powerless as they are when attempting to identify, describe and understand them with finesse and precision. Paralyzed by the emergence of a global world, global cities and 'creative cities', urban research alternately limits itself either to sweeping generalities and totalizing assertions or to highly-specialized, fragmented analyses whose teachings struggle to produce a general theory of the urban phenomenon. The analytical limits of theories on the city and the urban are all the more regrettable given that many highly-urbanized countries are facing problems of considerable magnitude. To address these crises, the social sciences take the stance of the arsonist-firefighter; by trying to solve the problems, it has made a business of 'inventing', without bothering to maintain a clear, objective and analytical perspective.

Undaunted by this state of affairs, and utilizing the approaches outlined by the authors, we propose an agenda based on three lines of research:

Analyzing the extraordinary

While the study of the ordinary character of the city is a first step in describing the nature of what makes the city, it is nonetheless insufficient. Several of the texts in this book indicate that we must go one step further. The normalizing and standardizing of cities through the pacification of space is gradually becoming their hallmark, from Dubai to Los Angeles to Paris. At the local scale, this trend takes on specific forms related to context. However, sustainable development applied to urbanism, citizen participation, large urban projects and the beautification of downtown areas is becoming a watered-down, common version of the globalized benchmarking of good practices.

Urban research is too focused on these productions, trying to dissect the logics involved and thereby contributing to their optimization. The overall stance and arguments in this book suggest that researchers' *should* be focusing on the extraordinary, on expressions of spontaneity, on the use (or misuse) of spaces and objects, on unplanned appropriations and on DIY, inhabiting containers like building blocks of urbanity but always starting from the infinitesimal, the hyper-ordinary. Nowadays, however, such phenomena find conducive environments outside of city centers. Urban mass tourism and museumification go hand in hand with the pacification of public spaces, which is increasingly incompatible with appropriation by inhabitants and users in urban hypercenters. The loss of urbanity in downtown areas is mitigated by its development in urban fringes. Like an old tree whose trunk has become hollow but whose roots still draw vital energy, sometimes far from the tree itself, the city's life no longer comes from its old, senile center, but rather from its peripheries. It is in these areas, ripe with opportunity (both socially and for those who study them), that research must ground itself.

Focusing research investigations on the extraordinary means exploring the fundamental ambivalence of how the city is appropriated. The chapters in this book effectively invite us to look both at how inhabitants intervene in the public space to make it familiar, thus strengthening their ontological security, as well as at power struggles and other criminal or Mafioso logics of domination. Understanding the fundamental ambivalence of the urbanity of contemporary cities based on what lies outside the framework is essential for those seeking to discover the essence of the city and the urban phenomenon, thus ensuring both its ordinary (hence structural) character *and* its extraordinary (hence dynamic) character.

Analyzing tensions

Because of their wealth of actors and the activities undertaken in them, cities are places of potential tension. The activation of these tensions in the form of various conflicts depends on a number of factors, particularly those relating to inequalities and the scope of opportunities specific to each context. This second point is critical. In the conclusion of a recent book on governance in major cities in the global South, Dominique Lorrain writes that major cities are ungovernable (Lorrain, 2011). However, he goes even further in this: *were* they totally governable, they would no longer be cities. Cities provide mobility in the fullest sense of the term; in other words, they make it possible to change and transform one's context in infinite ways. Here again we find the spontaneous expressions, uses and misuses mentioned in the first line of potential research. Once again, it is extremely reassuring to note that, despite the desire to control, cities elude laws and norms, and its actors do unexpected, undesirable things in places where we least expect them.

The ungovernable nature of the city also reveals what constitutes the city because it showcases both meaningful tensions – from the actors' points of view – and how to settle them. Our book raises several important questions on this point that are likely to pose problems for researchers in the future.

The first is related to cohesion. Several of the examples developed show that social cohesion in large cities cannot really be built on the urbanization of spectacle. Urban planning and the construction of emblematic buildings nd/or urban facilities make reference to an aesthetic of the global city in ich residents do not see themselves, as they do not take into account daily nd its small requirements. Many of the examples presented in this book ize the dialectical tension between formal and informal planning. This 'y a topic for further investigation.

A second approach has to do with policy. Trends towards standardization and the technicalizing of urban policy puts an end to debates and political clashes around urban issues. The result is a loss of creativity in the projects, as well as disregard for certain modes of action (i.e. everything relating to emotional attachment and collective memory, certain forms of sociability in public space, etc.). In-depth study of these issues calls for the use of critical sociology.

Finally, a third approach, already well established but in need of revisiting, concerns domination and inequalities. The city is a stage for inequalities, and contrary to the idea of mutual disengagement between the dominators and the dominated, it is in many ways proof of the persistence of a strong social hierarchy. Illegality, for instance, is indispensable to the economic activity of entire sectors including the hospitality, construction and restaurant industries. Clandestineness is a creator of urbanity, just as ostentatious displays of wealth are a driving force behind the dreams of the poor. Detailed study of forms of domination and the tensions they reflect is a very old-fashioned but extremely effective way of working on the social essence of the city. However, with changes in spatial relationships, it needs to be revisited, leading to a third research approach.

Studying proximity

While we now know that the city is not on the verge of disappearing, we have noted through the different chapters of this book (most notably that of H. Maksim, E. Ravalet, X. Oreiller and Y. Zorro, and the debates to which the authors make reference) that the urban phenomenon is nonetheless in the throes of profound change, largely as a result of the speed of transportation and telecommunications systems, which have had a major impact on societies and their territories. These systems are intensively used by populations, and often in ways that differ from their intended use. Nowadays, the spatial and temporal organization of cities and territories is traversed at variable speeds, from the slow pace of walking to the immediacy of telecommunications (Vincent-Geslin and Kaufmann, 2011).

Many essays and other theoretical writings have described this transformation of the city in terms of architecture, urbanism, geography, sociology, economy and political science, using a host of qualifiers. Hence, the city in transformation is emerging, fragmented, diffuse, franchised, global, generic, segregated and privatized – a metropolis and a metapolis – and is character- ized by the fact that it is 'without places or boundaries'. Beyond this mosaic of terms, and a variety of approaches that generally relate to a comprehensive understanding of a specific phenomenon, research teaches us that the spatial and social differentiations inherent to the city and urbanity do not go away; on the contrary, they seem to increase and build themselves around new dimen- sions. However, the literature does not address in a direct manner the issue of the relationships between what is connected, what moves and what is nearby. The city lives on but is no longer necessary, functionally speaking, meaning that the modes of production can easily do without it (Kaufmann, 2011).

Among the many ingredients that form the essence of a territory, there are three whose relationships have changed: function centrality (meaning a city radiates into its surrounding areas, of which it acts as the functional center); the built morphology (a city is characterized by a certain density of buildings, forms and infrastructures); and lifestyles (people are bearers of spe- cific social practices). These factors are behind the current transformations taking place in the city.

Contemporary cities are characterized by the fact that relationships have changed between what is close, what moves and what is connected. Sev- eral examples developed in this book illustrate this. Being nearby does not necessarily mean being connected. Moving is no longer the natural result of a lack of proximity. Being connected longer necessarily means being near or moving. The city remains the place with the greatest number of possible relationship combinations for being close, moving and being connected. On a more general level, the city contains the fundamental tension between what moves and what does not, between roots and mobility. In 1925, Robert Ezra Park made the 'man endowed with locomotion' the object of urban research. Our book shows that his proposal is at the heart of thinking on contempo- rary cities, whose characteristics favor or complicate (even prohibit) the free movement (spatial and social) of the people who live there.

References

Breviglieri, M. (2013) in Cogato Lanza E. *et al.*, eds. Une brèche critique dans la 'ville garantie'? Espaces intercalaires et architectures d'usage. *De la différence urbaine. Le quartier des Grottes/Genève.* MētisPresses, Geneva, 213–236.

Cogato, Lanza E. *et al.*, eds. (2013) *De la différence urbaine. Le quartier des Grottes/ Genève.* MētisPresses, Geneva.

Kaufmann, V. (2011) *Re-thinking the City – Motility and urban dynamics.* Routledge, London and New York.

Koolhaas, R. (2002) Junkspace. *October* 100: *Obsolescence.* MIT Press, Cambridge, 175–190.

Lorrain D. (éd.) (2011) *Métropoles XXL en pays émergents.* Les Presses de Sciences Po, Paris.

Robinson, J. (2006) *Ordinary Cities.* Routledge, London and New York.

Storper, M. (2013) *Keys to the City.* Princeton University Press, Princeton and Oxford.

Vincent-Geslin S. and Kaufmann, V. (2011) *Mobilité sans racines. Plus vite, plus loin... plus mobiles?* Descartes et compagnie, Collection Cultures mobiles.